PRINCIPLES
OF
MARKETING
ENGINEERING

2ND EDITION

PRINCIPLES OF MARKETING ENGINEERING

2ND EDITION

Gary L. Lilien
The Pennsylvania State University

Arvind Rangaswamy
The Pennsylvania State University

Arnaud De Bruyn
ESSEC Business School, France

State College, PA 16801
Phone: 814-234-2446
Fax: 814-234-2447
Email: sales@decisionpro.biz

ISBN: 978-0-9857648-0-7

CONTENTS

Chapter 2
Customer Value Assessment and Valuing Customers 27

Chapter 3
Segmentation and Targeting 61

PREFACE

Every generation of marketers finds new opportunities and challenges, as well as concepts and tools to handle them. Looking back even a decade or so, few marketers would have imagined that Internet advertising would pose such a serious threat to conventional advertising. Fewer still expected marketing investments to be held to the same standards of financial accountability as investments in more tangible aspects of the firm, like operations. And we would be willing to wager that very few visionary firms prepared themselves to exploit the deluge of data and information that often overwhelm today's marketing decision-making environment.

As a profession, marketing must evolve beyond relying almost exclusively on conceptual content to drive decisions and actions. Concepts that have been honed by experience will always have an important role to play in marketing, but today's marketing also requires more systematic analyses and processes. Marketing decision making resembles design engineering—putting together concepts, data, analyses, and simulations to learn about the marketplace and design effective marketing plans. Although many people view traditional marketing as an art and others regard it as science, modern marketing increasingly looks like engineering—a combination of art and science to solve specific problems. In this context, several key forces are working to alter the marketer's job.

High-Powered, Networked Computers

For better or worse, marketers today have 24/7 access to huge amounts of real-time data, reports, and expert opinions, and they can combine and process that information in new ways to enhance decision making. Basing decisions on such information therefore has become a minimum requirement to be a successful player in many industries.

Exploding Volumes of Data

As in financial markets, activities in other marketplaces leave behind data traces that astute marketers can use to improve their understanding of their customers and competitors. The data explosion accompanying the growth of e-commerce, database marketing, and direct marketing challenges the severely limited data processing capabilities of the human brain. More data cannot lead to better decision making unless managers learn how to generate actionable insights from them. If data are a burden, insights provide relief.

Reengineered Marketing Activities

All over the world, organizations face increasingly well-informed customers who seek greater and greater value. As a result, they must carefully scrutinize the productivity of all their management processes. To reduce costs and improve productivity, they have reengineered many marketing functions, processes, and activities for the information age. At the same time, mass marketing is giving way to micromarketing, fine-tuned to individual customers and well-defined customer segments. Simultaneously, global competition is driving organizations to do more with fewer employees. Marketing managers are finding themselves empowered—meaning they have little support staff. However, they have access to hardware, software, and data and must use these tools themselves to find and deliver value to micromarkets through fragmented media and channels.

As a result of these trends, marketers need much more than just concepts to exploit their available resources; they must move from conceptual marketing to Marketing Engineering. In this book, we integrate concepts, analytic marketing techniques, and operational software to help the new generation of marketers become marketing engineers.

OVERVIEW

The several editions of *Marketing Engineering* that we have published since 1998 have been aimed at a fairly narrow, somewhat technical audience interested in bringing more scientific rigor to the marketing discipline. Its use throughout industry and in more than 150 business schools on five continents demonstrates a certain degree of success.

But the issues central to Marketing Engineering extend well beyond the community that consists (mainly) of graduate students. Peter Drucker once pointed out that "marketing is too important to be left to marketers." Equally important, the realm of Marketing Engineering is too important to designate solely to those with deep analytic and technical skills. With this in mind, we have designed this book primarily for the business school student or marketing manager, who, with minimal background and technical training, must understand and employ the basic tools and models associated with Marketing Engineering.

This book is like the tip of an iceberg; more hides underneath than appears in plain view. The supplementary materials available at the website associated with this text, www.decisionpro.biz, provide technical details, cases, and software that will help you learn to implement the concepts described in the book. Our goal for this book is to convey the importance and value of the Marketing Engineering concepts and tools (i.e., the "why"); we offer the supplementary materials to clarify the "how to" of Marketing Engineering. Therefore, this book is designed to provide a self-contained introduction, with the hope that those readers looking for an initiation to Marketing Engineering will become intrigued enough to pursue this topic further via additional materials. Thus, we offer a general explication of the important issues that marketers face in their attempt to improve their decision-making skills in IT-intensive environments.

In turn, our specific objectives for this book are as follows:

- To help you understand the role of analytical techniques and computer models and how they enhance marketing decision making in modern enterprises.
- To improve your ability to view marketing processes and relationships systematically and analytically.
- To expose you to various examples that demonstrate the value of Marketing Engineering in real managerial contexts.

Most of the concepts we describe have software implementations and at least one problem or case you can explore and resolve by using the software available at our website. Reading the concepts in this book is like watching a movie about horseback riding; though watching (reading) gives you an idea, only riding (using the software and cases) can provide the butt-in-the-saddle experience that many of you will want and need.

Decision tools range from large-scale, enterprise-wide applications to those that can be quickly put together by anyone who has at least a general understanding of basic Marketing and Marketing Engineering. We emphasize end-user modeling here and therefore offer a prescription. End-user modeling shares the characteristics of good engineering: Do as good a job as you can with the time and resources you have available. We firmly embrace this perspective.

Even good managers rarely have all the answers, but they should be good at asking the right questions. We hope Marketing Engineering, as we describe and clarify it in this book, will help in this critical task.

WHAT'S INSIDE

The book is organized into eight chapters.

Chapter 1 defines Marketing Engineering and introduces its core building block: market response models.

Chapter 2 deals with gaining a more precise understanding of customers and customer groups. Understanding both the functional and psychological needs of individual and organizational customers is critical to convey the value of any firm's offerings to its customers, as well as the value of customers to the firm.

In Chapter 3, we address a central marketing question: Which customers should a firm choose to serve? To address this question, we describe the techniques of customer segmentation and targeting.

Chapter 4 deals with the issue of how firms can succeed in competitive markets by differentiating and positioning their offerings; we provide specific tools to address these issues.

With Chapter 5, we address forecasting, one of most important tasks a marketing manager undertakes, for both new and existing products and offer specific techniques to address these issues.

Chapter 6 deals with ways to enhance the new product development process using data and analytics. In particular, we provide specific approaches to enhance idea generation and evaluation, as well as product design through conjoint analysis.

Our main focus in Chapter 7 is the marketing mix—marketing budgeting, resource allocation decisions, communications, promotion spending, and pricing.

Finally, in Chapter 8, we summarize state-of-the-art knowledge about the implementation of Marketing Engineering in an organizational context, focusing on the determinants of success, as well as what can lead to failure. We also consider the future of Marketing Engineering.

The website, www.decisionpro.biz, offers access to additional materials that expand on the techniques described in each chapter and provides cases and problem sets keyed to major concepts. The Marketing Engineering software that operationalizes the concepts described in this book is also available at the website; it contains integrated help files, tutorials, and other key resources.

The website contains many useful resources for both students and instructors. Instructors in particular should peruse the site for sample course outlines, resources, and videos describing examples of successful applications of Marketing Engineering.

We wish you luck as you embark on your Marketing Engineering journey!

What's New in the 2nd Edition

While much has changed in the nearly five years since the first edition of *Principles of Marketing Engineering* was published, much has remained the same. Hence, we have not changed the basic structure or contents of the book. We have, however

- Updated the examples and references.
- Added new content on customer lifetime value and customer valuation methods.
- Added several new pricing models.
- Added new material on "reverse perceptual mapping" to describe some exciting enhancements to our Marketing Engineering for Excel software.
- Provided some new perspectives on the future of Marketing Engineering.
- Provided better alignment between the content of the text and both the software and cases available with Marketing Engineering for Excel 2.0.

ACKNOWLEDGMENTS FOR SECOND EDITION

This book builds on several earlier editions of *Marketing Engineering* and the first edition of *Principles of Marketing Engineering*. The book does not stand alone; it involves, in addition to this text, a suite of software tools, tutorials, help files, technical notes, problem sets, a website, and other supplementary material. Such a major undertaking could not have been accomplished without the support of many people and institutions, many of whom we recognized in the Preface to the First Edition.

In addition, we would like to thank the students in our classes at Penn State, ESSEC, the Indian School of Business and elsewhere who have consistently persisted in their demands to make the text and software more accessible.

The continuing enhancements to the software that complements and implements the concepts in this book require substantial development effort. Our chief software developer, Andrew (Nuke) Stollak continues to write, maintain, and manage the core code and we are indebted to him for his efforts.

The production of the book required the support of many people. Lori Nicolini was instrumental in keeping things on track. Steve Hoover managed the entire production process, including design, and layout of the book, the exhibits as well as printing and distribution.

Mike Clitherow and Allan Darr, through our link with DecisionPro, Inc. have provided the management structure and disciplined environment needed to make this book and the associated software developments a reality.

But behind every book is a generous group of family and friends, and without exception, so it is in our case. In particular, our wives, children (and Lilien's grandchildren) let us be who we are, and for that we are eternally grateful.

This book and the related material represent the continuation of our collaboration, and our contributions are intimately intertwined. We continue to enjoy the collaboration, learn from one another, and marvel at the value of positive synergies.

Gary L. Lilien, State College, PA
Arvind Rangaswamy, State College, PA
Arnaud De Bruyn, Paris, France

July 2012

ABOUT THE AUTHORS

Gary L. Lilien

Gary L. Lilien is Distinguished Research Professor of Management Science at the Smeal College of Business at Penn State. He is also cofounder and Research Director of the ISBM. Previously, Prof. Lilien was a member of the faculty at the Sloan School at MIT. His research interests include B2B marketing, Marketing Engineering, market segmentation, new product modeling, marketing mix issues for business products, bargaining and negotiations, modeling the industrial buying process, the implementation of marketing science and innovation diffusion modeling.

He is the author or co-author of twelve books (including *Marketing Models* with Phil Kotler, *Marketing Engineering* and *Principles of Marketing Engineering),* as well as over 100 professional articles. He was departmental editor for Marketing for *Management Science*; is on the editorial board of the *International Journal for Research in Marketing*; is functional Editor for Marketing for *Interfaces*, and is Area Editor at *Marketing Science.* He was Editor in chief of *Interfaces* for six years. He is the former President as well as Vice President/Publications for The Institute of Management Sciences. He is an Inaugural INFORMS Fellow, was honored as Morse Lecturer for INFORMS and also received the Kimball medal for distinguished contributions to the field of operations research. He is an Inaugural Fellow of the European Marketing Academy, is VP External Relations for the INFORMS Society for Marketing Science (ISMS) and is an Inaugural ISMS Fellow. He is on the Board of Directors of the American Marketing Association.

He received a BS, an MS and a PhD from Columbia University in Operations Research. He has received honorary doctorates from the University of Liege, the University of Ghent and Aston University and received the 2008 AMA/Irwin/McGraw Hill Educator of the Year award. In 2010, the ISMS-MSI Practice Prize for the best applied work in marketing science globally was renamed the Gary Lilien ISMS-MSI Practice Prize in his honor.

In addition to his teaching and research, Prof. Lilien consults for many companies, including Arcelor, AT&T, BP, CTCA, Dow, DuPont, Eastman Chemical, Exelon, the Federal Reserve Bank, GE, Goodyear, IBM, Pillsbury, Pfizer, Pitney Bowes, PPG, Sprint, and Xerox. He serves as well as a principal of the Marketing Engineering consultancy DecisionPro (www.decisionpro.biz).

Prof. Lilien is three-time winner and seven-time finalist in the Penn State Squash Club Championship and has substantial collections of fine wines and unusual porcine objects.

Arvind Rangaswamy

Arvind Rangaswamy is Senior Associate Dean and Anchel Professor of Marketing at Penn State. He received his doctorate in marketing from Northwestern University; an MBA from the Indian Institute of Management, Calcutta; and a B.Tech from the Indian Institute of Technology, Madras. Before joining Penn State, he was a faculty member at the J.L. Kellogg Graduate School of Management, Northwestern University, and the Wharton School, University of Pennsylvania. He is actively engaged in research to develop concepts, methods, and models that will improve the efficiency and effectiveness of marketing through the use of information technologies, as well as investigations of topics such as marketing modeling, online customer behavior, networked markets, and Internet business models. He currently teaches graduate courses in Marketing Engineering and e-Marketing.

Prof. Rangaswamy has published numerous articles in such leading journals as *Marketing Science, Journal of Marketing Research, Journal of Marketing, Management Science, Information Systems Research, Service Science, International Journal of Research in Marketing, Marketing Letters, Psychometrika, Multivariate Behavioral Research*, and *Journal of Economics and Statistics*. He was an Area Editor for *Marketing Science* (1997–2011) and serves on the editorial boards of the *Journal of Interactive Marketing; International Journal of Intelligent Systems in Accounting, Finance and Management; Journal of Service Research; Journal of Business-to-Business Marketing;* and *Journal of Electronic Commerce.*

He has consulted for many companies, including recent engagements at Abbott Labs, ImpactRX, J.D. Power Associates, Pfizer, Xerox, and Unisys. He is a Fellow of the IC^2 Institute, is a Principal and co-founder of DecisionPro, Inc., and was an IBM Faculty Partner (2000–2001). Prof. Rangaswamy is an avid and successful trader on eBay and other auctions, where he blends his research with his personal interest in rare Indian stamps, coins, and postal history.

Arnaud De Bruyn

Arnaud De Bruyn is Professor of Marketing and Head of the Marketing Department at ESSEC Business School, Paris, France, and Associate Director for the Marketing Engineering Program at the Institute for the Study of Business Markets at Penn State.

He received a Ph.D. in marketing from Penn State and a Master in Economics from the University of Liège, Belgium. His research interests, teaching, and consulting practice coincide at the frontier of marketing, operations research, and computer science, particularly in the domains of customer relationship management, database marketing, and Marketing Engineering. These domains encompass various applications for customer segmentation, targeting, positioning, lifetime value analysis, direct marketing, conjoint analysis, and online recommender systems. He also develops computer programs and Web applications.

His work has been published in *Marketing Science, Management Science, International Journal of Research in Marketing, Information Systems Research*, etc., and serves on the editorial board of *IJRM, Journal of Interactive Marketing* and *RAM*. His work on the quantitative analysis of viral marketing behavior, co-authored with Gary Lilien, has won the IJRM Best Paper Award.

Over the last 10 years, Prof. De Bruyn has accumulated north of 1,000 teaching hours covering how to apply tools and concepts of Marketing Engineering to guide managerial decision-making, coaching both undergraduate and graduate students as well as marketing managers, fundraisers, and instructors.

Prof. De Bruyn has consulted for several companies and nonprofit organizations in the areas of direct marketing fundraising, database marketing, and marketing campaign optimization; his recent consulting engagements in the nonprofit sector include the WWF, the Salvation Army, CARE, the Gustave Roussy Institute, the Curie Institute, and Amnesty International.

He is a passionate player of role-playing, diplomatic, and strategy games, and is a student of the *Tenshin Shoden Katori Shinto Ryu*, a 600-year old traditional swordsmanship school from Japan.

CHAPTER 1

The Marketing Engineering Approach

A good decision requires a reasoned choice among competing alternatives. Good decision making is essential in business and does not happen by accident. Business leaders in today's unpredictable but data rich decision environments who want to develop effective decision-making skills must learn the art and science of decision making and then apply those lessons in practice. This book is designed to help readers become more effective marketing decision makers by providing them with the necessary concepts and tools, as well as the opportunities to apply them.

Marketing managers make frequent decisions about product features, prices, distribution options, and sales incentives. In making these decisions, managers choose from among many alternative courses of action in a complex and uncertain world. Like most decisions, marketing decisions follow an intuitive decision-making process comprised of judgment calls based largely on managers' mental models of the world, developed through their own experiences. In many cases, such mental models, perhaps backed by market research data, may be all that managers need to feel confident about their decisions. Yet mental models are prone to systematic errors. Although everyone recognizes the value of experience, any experience is unique to each person and can be skewed toward particular points of view: Sales managers might lower advertising budgets to achieve higher personal selling expenditures, whereas advertising managers might prefer larger advertising budgets.

An alternative approach to making decisions about advertising expenditures can employ a spreadsheet decision model of how the market should respond to various expenditure levels. Managers can use this model to explore the sales and profit consequences of alternative expenditure levels before making a decision.

The systematic translation of data and knowledge (including judgment) into tools used for decision support is what we call **Marketing Engineering**. In contrast, when a decision maker relies solely on his or her mental model, without using any support system, we refer to it as **conceptual marketing**. A third option is to automate the decision process using a sophisticated information system, an increasingly popular approach we call **automated marketing**.[1] However, the intrinsic complexity of many marketing problems defies easy solutions or automation; often, a combination of decision support tools and the judgment of the decision maker provides the best results. That is, an approach that systematically combines managerial judgment with formal decision models is **Marketing Engineering**: *a systematic approach to harness data and knowledge to drive effective marketing decision making and implementation through a technology-enabled and model-supported interactive decision process.* In an organizational setting, the Marketing Engineering approach requires the design and construction of decision models and the implementation of those models in the form of marketing management support systems (MMSSs).

Marketing Engineering: A systematic approach to harness data and knowledge to drive effective marketing decision making and implementation through a technology-enabled and model-supported decision process.

The purpose of Marketing Engineering is actually to simplify the decision context and create a decision architecture to help managers focus on the key issues. Without simplification, noise rather than insights will drive people's decisions. A good decision model therefore focuses attention and limited resources on the decision at hand.

In addition, Marketing Engineering aids managers by providing a platform to ask "what if," enabling them to assess the **opportunity costs** associated with their decisions and determine the potential value of alternatives they choose to reject. For example, if a marketing manager must select between two pricing policies and chooses the lower-priced option, the Marketing Engineering approach can help assess the foregone profitability of the higher-priced option. This capability of Marketing Engineering is

[1] *The widely used term Marketing Analytics corresponds roughly to what we call Marketing Engineering PLUS automated marketing. This distinction is not critical for our discussions here.*

critical. In reality, managers can observe only the consequences of actions they have actually taken; however, Marketing Engineering helps them understand whether they might have made better decisions to begin with.

THE EMERGING MARKETING DECISION ENVIRONMENT

Although there have been attempts to employ aspects of Marketing Engineering in organizations since the 1950s, the pace has accelerated in the past decade, largely because of the range of technologies that make the approach imperative in competitive markets. Prior attempts to engineer marketing have generally led to short-lived successes, not because of poor models but because of the lack of technology available to embed that success into the fiber of the organization. During the past decade, technology has advanced to a stage that model-based decisions can be integral parts of the repertoire of skills marketing managers possess.

For several decades, researchers and practitioners have developed and implemented powerful systems that facilitate decision making in real-world marketing settings. Yet until recently, much of the knowledge about marketing decision models resided primarily in specialized academic journals or required considerable technical expertise to comprehend, becoming accessible to marketers only with the help of consultants. Major changes began with the development of stand-alone models, embedded within hundreds of commercially available software packages that support marketing analytics. With the advent of enterprise-wide systems for resource planning (ERP) and customer relationship management (CRM), marketing analytics is becoming an integrated aspect of the decision-making architectures that leading firms employ. As an indication of this trend, IDC (2010), a market intelligence consulting firm, reported that the business analytics market grew by more than 6 percent in 2010. And a Forrester Research study (2010) reports that business analytics is the fastest growing category of global IT software expenditures.

Exhibit 1.1 shows how the Marketing Engineering approach transforms objective and subjective data about the marketing environment into insights, decisions, and actions.

Exhibit 1.2 sketches how Marketing Engineering can become an integral part of the information and decision architectures that support marketing decision making.

EXHIBIT 1.1

The Marketing Engineering approach to decision making helps transform objective and subjective data about the marketing environment into decisions and decision implementations.

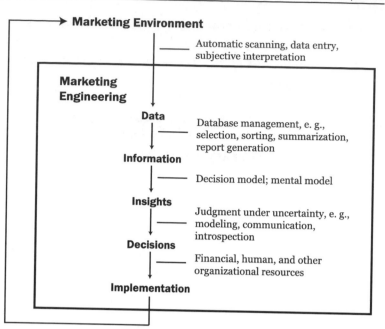

EXHIBIT 1.2

The Marketing Engineering approach offers several opportunities for using information technologies to develop a marketing decision platform throughout an organization. It supports the identification of new business opportunities, offers a common analytic foundation for driving marketing decisions, incorporates the latest insights and practices associated with a particular area of marketing decision making (e.g., segmentation), and integrates actions with decisions, all of which can serve to enhance achievement of strategically important metrics.

Trends that Favor Marketing Engineering

Although Marketing Engineering encompasses all the elements shown in Exhibits 1.1 and 1.2, in this book, we focus more narrowly on how Marketing Engineering helps transform data, information, and insights into effective decisions. Several trends, both on the supply side and the demand side, favor the wider acceptance of Marketing Engineering approaches among companies.

The ubiquity of high-powered personal computers connected to networks

Like other professionals, marketing managers depend increasingly on computers to perform their jobs. A senior marketing executive once told us, "We used to have lots of people and very little software in our office. Today we have lots of software and very few people." For example, more than 500 million copies of Microsoft Excel currently are in use[2]. Excel, similar to other model-building software such as Java, enables companies to embed models into their information and decision systems, increasing their ability to gather, process, and share information and then apply marketing models at the point of decision making.

An exploding volume of data

The automatic electronic capture of data related to transactions with customers and the growth of interactions and exchange via the Internet have generated massive amounts of potentially useful information about the preferences and behavior of customers. In a sense, an abundance of data can be a bigger problem than a lack of data. Today, several companies have databases that are 1,000 times larger than the most massive database 10 years ago. It requires strong managerial skills, advanced analytical capabilities, sophisticated information technology, and superior organizational capabilities to transform these data into actionable marketing knowledge. A recent IBM study of 1,700 Chief Marketing Officers reports that 71% of them are unprepared for managing the data explosion. As one CMO put it, "We're drowning in data. What we lack are true insights."[3] Marketers demand decision tools and processes that can quickly transform data into insights and actions. Outdated data or analyses leave managers just as dependent on intuition and experience as in the past—and at a disadvantage compared with more nimble competitors.

Reengineering marketing

Today's firms use flat organizational structures, ad hoc teams, outsourcing, strategic relationships, and reduced cycle times. In this environment, firms are reengineering marketing functions, processes, and activities for the information age. In the reengineered firm, centralized decision making, a characteristic of traditional hierarchical organizations, is giving way to the decentralized decision making that is characteristic of entrepreneurial or-

---

[2] *http://www.askpedia.com/q/525/Install_Base_of_Microsoft_Office_Worldwide_and_in_the_US (retrieved December 15, 2011).*
[3] *http://www.smartplanet.com/blog/business-brains/marketing-chiefs-not-prepared-for-data-explosion-ibm-study/19518 (retrieved December 15, 2011).*

ganizations. As a consequence, marketing managers increasingly deal directly with market information and use computers to complete tasks that were once done by support staff.

Higher standards of accountability

Several factors, including the pressures of the most recent recession, the increasing levels of competition in major markets, and the improved ability to associate market response with marketing activities (e.g., Direct Response TV, websites), have focused senior management's attention on marketing's contribution to the top and bottom lines. Senior management now demands that marketing expenditures be justified in the same way as other firm investments. The Fortune 1,000 companies spend over $1,200 billion on Marketing annually (Business Week 2009), yet, most companies report low use of marketing analytics to support marketing decision making. In 2009, McKinsey & Co. interviewed more than 600 C-level executives who represented all industries in the US and found that only 14% of the firms interviewed use a comprehensive set of quantified marketing priorities to determine how to allocate their marketing investments (McKinsey & Co. 2009). Yet a recent Forrester Research study (2010) showed that approximately 69 percent of businesses are interested in using analytics. Hence, there is both an opportunity and increasing interest in deploying systematic, analytic processes to generate insights, guide creative thinking to develop more effective marketing programs, and measure outcomes.

Marketing Engineering capitalizes on these trends, which favor both the supply of and demand for marketing analytics. Not only does Marketing Engineering enable marketers to capture the essence of marketing problems in well-specified models, it also improves their ability to make decisions that influence market outcomes. But the mere availability, or use, of marketing analytics does not necessarily affect managerial or organizational performance; rather, analytics must become part of the company's core managerial decision-making capabilities.

Managers recognize that a model does not provide the complete answer and therefore correctly believe that model results cannot be implemented without modifications by judgments. If model results are tempered by intuitive judgments, why not rely on judgments in the first place? This question reflects a non sequitur—it simply does not follow. As Hogarth (1987, p. 199) notes, "When driving at night with your headlights on, you do not necessarily see too well. However, turning your headlights off will not improve the situation."

Decision support tools and mental models must be used in conjunction so that each strengthens the areas in which the other is weak. Mental models can incorporate idiosyncratic aspects of a decision situation, but they may force-fit new cases into old patterns. Decision models may be consistent and unbiased, but they can underweight or ignore idiosyncratic aspects of the situation. Blattberg and Hoch (1990) find that forecasting accuracy improves when managers combine the forecasts generated by decision models with those from mental models; a 50–50 (equal weighting) combination of these two forecasts was best.

In this sense, Marketing Engineering can be both data-driven and knowledge-driven. A data-driven support tool answers "what if" questions on the basis of a quantified market response model. A knowledge-driven decision support tool captures the qualitative knowledge available about a particular domain.

But there are yet other benefits to a Marketing Engineering approach. Managers can explore more decision options, consider decision options that are more distant from the "base solutions," assess the relative impact of different marketing decision variables more precisely, facilitate group decision making, and enhance their own subjective mental models of market behavior. In essence, the Marketing Engineering approach leads to better and more systematic marketing decision making.

Examples of Marketing Engineering Success

Various well-documented examples have demonstrated that companies can derive substantial benefits from the application of the Marketing Engineering approach to decision making. We outline just a few here.

EXAMPLE

ABB Electric, a manufacturer and distributor of power generation equipment, wanted to increase its sales and market share in an industry that was facing a projected 50% drop in demand. By carefully analyzing and tracking customer preferences and actions, it determined which customers to focus its marketing efforts on and what features of its products were most important to those customers. It credits its ability to go from just 4% to over 40% market share, while raising its profitability in a declining market, to its ME application of choice models (Gensch, Aversa, and Moore 1990).

EXAMPLE

The *German Railroad Corp.* (a $15 billion company) historically priced transportation between any two points as a simple multiple of the distance between them. However, this price structure was not competitive with automobile usage. On the basis of a large-scale conjoint analysis, the company launched a "BahnCard" that allows customers to buy tickets at large discounts off the standard per kilometer fares. With the card, many more passengers found the train an attractive alternative to driving. With 3.5 million cardholders, the BahnCard has increased the firm's profits by more than $200 million per year (Dolan and Simon 1996).

EXAMPLE

Rhenania, a medium-sized German direct mail-order company, used a dynamic, multilevel response modeling system to answer the most important direct marketing questions: When, how often, and to whom the company should mail its catalogs. This model dynamically evaluates customers on the basis of their past purchase histories and derives the threshold sales per customer needed to maximize profits across time periods and multiple customer segments. The model helped the company increase its customer base by more than 55% and quadrupled its profitability in the first few years after its implementation. The application of the modeling approach also helped propel the company from fifth to second in terms of market position in the German marketplace. In terms of costs, the model paid for itself in a few weeks (Elsner, Krafft, and Huchzermeier 2004).

EXAMPLE

Telering, a leading Austrian cellular phone supplier, was severely threatened by competitive activities. By undertaking a detailed segmentation study, Telering identified a new market opportunity, offering no upfront subscription charges, that competitors had trouble mimicking. A sophisticated perceptual mapping study not only made the resulting service innovation credible to senior management and overcame internal barriers to its launch but also provided ideas as to how the product could be introduced through a compelling and relevant advertising campaign. The new service returned over $20 million in incremental revenue to Telering (Natter et al. 2008).

EXAMPLE

J.D. Power and Company developed a promotional analysis decision model that enabled automobile manufacturers to improve the timing, frequency, and components of their promotional activity to maintain sales but reduce margin loss. They report savings of about two billion dollars across the auto industry, with Daimler Chrysler executives alone claiming annual benefits of $500 million (Silva-Risso and Ionova 2008).

EXAMPLE

National Academies Press was concerned about the best way to price and distribute multiple formats for their books via the internet: print and pdf. They built a pricing model that allowed for both substitution between the two forms as well as complementarity (customers buying both forms) and calibrated the model via a sophisticated choice modeling experiment. The results permitted National Academies Press to launch their entire range of digital products with a variable pricing scheme that allowed them to meet their profit objectives as well as to maximize the reach of their authors' work (Kannan, Kline Pope, and Jain 2009).

These examples represent published reports of Marketing Engineering applications that were both technical and organizational successes. (See Lilien, Roberts, and Shankar [2011] for a number of others). But for every such highly visible, large-scale organizational success, thousands of small successes use many of the same Marketing Engineering principles. Imagine—only a few hundred, highly visible professionals make the rounds at golf tournaments, but more than 25 million Americans play the game. Golf professionals serve as exemplars for the golfing public—in much the same way these Marketing Engineering exemplars should inspire marketing practitioners in large and small organizations alike.

TOOLS FOR MARKETING ENGINEERING

The wide availability of spreadsheet software, such as Excel, has made it easier to work with mathematical representations of marketing phenomena. For example, marketing spreadsheets typically include planned marketing expenditures and the associated gross and net revenues. However, in most cases, the model developer does not establish a spreadsheet relationship between marketing inputs (e.g., advertising) and sales revenues. Thus, marketing inputs impact net revenue only as cost items. We refer to such spreadsheets as "dumb" models: They make little sense as marketing models because they are silent about the nature of the relationship between marketing inputs and outputs. For the spreadsheet model to make sense, the model developer must define objectives and variables explicitly and specify the relationships between variables. In a "smart" model, the spreadsheet embeds an equation or "response model," which the manager uses to consider the effect of advertising on both sales and revenues and determine if increases or decreases in advertising are justified. Hence, the design environment (knowledge, software, data) facilitates Marketing Engineering.

Market Response Models

Market response models are the basic tools of Marketing Engineering, the ingredients that can transform a dumb spreadsheet model into a smart one. Response models are critical for systematically addressing many recurring strategic and tactical decision problems in marketing, such as marketing budgeting and mix allocations, customer targeting, and product/company positioning. Without models that describe how customers and markets might respond to marketing actions, it is very difficult to assess the opportunity costs of the decision at hand. And poor response models that lead the decision process astray—just like a golfer who does not stand square to the ball—will likely slice far away from the target.

Market response models require that the following be made explicit:

- *Inputs:* Marketing actions that the marketer can control, such as price, advertising, selling effort, and the like (the so-called marketing mix), as well as noncontrollable variables, such as market size or the competitive environment.
- *Response model:* The link from inputs to measurable outputs of concern to the firm (e.g., customer awareness levels, product perceptions, sales levels, profits).
- *Objectives:* The measure the firm uses to monitor and evaluate actions (e.g., sales in response to a promotion, percentage of a target audience that recalls an ad).

Response models function within the framework of marketing decision models (Exhibit 1.3). A firm's marketing actions (arrow 1), along with the actions of competitors (arrow 2) and environmental conditions (arrow 3), combine to drive the market response, leading to key outputs (arrow 4). Those outputs must be evaluated relative to the objectives of the firm (arrow 5), and the firm then adapts or changes its marketing actions, depending on how well it is doing (arrow 6) — the decision–modeling link.

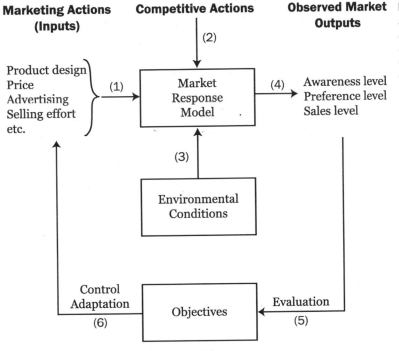

EXHIBIT 1.3

Market response models translate marketing inputs, competitive actions, and environmental variations into observed market outputs within the framework of a marketing decision model.

The Marketing Engineering approach enables managers to be more systematic about how they make decisions in partially structured decision situations. Without Marketing Engineering, firms resort to statements such as the following: "Sales in Minneapolis are down 2.3% relative to forecast [was the goal to meet or exceed the forecast?]; I suggest that we increase our promotional spending there by 10% over the previous plan. [Note the assumption: An increase in current promotional spending (input) will lead to a (short-term?) sales response of at least +2.3% and will be cost effective.]" With Marketing Engineering, this statement instead might appear as follows: "Sales are down 2.3% in Minneapolis. After including that information in our database and recalibrating our Minneapolis response model, it looks as if a promotional spending increase of 12.2% will maximize our profit in that market this quarter."

Types of Response Models

To a craftsperson with a hammer, the entire world looks like a nail, but the availability of a screwdriver introduces a host of opportunities. So it is with marketing models, which can be characterized in several ways:

- *By the number of marketing variables:* Do we consider the relationship between advertising and sales alone (a one-variable model), or do we include price as well (a two-variable model)?
- *By whether they include competition:* Does the model explicitly incorporate the actions and reactions of competitors, or is competition considered simply part of the environment?
- *By the nature of the relationship between input and output variables:* Does every dollar of advertising provide the same effect on sales (a linear response), or are there ranges of spending in which an additional dollar causes larger or smaller returns (an S-shaped response)?
- *By whether the situation is static or dynamic:* Do we want to analyze the flow of actions and market response over time or simply consider a snapshot at one point in time?
- *By whether the models reflect individual or aggregate response:* Do we want to model the responses of individuals (for direct marketing or to target specific sales efforts) or overall response (the sum of individual responses)?
- *By the level of demand analyzed:* To determine the sales of a brand, should we analyze brand sales directly (the most common approach) or consider brand share and total market demand, whose product is brand sales, separately?

In addition to these characteristics, several common terms are important to understand when dealing with market response models.

Parameters are the constants (usually a's and b's, not x's and y's) in the mathematical representation of models. To make a model form apply to a specific situation, we must estimate the parameter values, which infuse life into an abstract model. Parameters often have direct marketing referents (e.g., market potential, price elasticity).

Calibration is the process of determining appropriate values for the parameters. To calibrate a model, a marketer might use statistical methods (i.e., estimation), some sort of judgmental process, or a combination of approaches. For example, a simple model is:

$$\text{SALES} = a + b \times \text{ADVERTISING}$$

In this equation, *ADVERTISING* is an independent variable, *SALES* is a dependent variable, the model form is linear, and *a* and *b* are parameters. Note that *a* is the level of *SALES* when *ADVERTISING* equals zero, or the base sales level. For every dollar increase in advertising, the equation says that we should expect a change in sales of *b* units. Here, *b* is the slope of the sales/advertising response model. If we can determine that the appropriate values of *a* and *b* are 23,000 and 4, respectively, we place those values in the equation to get:

$$\text{SALES} = 23,000 + 4 \times \text{ADVERTISING}$$

so we may say we have calibrated the model (i.e., given values to its parameters).

But how do we perform this calibration, that is, select "good" parameters? We want estimates of *a* and *b* that make the relationship *SALES* = *a* + *b* × *ADVERTISING* a good approximation of how *SALES* varies with the values of *ADVERTISING*, which we may obtain from data or intuition.

People often use least squares regression to calibrate a model. In effect, if we have several observations of *ADVERTISING*, the **X-values** (call them x_1, x_2, etc.), and the associated observations of *SALES*, the **Y-values** (called y_1, y_2, etc.), the regression estimates of *a* and *b* are those values that minimize the sum of the squared differences between each of the observed *Y* values and the associated "estimate" provided by the model. For example, $a+bx_7$ would be our estimate of y_7, and we want y_7 and $a + bx_7$ to be close. We may have actual data about these pairs of *X*'s and *Y*'s, or we may have to use our best judgment to generate them ("What level of sales would we get if our advertising was 10 times what it is now? What if it was half of what it is now?").

When the data that we use for calibration are actual experimental or market data, we call the calibration task "objective calibration" (or objective parameter estimation). In many cases, managers do not have relevant historical data for calibrating the model. If the firm always spends about the same amount for advertising (say, 4% of sales in all market areas), it has no objective information about what would happen if it changed the advertising-to-sales ratio to 8%. Alternatively, the firm may have some historical data that are no longer relevant because of changes in the marketplace, such as new competitive entries, changes in brand price structures, varying customer preferences, and the like. (Imagine using year-old data in the smartphones market to predict future market behavior!)

For subjective calibrations, we must rely on judgment calls. For example, a judgmental calibration mechanism might consist of the following questions:

Q1: What is our current level of advertising and sales?

(A: advertising = $8/capita; sales = 25 units/capita)

Q2: What would sales be if we spent $0 in advertising?

(A = $0/capita)

Q3: What would sales be if we cut 50% from our current advertising budget?

(A = $4/capita)

Q4: What would sales be if we increased our advertising budget by 50%?

(A = $12/capita)

Q5: What would sales be if advertising were made arbitrarily large?

(A = $XXX/capita)

Whether we use an objective or subjective calibration, we need an idea of how well the model represents the data. One frequently used index is R^2, or R-square. If each of the estimated values of Y equals the actual value of Y, then R-square has a maximum value of 1; if the estimates of Y only perform as well as the average of the Y values, then R-square has a value of 0. If R-square is less than 0, the model performs worse than if we simply assigned the average value of Y to every value of X. In that case, we have a very poor model indeed.

The equation or relationship between advertising and sales that we discussed above is one every marketer knows—it is a straight line within a reasonable range. But we are not limited to straight-line relationships for response models; there are many types that are in common use and more appropriate than straight lines for certain marketing situations. (See the Technical Notes at www.decisionpro.biz for technical details on the issues we discuss here.)

Dynamic Effects

Responses to marketing actions rarely take place instantly. For example, the effect of an ad campaign does not end when that campaign is over; part of it will continue in a diminished way for some time. Similarly, many customers purchase more than they can consume of a product during a short-term price promotion, which causes an inventory buildup in their homes and therefore lowers sales in subsequent periods. Furthermore, the effect of a sales promotion depends on how much inventory buildup has occurred in prior periods (i.e., how much potential buildup is left). If customers stocked up on Brand A cola last week, a new promotion this week probably would be less effective than one several weeks in the future.

Carryover effects refer to the influence of a current marketing expenditure on sales in future periods. There are several types of carryover effects. The **delayed-response effect** arises from delays between when marketing dollars are spent and their impact. Delayed response is especially evident in industrial markets, in which the delay, especially for capital equipment, can be a year or more. Another type of effect, the **customer-holdover effect**, arises when new customers created by marketing expenditures remain customers for many subsequent periods, so their later purchases should be credited to some extent to the earlier marketing expenditures. Some percentage of these new customers will be retained in each subsequent period; this phenomenon gives rise to the notion of the **customer retention rate** and its converse, the **customer decay rate** (also called the attrition or erosion rate). **New trier effects**, in which sales reach a peak before settling down to a steady state, are common for frequently purchased products, for which many customers try a new brand but few become regular users. **Stocking effects** occur when a sales promotion not only attracts new customers but also encourages existing customers to stock up or buy ahead. The stocking effect often leads to a sales drop in the period following the promotion.

Market Share and Competition

Marketing Engineering models can be built at many levels. Managers use models of brand sales, models of the total market, and models of market share, among others. These three types of models have an intimate and important relationship, by definition:

$$\text{Brand Sales} = \text{Market Sales} \times \text{Brand Market Share}$$

This equation is a powerful reminder that marketers obtain (brand) sales by extracting market share from the market in which they operate. Thus, a firm's action may influence sales by affecting the size of the market, share of the market, or both. Thus, a marketing action might result in zero incremental sales for at least two reasons. First, it might have no effect at all. Second, it might provoke a competitive response, which increases total product class sales but lowers the firm's share in that market. The preceding equation helps disentangle such effects.

Models of market or product class sales have several common functional forms and can use forecasting methods or demand build-up procedures that rely on environmental variables (e.g., population size, growth, prior sales levels). Market share models are a different story. To be logically consistent, regardless of what any competitor does in the marketplace, each firm's market share must be between 0 and 100% (range restriction), and market shares summed over brands must equal 100% (sum restriction).

A class of models that satisfies both the range and the sum restrictions are **attraction models**, which determine the attraction of a brand on the basis of its marketing mix. Essentially, these models say:

$$\text{Share} = \frac{\text{Attractiveness of Offering}}{\begin{array}{c}(\text{Attractiveness of Offering} + \\ \text{Attractiveness of Competitive Offerings})\end{array}}$$

where attractiveness is measured from the perspective of potential customers.

Response at the Individual Customer Level

Thus far, we have looked at aggregate market response at the level of the entire marketplace. However, markets are composed of individuals, so we can analyze the response behaviors of those individuals and either use them directly (at the segment or segment-of-one level) or aggregate them to form total market response. In Chapter 2, we describe how individuals and groups of individuals can be modeled in a Marketing Engineering framework.

Objectives

To evaluate marketing actions and improve the performance of the firm in the marketplace, managers must specify objectives. (See Exhibit 1.3.) Those objectives may have different components (e.g., profit, market share, sales goals) but must specify the time horizon, deal with future uncertainty, and address the issue of which objectives to pursue.

Short-run profit

The simplest and most common tactical objective is to maximize short-run profit. The equation focusing on that single marketing element in a static environment is:

$$\text{Profit} = (\text{Unit price} - \text{Unit variable cost}) \times \\ \text{Sales volume} - \text{Relevant costs}$$

$$= \text{Unit margin} \times \text{Quantity} - \text{Costs}$$

Response models characterize how the sales volume is affected by marketing actions. If our focus is on price, then (assuming costs are fixed) as price increases, the unit margin goes up and sales generally go down. If we focus on another marketing instrument, such as advertising, the margin is fixed and quantity goes up, but costs go up as well.

Relevant costs generally consist of two components: fixed and discretionary. **Discretionary costs** are those associated with the marketing activity under study and should always be considered. **Fixed costs** include plant and overhead expenditures that should be allocated appropriately to marketing activity. Allocating fixed costs is thorny and difficult; it keeps accountants employed and frequently frustrates managers of profit centers.

For our purposes, only two questions are relevant regarding fixed costs:

- *Are the fixed costs really fixed?* Suppose that tripling advertising spending leads to a 50% sales increase, leading in turn to the need to increase plant size. Capacity expansion costs then must be taken into account. Normally fixed costs are locally fixed; that is, they are fixed within the limits of certain levels of demand and shift to different levels outside those regions. As with our response models, as long as we focus our attention to a limited range of independent variables, most fixed costs are indeed fixed.

■ *Are profits greater than fixed costs?* If the allocated fixed costs are high enough, actual profitability may be negative. In this case, the decision maker may want to consider dropping the product, not entering the market, or some other action.

Long-run profit

If a marketing action or set of actions causes sales that are realized over time, we may want to consider profit over a longer time horizon. If we look at the profit stream over time, an appropriate way to deal with long-run profits is to take the present value (PV) of that profit stream:

$$PV = Z_0 + Z_1 r + Z_2 r^2 + Z_3 r^3 \ldots,$$

where Z_i is the profit for period i, and $r = 1/(1 + d)$, with d being the discount rate (typically 20%—d=0.2—or more per year, depending on the firm and the nature of the marketing investment). The discount rate d is often a critical variable; the closer d is to 0, the more oriented toward the long term the firm is, whereas a high value of d (over .25 or so) reflects a focus on more immediate returns. In practice, the more certain the earnings flow, the lower is the discount rate that firms use.

Multiple goals and multiple decision makers

Although profit of some sort is an overriding goal of many organizations, it is not the only factor managers consider in trying to decide among possible courses of action. Managers may say, "We want to maximize our market share and our profitability in this market!" or "We want to bring out the best product in the shortest possible time." Such statements are attractive rhetoric but show faulty logic. For example, firms can almost always increase market share by lowering the price; after some point however, profits decrease while market share continues to increase. And when prices become lower than costs, profit becomes negative even though market share is still increasing!

If a firm has two or more objectives that conflict, how can the decision maker weigh those objectives to rank them unambiguously? The simplest and most common approach is to choose one (the most important) objective—say, profit—and make all the others constraints (e.g., market share must be at least 14%). However, whether companies use a simple formal method, such as a single objective plus constraints, or a more sophisticated method to measure the trade-offs among goals, it is critical that they neither ignore nor poorly assess important objectives.

Various stakeholders in an organization may not agree about the goals. Marketers typically are more concerned about market share and sales growth than are financial analysts; time horizons also vary according to those involved in the decision. Therefore, it is important that some level of understanding about (if not agreement on) stakeholder differences in goals be incorporated into the decision-making process. (See Chapter 2.)

After the firm has specified its goals or objectives, the Marketing Engineering approach facilitates the process of decision making by suggesting the values of the independent variables (e.g., advertising, selling effort, promotional spending) that will offer the best opportunity to achieve these goals.

Shared Experience and Qualitative Models

Our preceding discussion focuses on quantitative response models—equations that develop a formal analytic structure of the marketplace. We now introduce two other forms of modeling that have proved valuable: shared experience and qualitative models.

Shared experience models

If we lack data about the way a market responds, it may be valuable to pool the experience of a wide range of businesses and develop norms or guidelines for response behavior from these pooled data. There are many ways that such pooling takes place, including benchmarking (comparing operations against acknowledged good alternatives), which facilitates systematic comparisons with an exemplar or strong outside comparison point.

Qualitative response models

Some decision situations call for qualitative insights (e.g., new copy for an advertising campaign, structuring a negotiation between a buyer and a seller from different cultures). The experience attained by knowledgeable practitioners and the guidelines generated by academic research can be useful in these situations. Qualitative response models help represent qualitative knowledge and insights.

If a particular phenomenon can be described best in a qualitative fashion, a precise numerical model may be inappropriate for representing what is known. For example, if we can characterize consumer response to an ad only as positive, neutral, or negative, a precise numerical model is inappropriate.

EXAMPLE

The possible responses to a price reduction by a competitor might be (1) match the new price, (2) maintain the current price, (3) change TV advertising, (4) increase trade promotion, or (5) fire the brand manager. These options do not fall along an easily characterized continuum.

EXAMPLE

A retailer might react to a trade promotion by always accepting the deal, but what it does with that promotion may depend on coop (shared) advertising dollars. If the deal includes coop money, the retailer accepts the deal and passes on the entire discount to the consumer. If the discount is greater than 30%, it puts up a big display. Otherwise, the retailer leaves the item at its regular price and does not use an ad feature or a display.

We can use qualitative response functions in decision models by adopting nonmathematical representation schemes. One approach is to use a rule-based representation, which states the response model in the form of rules, or statements joined by the connectives AND, OR, and NOT, and properly specified by the qualifiers FOR ALL and THERE EXISTS. Using this representation, the retailer example becomes a set of rules in computer representation form:

If the deal includes coop money,
    Then the retailer will accept the deal.

If the deal includes coop money,
    Then the retailer will pass on the entire discount to the consumer.

If the deal discount is greater than 30%,
    Then the retailer will put up a big display.

If NOT (the deal includes coop money) AND NOT (discount is greater than 30%),
    Then the retailer will sell the item at regular price.

If NOT (the deal includes coop money) AND NOT (discount is greater than 30%),
    Then retailer will use ad feature = No.

If NOT (the deal includes coop money) AND NOT (discount is greater than 30%),
> Then retailer will use display = No.

When a response model consists of a set of rules, artificial intelligence techniques, particularly logical inference, can derive recommendations in specific decision situations. Such rule sets also can help develop knowledge-based systems to support marketing decisions.

Choosing, Evaluating, and Benefiting from a Marketing Engineering Model

Response models are approximations of likely market or customer behavior and thus may vary, sometimes substantially, from the unknown, true response behavior. In some sense, all models are wrong, but many are useful. Model users must choose among those that are useful and those that are not. One model form is not better than another; rather, each is useful in some situations and for some purposes. Although various criteria dictate which model to select, here are four that apply specifically to response models.

Model specification
- Does the model include the right variables to represent the decision situation?
- Are the variables, as represented, managerially actionable?
- Does the model incorporate the expected behavior of individual variables?
- Does the model incorporate the expected relationships between variables?

Model calibration
- Can the model be calibrated via managerial judgments or historical data?
- Can the model be calibrated through experimentation?

Model validity and value
- Does the level of detail in the model match that in the available data?
- Does the model reproduce the current market environment reasonably accurately?
- Does the model provide value-in-use to the user?
- Does the model represent the phenomenon of interest accurately and completely?

Model usability
- Is the model easy to use? (Is it simple, does it convey results in an understandable manner, and does it permit users to control its operation?)
- Is the model, as implemented, easy to understand?
- Does the model give managers guidance that makes sense?

When we select a model, we can summarize these criteria into one overriding question: "Does this model make sense for this situation?" That is, does the model have the right form, can it be calibrated, is it valid, and is it useful? If the answers to these questions are all yes, then the model is appropriate.

BUSINESS VALUE OF MARKETING ENGINEERING: FROM PROMISE TO REALITY

Marketing Engineering succeeds because of sophisticated managers, not because of sophisticated models. Such managers recognize that decisions affect many stakeholders and that most people resist change and will not embrace decision processes they do not understand or decisions unfavorable to their interests. Therefore, developing good decisions is only half the battle. It is just as important to make those decisions acceptable to stakeholders within a firm; in many situations, model users and decision makers are different people.

Germann, Lilien and Rangaswamy (2012) therefore suggest that an organizational culture is a key determinant of the effective deployment of marketing analytics/engineering. In turn, since the organizational culture is largely shaped by the top management team (TMT) of a firm, they show that TMT advocacy of marketing analytics/engineering is critical for the widespread deployment of marketing analytics within the firm. Hence, support by top management and an organizational culture supportive of analytics are keys to reaping benefits from Marketing Engineering.

Here's how such benefits arise. By clearly stating model assumptions and explaining the results, managers can replace positions with principles. Instead of saying "Let's do X," a manager might say, "I believe that our objective should be A, and according to the model, X is a good way to achieve that objective." If the process of articulating model assumptions is well orchestrated, the ensuing discussion will focus on the merits of those assumptions rather than the appropriateness or validity of the model output. Models are particularly useful when they help change mental models by challenging the assumptions or beliefs that underlie those mental models. A model also provides an explicit mechanism for including stakeholders in the decision process. In the ABB example mentioned earlier, various stakeholders participated by linking the results of the model to their business problems (bidding for contracts, developing value propositions for new offers and planning for in-process inventory) and helping implement model results. Interested parties are more likely to accept decisions resulting from a model if they know their inputs and judgments are part of the process. In Chapter 8, we pull together a few critical lessons on the successful implementation of Marketing Engineering.

STRUCTURE OF THIS BOOK

For the reader who wants a broad perspective on Marketing Engineering, this book is designed to be read like any other. For the reader who wants to gain deep understanding and experience with Marketing Engineering, we provide substantial additional material on our website, www.decisionpro.biz, including software, software tutorials, and technical appendices that provide more details about the models described herein. Although readers can work directly with the Marketing Engineering models using our software, we have not written this book for marketing analysts or modelers. Rather, our main goal is to help you become an astute user of well-established models and a knowledgeable consumer of the modeling results generated by others. In particular, we hope this book will enable you to recognize decision situations that could benefit from a Marketing Engineering approach and help you focus your modeling efforts and your interpretation of results to facilitate the decision-making process. Specifically, we attempt to provide a basic understanding of the most successful marketing decision models, offer examples that show why they are successful, and give you some real experience with Marketing Engineering. In general, it is best to get the basic ideas from the text, refine that understanding through the use of the cases and software, and then use the technical notes mainly as backup.

We chose the models in this book to be both theoretically sound and practically useful, as the cases, exercises, and software on our Web site demonstrate. The models we describe here are all widely used in industry, which means they are robust and have been tested in field settings.

Chapter 2 deals with understanding customers and customer groups. We discuss how customers gather information, form preferences, and make decisions, both individually and in groups (i.e., organizational buying situations). Understanding both functional and psychological needs is critical. Such an understanding provides the basis for creating Marketing Engineering models that describe what customers' value and how they might respond to marketing actions. We also explore the value that customers provide to companies and develop several key ideas and methods associated with Customer Lifetime Value (CLV).

In Chapter 3, we focus on Marketing Engineering approaches that address a core strategic marketing issue: Which customer segments should we choose to serve? To answer this question effectively, marketers need tools to understand how a market is segmented and determine which segments are most attractive.

Chapter 4 deals with another core strategic marketing issue: How should we position our offerings in competitive markets, so that they are perceived as superior by those customers and segments we choose to serve? Again, Marketing Engineering approaches provide insight into this question that helps marketers avoid inefficient allocations of their limited resources.

Chapter 5 deals with methods of forecasting, for both new and established products. We cover both judgment-based and data-based approaches and show why combining the two is often a very effective strategy.

In Chapter 6, we describe concepts and tools for marketing new products or, more generally, new offerings. We focus heavily on methods that support the design of new products and conjoint analysis in particular.

Chapter 7 addresses the marketing mix—pricing, advertising, sales force and promotion decisions—as well as marketing budgeting and resource allocation decisions: how much to spend and where (what marketing mix elements, what programs?) and when to spend it.

Finally, Chapter 8 discusses what we know about the implementation of Marketing Engineering in an organizational context, focusing on the elements necessary for success, as well as those that can lead to failure. It then considers the future of Marketing Engineering.

SUMMARY

In this chapter, our primary objective was to introduce the field of Marketing Engineering—the use of interactive computer decision models to facilitate marketing decisions. More and more marketing managers are functioning in decision environments characterized by increasing amounts of data, information (summarized data), and computing resources. Such managers need various concepts and tools to survive and thrive in such environments.

The Marketing Engineering approach centers around interactive decision models, which are customizable, computerized representations of marketing phenomena that enhance managerial decision making. We provide a basic overview of the types of models and how they are constructed. We also describe some of the many potential benefits of using decision models, including improving decision consistency, gaining an ability to evaluate more decision options, assessing the relative impact of different factors on a decision, and updating mental models of market behavior. Finally, we summarize several reasons many managers cite for choosing not to use decision models, despite their potential benefits, with the hope that this book and related material can deflect those concerns. The real value of Marketing Engineering is to permit companies to move beyond an intuitive approach to marketing, or reasoning by historical analogy, toward smart marketing driven by clear metrics, profitability and exploitation of market opportunities.

CHAPTER 2

Customer Value Assessment and Valuing Customers[1]

In this chapter, we deal with two related topics: First, we address how to determine the value customers' associate with the products or offerings that a firm might provide. We call this first issue **customer value assessment**. Second, if customers find more value in a firm's products, those customers become more valuable to the firm. This second issue, a mirror image of the first, we refer to as **customer valuation**.

The core of the Marketing Engineering (ME) approach—recall the market response model in Exhibit 1.3—consists of customers and their responses. Marketing Engineering starts with an understanding and assessment of customer responses to actual and possible marketer actions. This chapter provides an approach by which you can gain such an understanding.

Throughout this book, we use the words *product* (or more generally, offering), *market,* and *customer*. Given their pivotal roles, we briefly define each term here.

From a marketer's perspective, a product or offering is a set of designed attributes that satisfy specific needs of specific customers. Typically, attributes can be organized into as many as three components: physical, service, and perceptual. When buying a BMW, a consumer obtains a car with all its physical attributes,

Product/offering:
Anything that can satisfy human needs. A need is the difference between a person's (or organization's) present state and a desired state. Thus, a need includes a gap, a barrier, a problem, or a specific want.

---

[1] *We are indebted to Grahame Dowling and Robert Thomas for their contributions to this chapter.*

a warranty, and other service offerings, plus the perceptions and feelings associated with the "Ultimate Driving Machine."

We deal primarily with physical products (almost all of which also have some service components) and services (almost all of which also have some physical components). Pure services exist, of course, characterized by simultaneous manufacture and consumption; for example, an airline seat for a specific flight cannot be inventoried or resold if unused. In addition, physical products may be classified as durables (e.g., razors used for a significant period of time after purchase) and consumables (e.g., razor blades used just a few times). We also focus on products for both consumer use (i.e., personal consumption) and business consumption (i.e., for use as inputs in other products and services).

Thus, our product definition includes consumable and durable physical products and pure services involved in consumer as well as business-to-business (B2B) use. We also recognize that all products have an associated perceptual component along with their tangible and service aspects.

Markets: *Depending on the perspective (supply or demand), either the competitive arena in which a particular product or service is sold or the segment of customers who require particular benefits and solutions from the product or service.*

Different people use the term "market" differently, but these definitions all take either a supply or a demand perspective. When a market is defined in terms of the needs of customers and the benefits and solutions to customer problems that the product or service provides, the definition takes a *demand* perspective. This point of view can lead to some novel descriptions of markets. For example, a market research study by a camera manufacturer suggested that when 18–25-year-old consumers bought its least expensive camera, the company was competing in an entertainment market: The cameras were bought to provide fun. If these customers did not purchase cameras, they spent their money going to the movies or engaging in other forms of entertainment, not on another type of camera at the same price point.

However, for practical reasons associated with the way firms manage their transaction databases, they usually adopt a product or *supply*-side view of their market. Thus, if the camera manufacturer declares itself to be in the camera market, the company has adopted a supply perspective of its market. This definition traditionally focuses on any competitors who supply physically similar (versus functionally superior, which would imply a focus on customer needs) products or services. This perspective also explicitly considers manufacturing processes, cost structures, technology development and utilization, marketing and distribution strategies, entry and exit costs, and so forth. Therefore, a market in this context is a competitive arena, which can make it easy to lose sight of customers, who often become volume or market share statistics rather than opportunities for companies to satisfy needs with products and services.

Consequently, we consider both demand (needs of customers) and supply (products and services offered to customers) perspectives of a market. In so doing, we recognize the benefits of Amazon.com's rule: "Watch customers, not competitors" (*BusinessWeek* 2006).

Customers: Persons who interact with the company to purchase and use products and services.

Marketers must take a broad view of customers. Sometimes they need to focus on those who are seeking products and services to satisfy their own personal needs, whereas at other times, they must consider the customer to be the person buying a gift, buying items for a household, or participating in a purchase decision for an organization. Thus, it is worthwhile to explore the broad nature of the customer concept. By considering both consumer and organizational buying processes, we develop our preceding definition and distinguish two types of "buying centers."

The consumer buying center involves five possible customer roles:

- *Initiator:* The person who suggests the idea of buying an offering.
- *Influencer:* A person whose advice influences the purchase.
- *Decider:* The person decides what, when, where, or how to buy.
- *Buyer:* The person who makes the actual purchase.
- *User:* The person who uses the product or service.

Although organizational buying centers may seem drastically different from personal purchasing, the categories of persons who play roles are similar:

- *Influencers:* Those who influence the buying decision by providing information or advice or defining the specifications for the product or service. (These people are not necessarily employees of the firm; they might be consultants or members of competitor, supplier, or buyer organizations.)
- *Approvers:* People who authorize the purchase, either financially or technically.
- *Deciders:* Often referred to as the buying center, the people who make a (group) purchase decision.
- *Buyer:* The person who actually places the order (often a professional purchasing officer or possibly an automated computer program).

- *Gatekeepers:* People who have the power to sanction or block a supplier or prevent the flow of information among buying center members.
- *Users:* The people who actually use the product or service.

In either case, one person may assume multiple roles, and different people often play different roles in high-involvement purchase situations. The customer values that motivate buying decisions often depend on the role played by a specific influencer at a particular time or stage of the decision process.

Therefore, ME must begin with a clear understanding of customer needs and how those needs translate into the value that these customers ascribe to potential offerings. For this purpose, firms must clearly identify their customers and prospects—that is, their target market segment. We address this issue in detail in Chapter 3; for now, we focus on customer value assessment and customer valuation methods for a defined target segment, which may be as specific as the individual customer.

THE CONCEPT OF CUSTOMER VALUE

Value means different things to different people; we must define and measure it carefully if it is to be used as a basis for ME. Subsequently in this chapter, we develop four specific and practical techniques: value-in-use, conjoint analysis, choice modeling and Markov chain analysis.

Value: The customer's estimate of a product's or service's overall capacity to satisfy his or her needs.

Value can be measured by what a customer exchanges (in economic terms) for various options that can satisfy a want or a need. This is a behavioral measure of value, in that it requires a transaction to take place ("what a customer exchanges"). Alternatively, we could measure value in terms of customer intentions, or what a customer *intends* to exchange. These definitions are related and depend on the point in the purchase process at which we assess value. Finally, we might assume that the customer is a rational economic agent and therefore define value as what a customer *should* (if he or she had all the facts and the ability to understand them) be willing to exchange. These different perspectives reflect the need for different value assessment methods. All three methods recognize that value is hidden in the minds of customers and must be revealed or inferred through systematic measurement.

Although the general concept of customer value remains the same for consumers and organizations, the needs that drive value may differ considerably in these two contexts. For example, individual consumers value products and services for their personal consumption, whereas organizations value products and services for the competitive advantage they provide in the marketplace. That is, organizations face a competitive market in which they are offering products and services to customers, who are in turn seeking to offer the best value to their customers. Thus, organizations are often driven, through the discipline of the marketplace, to use the rational, "should do" approach, whereas the concepts related to what consumers plan to or have exchanged are more generally applicable to individual consumers.

For most customers (whether individuals or organizations), value is a function of the (perceived or expected) benefits relative to the price (to be) paid, namely:

$$\text{Value} = \text{Benefits} - \text{Price}.$$

We must examine both parts of this equation:

Benefits .....functional (e.g., the product "does the job").
.....psychological (e.g., Nike shoes provide social status).
.....economic (e.g., Wal-Mart offers branded products at everyday low prices).

Price .....monetary (e.g., $, £, euro).
.....perceived risk.
.....inconvenience.

EXAMPLE

Consider the development and launch of the Lexus automobile. First, Toyota identified a segment of potential customers who would like to buy a European brand (such as BMW or Mercedes) but thought they were overpriced. If they could build a car to the design standards of a Mercedes and sell it at a significantly lower price, it should appeal to these customers. With this goal in mind, and this "smart buyer" as the target segment, Toyota developed the Lexus. On the benefit side of the value equation, the engineering, safety, style, fit, and finish of the Lexus were at least equivalent to that of Mercedes. On the price side of the equation, the car sold at a major discount relative to the Mercedes. To reduce the perceived risk of buying an expensive luxury car from Toyota, the car avoided the Toyota name badge and was not sold through Toyota dealers. Establishing a separate dealer network and training salespeople to sell to this specific target segment increased the prestige of the brand (psychological benefit) and reduced the inconvenience of buying and servicing the car. This great car value thus became an outstanding success in the market.

Value can range from negative to positive numbers, such that customers prefer those products with high value more than they do those with low value. A negative value score applies to a product that a customer would not accept for free. Consider a famous ad, attributed to the great polar explorer Ernest Shackleton, which allegedly appeared in London newspapers in the early 1900s:

Men wanted for hazardous journey. Small wages, bitter cold, long months of complete darkness, constant danger, safe return doubtful. Honor and recognition in case of success.

Many people would find that Shackleton's value equation (benefits = honor and recognition; costs = low wages, cold, darkness, danger) returned less than zero value for them. More than 500 responded, however, indicating that they found positive value in Shackleton's ad.

In some cases, a customer will have almost unlimited value for a product; a donor's kidney has immeasurable value to the recipient who wants to stay alive. Many factors determine where value falls along a scale, including the characteristics of the individual's or organization's need and the availability (or scarcity) of options to satisfy that need.

Customer Needs and Value

In Exhibit 2.1, we consider customer value from the perspective of an individual (or a single organization), albeit in a specific need/product context rather than as a system of beliefs. The upper set of boxes represents needs and the purchase process, whereas the lower set reveals the parallel process of customer value measurement. In the top set of boxes, customer value is driven by customer needs and the availability of options. In this figure, we also distinguish between a *functional* need and a *perceived* need, because what is actually required to complete a job or perform a function is rarely the same as what the customer perceives as required. This distinction is important in differentiating among various measurement approaches.

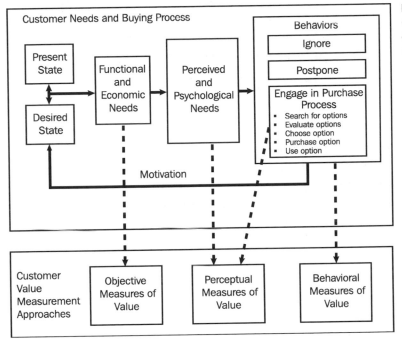

EXHIBIT 2.1
Customer needs and customer value measurement.

Once the customer perceives a need, three general behavioral possibilities exist: ignore the need, postpone it, or engage in a purchase process to identify options to satisfy it. These options appear in the "behaviors" box in Exhibit 2.1. The customer searches for options to satisfy the need, evaluates them, chooses one, purchases it, and uses it. Although stated simply here, this process can be quite complex. As the customer goes through the process, the perceived need remains subject to change (the two-way arrow) as the customer gathers information about various alternatives. The phase of the process that involves an evaluation of options occurs when the customer formulates more concrete notions of value associated with satisfying the need.

A customer's needs determine the value a market offering possesses in terms of satisfying them, such that the closer the fit between an identified offering and needs, the greater is the value of the offering to a potential customer. Therefore, confronted with an array of offerings, a potential customer generally chooses the option with the greatest (positive) value. That consideration is why customer value is so critical to marketers—it relates directly to customer choice. Of course, actual purchases are subject to various constraints, including availability, the customer's budget, and other factors that might redirect the customer from a preferred option to a secondary one. Thus, market measurements and analysis based on actual behavior may provide different results than those based on perceptions of needs.

Understanding Customer Needs

Understanding needs is central to an understanding of customer value. A need can be characterized by its subject and importance, its temporal aspects, and its information requirements.

Subject and importance of need

The *subject and importance* of a need are the primary bases for a person's perception of that need. Maslow's famous hierarchy of needs vary in terms of their importance to the individual's survival: physiological, security, social, status, and self-actualization. Needs higher up in the hierarchy are more crucial than those farther down, so NEC positioned its early mobile phone as a safety device (especially for women) to place its importance higher in Maslow's hierarchy, often a very effective positioning. And many soap manufacturers emphasize how their product enhances the appearance and beauty of the user (a higher-order need) rather than cleanliness (presumably, a lower-order need), which is the primary function of most soaps.

Customers' processing of such internal and external stimuli generates *motivation* to fulfill the various need states (represented as the solid line in Exhibit 2.1 between behaviors and need states). This motivational connection not only influences customer perceptions of value but also reveals the importance of external communication (e.g., advertising, sales force, sales promotion) in helping position a brand or offering in their minds. From a consumer perspective, the object of a need can be defined by levels ranging from very general (e.g., thirst) to very specific (e.g., thirst to reduce body temperature or replenish lost fluids). A need such as thirst also can be described in terms of physical, social, status, and other dimensions. Physical dimensions might include factors such as sweetness, temperature, alcoholic content, smoothness, carbonation, and flavor; social dimensions recognize that thirst can be satisfied within a family setting, at a restaurant, at a bar, and so on. These factors thus characterize customer needs and the kinds of offerings that would satisfy them: Water may be a highly valued thirst-quencher in an outdoor setting, while beer may be valued more at a bar. Both the characteristics and importance of the specific need serve as the bases for customer judgments of the value of an offering that quenches thirst.

Temporal aspects of need

The *urgency, frequency,* and *duration* of a need define its temporal dimensions. The urgency of a need refers to the perceived amount of time within which the consumer believes the need must be resolved. People who get severe headaches if they do not eat when they feel hungry perceive such a need as urgent. Similarly, an organization that depends on reliable responses to customer telephone calls may deem upgrading or obtaining a new switching system as urgent once it reaches its calling capacity. The frequency of a need pertains to how often the same need occurs. Thirst may occur several times in a day, and an organization's need for a new telephone switching system may occur every five years. Finally, the duration of a need refers to how long the state of tension associated with that need lasts. Hunger or thirst may last for a few minutes before being satisfied, whereas the need for a new telephone switching system may exist for several months before the upgraded system is ready.

Information requirements associated with a need

The *newness, complexity,* and *clarity* of a need help define the customer's information requirements associated with having that need satisfied. New needs generally require more learning to make a purchase decision. Complex needs, with more facets or characteristics, also require more learning, involve longer buying processes, invite consultation with others, and require consumer consideration of more alternatives. The clarity of a need is the certainty with which a customer perceives the need and its facets. When needs are unclear, consumers may engage in a significant amount of information search, including evaluation and trial of the product, if possible, to better define the need and how well alternative offerings satisfy it. Customers with unclear needs also may be more susceptible to the marketing information they receive (e.g., salesperson's advice).

Taken together, the subject/saliency, temporal, and information characteristics of a need help determine both the process the customer uses to satisfy the need and the value of the various options available to satisfy it. For example, the more important and urgent a need, the more the customer values offerings that satisfy it immediately. Customers who require significant information may favor offerings that provide the necessary communication, even if they are not objectively superior. Thus, the value of various options to satisfy a need are driven by customer perceptions of that need, combined with how well marketers can tailor the 4Ps of the marketing mix to satisfy it (with a Product), accommodate the customer's budget (in Price), and make the search process easy (through Promotion and Place).

The factors that describe the type of buying process in Exhibit 2.1 are critical in developing a sound, fact-based marketing program. For example, in organizational buying, the temporal and informational characteristics of needs define the buying situation as a new task, modified rebuy, or straight rebuy. Similarly, when individual consumers buy, the characteristics of their need determine their level of involvement in the purchase decision process. High- (vs. low-) involvement purchases address needs that are important, complex, new, and less clear. Personal customer characteristics influence the purchase process as well; customers who differ in how they perceive the risk associated with various offerings that may satisfy a need consider the value of those offerings differently.

Exhibit 2.1 thus shows that the evaluation process is based largely on the perception of a need and the characteristics of offerings that satisfy that need, which may or may not be based on accurate or objective criteria. For example, the original IBM personal computer (PC) became the market leader soon after its release. A technical assessment of this PC indicated it did not offer the best objective value on the market, but IBM's corporate reputation among business customers was so good at the time that the IBM PC became the risk-free choice. A big factor in the IBM PC's rise to prominence was that "nobody got fired for buying IBM." In effect, perceptions dominated objective value.

This discussion underscores the importance of measuring customer value from all three perspectives: objective (functionality and economic), perceptions (psychology), and behaviors. Following the dotted arrows downward in Exhibit 2.1 reveals the three major measurement approaches for assessing customer value, which correspond to the three motivational states of customers.

APPROACHES TO MEASURING CUSTOMER VALUE

Objective Customer Value: *Should-Do Measures*

Objective value measures attempt to estimate the objective or *true* customer value of a product or service offering. Thus, it is not the *perception* of value by the consumer or other market stakeholders (despite the importance of these perceptions) but rather the objective worth of the product in terms of satisfying the consumer's set of needs. If this value can be determined, it provides an important reference point for a better understanding of how perceptions can enhance or reduce the value estimates that consumers use to make choices.

Firms report using three types of objective customer value measures: internal engineering assessments, indirect survey questions, and field value-in-use assessments. These methods rely on a careful study of consumers' needs, as well as the entire purchase and usage process of available offerings. Although these measurement approaches are applied most widely in B2B marketing situations, they can be extended to consumer marketing as well.

Exhibit 2.2 illustrates several approaches to measuring customer value.

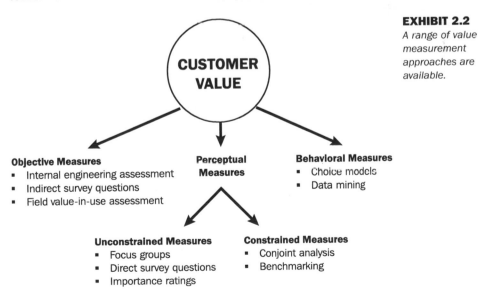

EXHIBIT 2.2
A range of value measurement approaches are available.

Objective Measures
- Internal engineering assessment
- Indirect survey questions
- Field value-in-use assessment

Perceptual Measures

Behavioral Measures
- Choice models
- Data mining

Unconstrained Measures
- Focus groups
- Direct survey questions
- Importance ratings

Constrained Measures
- Conjoint analysis
- Benchmarking

Internal engineering assessment

Some estimates of customer value rely on evaluations by the selling firm's own managers and engineers based on laboratory tests, use of the product by the firm's own employees (alpha tests), or computer simulations. Although the firm might not contact customers directly to ascertain the value they ascribe to the offering, it must obtain a very good understanding of the usage situation and, in B2B markets, the customer organization's production process.

The success of this method depends on how well a firm really understands its customers' buying behavior and usage patterns. Success also depends on how well the firm translates this understanding into economic estimates of customer value. In situations in which a firm cannot interrogate its customers directly or secrecy is crucial, such methods may be the only viable means to assess customer value.

Indirect survey questions

To overcome the limitations of little or no customer input in internal engineering assessments, firms often query customers about the value they place on satisfying a need or resolving a problem. With this approach, salespeople may ask company personnel about the effect of one or more changes in existing offerings on certain aspects of their needs or problems. This technique is indirect, in that the questions focus on the changes rather than the worth of the entire product offering. These answers, typically combined in some way with other known information, can create estimates of the customer value of each change to the product offering.

For example, a potential consumer of inkjet cartridges might simply be asked: "If we could increase the life of the cartridges that you are currently using by 20%, how much would it be worth to you?" The success of this method depends on how well the questions are framed, as well as how willing the customer is to provide valid and reliable responses.

Field value-in-use (VIU) assessment

A third method of customer value assessment requires the customer and the supplier to conduct a joint value assessment. Although most appropriate for B2B markets, it can be used effectively with individual customers. For a supplier's current product, value-in-use is defined as the price that would make a customer indifferent (e.g., economic breakeven) between continuing to use the current product versus switching to another option. For a (radically) new product, VIU is the maximum amount the customer would be willing to pay for the new product, given the extra benefits (beyond those provided by the current product) that it offers.

Value-in-Use (VIU): The price of the product that would equalize the overall costs and benefits to the user of utilizing the product (rather than the incumbent product or other alternative) in the user's specific circumstances.

To arrive at the VIU price, marketers must develop a complete list of cost elements associated with the use of the incumbent product compared with the new product. They then can calculate the values or costs associated with each element to arrive at a complete VIU estimate of the product offering for that application, usually on a cost-per-unit basis. The success of a VIU approach depends on identifying various cost elements, as well as the assumptions the firm uses to estimate costs and, in a B2B setting, its ability to understand the impact of these cost elements on customers' ability to create value for their own end-customers.

Determining the VIU of an offering may be the measure that comes closest to "true" customer value, because it represents what a consumer should be willing to pay. Value-in-use also requires the closest cooperation with the customer to determine how the product will be used. Joint value assessments by the supplier and the customer often reveal surprising and unanticipated cost savings. In this context, a VIU analysis offers the opportunity to "train the customer" to understand the value that may be realized from smart purchase decisions. Many supplier–customer collaborative arrangements have started with a VIU assessment.

EXAMPLE

Suppose a chemical plant uses 200 O-rings to seal valves on pipes that carry corrosive materials. The plant pays $5 for each O-ring and must change them during regular maintenance every two months. However, a new product has twice the resistance to corrosive materials. The supplier of the new product can determine the value-in-use (VIU) of the material according to different methods.

Solution 1:
Annual cost of incumbent product = 200 O-rings × 6 changes per year × $5 per O-ring = $6000.
Thus, the VIU of the new product, which must be changed only half as often, is:

200 O-rings × 3 changes per year × VIU = $6000,
and therefore, VIU = $10.

Solution 2:

The new material allows a longer time between maintenance shutdowns—four months versus two months—and the cost of a shutdown is $5,000. Therefore,

$$\underbrace{\underbrace{200 \times 6 \times 5}_{\substack{\text{Equipment}\\\text{Cost}}} + \underbrace{5000 \times 6}_{\substack{\text{Shutdown}\\\text{Cost}}}}_{\text{Incumbent}} = \underbrace{\underbrace{200 \times 3 \times \text{VIU}}_{\substack{\text{Equipment}\\\text{Cost}}} + \underbrace{5000 \times 3}_{\substack{\text{Shutdown}\\\text{Cost}}}}_{\text{New}}$$

and the new VIU = $35.

For a VIU calculation, it is extremely important to include all costs. For example, the equations in the Example fail to include switching costs, if any, the costs of changes to ordering policies, and new risk factors. Other costs to consider in such VIU calculations include, as just a partial list,

- Purchase costs.
- Fabrication costs.
- Finishing costs.
- Inventory costs.
- Maintenance/service costs.
- Scrap adjustment costs.
- Level-of-requirement adjustment costs.
- Changeover costs.

Multiyear VIU calculations also must include the user's cost of capital.

Clearly, VIU provides a practical tool for understanding customer value in selected markets, especially B2B. The basic steps to follow in conducting a value-in-use analysis are as follows:

1. Specify the product application under consideration and the incumbent product (or comparative alternative).
2. Identify all relevant cost/benefit components of the incumbent (including product, supplier, and switching costs, such as equipment rental and labor costs).
3. Define the criterion to compare equivalent functional benefits (e.g., the value of time saved).
4. Obtain the data necessary to estimate the various cost/benefit elements.
5. Calculate the value-in-use price as the point at which the customer breaks even while receiving equivalent long-run functional benefits compared with the incumbent product.

Although various commercial software packages facilitate VIU analysis, Excel provides an almost ideal platform to develop and test a VIU model with customers.

Perceptual Customer Value: *Plan-to-Do Measures*

Even with limited information, customers can evaluate one or more offerings to satisfy their needs. This form of perceived customer value often differs from an objective assessment of customer value, as we discussed previously. The difference is driven by psychological considerations, such as risk perceptions, and the particular information a customer has about the different offerings. Assessments of perceived customer value generally employ a series of customer measurements that question customers about their perceptions of and preferences for various offerings, as well as the attributes and benefits of these offerings. Such questions often appear as part of a questionnaire in a survey of customers.

As in Exhibit 2.2, perceptual measures can involve both *constrained* and *unconstrained* measures of customer value. Unconstrained measures place few boundaries on customer value assessments (everything can be rated as very important), whereas constrained measures establish parameters for customer value assessments (customers rank alternatives or allocate a fixed number of points across them), which means respondents have to give up gains along some dimensions to obtain gains on others.

Unconstrained question measures

Focus groups. In a focus group, five to ten (potential) customers convene for a several hour discussion with a trained moderator about their perceptions, attitudes, preferences, and usage of a (usually new) product or service. The moderator presents participants with potential product offerings or concepts and asks them about the value or worth of various options to them (or their firm). The goal of a focus group is to obtain a better understanding of the *common or shared* perceptions of a well-defined target group of customers.

For example, suppose a carpet manufacturer wants to know if potential customers will find value in a carpet with customizable color patterns. As a first indication of whether such value exists, the company could ask focus groups of potential carpet customers to discuss and evaluate alternative types of carpet for their homes. At a suitable point in the discussion, each customer might individually write down his or her answer to a question, such as,

"What would you be willing to pay for this carpet with color patterns customized for you (or your firm)?" Customers then discuss their answers, and the moderator probes for information about factors that influenced these valuations.

However, focus groups are limited for assessing customer value. In particular, the potential for "groupthink" can often lead to homogeneous results. A vocal naysayer in the group also may have undue influence on the value estimates. Consequently, focus group results should be viewed as exploratory. Nevertheless, they often provide valuable insights and hypotheses about various components of customer value, as well as the relative ranges of worth of an offering. Perhaps more important, with the results from a focus group, marketers can gain a better understanding of the language that customers use to describe the value they derive from a product category or offering.

Direct survey questions. Because focus group results are exploratory, they often suggest hypotheses about customer value that firms can test with a broader-based market survey. Such a survey usually involves a sample of customers who agree to complete a questionnaire that includes a description of one or more potential product offerings or concepts. Respondents indicate the value or worth of these concepts to them or their firm. A typical question in this kind of value assessment would be, "Given [a stated usage situation], how much more than a standard carpet would you be willing to pay for a carpet with customizable colors?"

As is the case with any survey data, the selected respondents must represent the buying population, have the knowledge to answer direct questions about the value of an offering, and be willing to share that knowledge. The wording of questions, their placement in the survey, whether the survey occurs over the telephone or by mail, and other such considerations all can introduce error into value measurement. Therefore, marketers must follow basic market research data collection procedures carefully to ensure that the resultant data are reliable and valid.

Importance ratings. Importance ratings are among the most popular approaches to measuring customer value. Typically, in a field research survey, respondents receive a set of attributes that describe a product offering and rate (or rank) them according to their importance to the respondent or the firm. Respondents also usually rate (or rank) competitive products on their performance pertaining to each of the attributes, which offers the firm a sense of the customer value provided by competitors.

This highly popular approach is easy to develop and execute and provides a simple, detailed assessment of the importance of the various components of customer value. However, it also has many critical weaknesses. First, respondents might not be able to discriminate effectively among the various benefits, and because the ratings are unconstrained, some respondents will give top scores to all the benefits listed. Second, the approach does not provide an easy means to determine willingness to pay for these important options, because there is no indication of relative value or any trade-off in the level of performance of one benefit in relation to another. Third, such surveys offer no direct link to behavior, because the items that survey respondents rank highly often do not drive choice behavior in the marketplace.

EXAMPLE

Suppose the customizable color carpet focus group identified several product attributes that deliver customer benefits, that is, components of overall customer value. The carpet manufacturer then asks customers to rate the importance of these identified benefits. Consider an example of an importance question for three such attributes:

How important is each of the following benefits of personally customizable color carpet to you? Please circle the number that best represents your rating, where "1" is not at all important, "5" is very important, and the numbers in between represent the range of importance to you.

Allows me to express myself	1	2	3	4	5
Easy to mix and match designs	1	2	3	4	5
Will be attractive to my friends	1	2	3	4	5

EXAMPLE

In a study of buying behavior for industrial heating and cooling equipment, all respondents, including technicians who worked with the systems (and thus were important buying center members) rated "reliability" as a critical buying criterion. However, closer inspection showed that those technicians strongly preferred newer technologies— state-of-the-art equipment—that they themselves rated as unreliable. They answered the survey in a way they thought was best for the company, which conflicted with their need for personal job satisfaction, which was not included in the survey. As it turns out, they were excited and challenged by the opportunity to work with new technologies—a need that drove their overall preference and product valuation.

Constrained question measures

Conjoint analysis. Conjoint analysis, one of the most widely used customer value measurement approaches, employs a field research survey to ask respondents to provide their overall ratings for each of a set of potential offerings. A set of attribute options or features describes each offering, and the levels of these options vary systematically. Then, statistical analyses decompose these resultant ratings into the value (partworth) that the respondent attributes to each option. The partworth values can be recombined to describe new product offerings and thereby estimate the total customer value of many possible offerings, such that each option of each attribute receives a valuation for each customer studied.

Conjoint analysis appears most frequently in new product development processes; we provide a more detailed explanation and illustration of this approach in Chapter 6.

Benchmarking. In a field research survey, respondents receive descriptions of a product offering that represents the best available competitive product or service, which thus serves as a benchmark. Respondents indicate how much more they (or their firm) would be willing to pay for added product attributes or features to this benchmark offering. Similarly, they might indicate how much less they would expect to pay if selected attributes or features disappeared from the offering.

In a simplistic (and nonrigorous way), the benchmarking approach attempts to determine consumers' willingness to pay for each attribute or feature. These valuations can be combined, like partworths in conjoint analysis, to reveal the worth of the entire product concept or offering, as it compares to the benchmark competitor. Although benchmarking is easier to implement than conjoint analysis, it lacks rigor for systematically examining trade-offs among attributes.

Behavioral Customer Value: *Have-Done Measures*

A major limitation of objective and perceived customer value measures is that they represent estimates based on information obtained or judgments made *before* a purchase. Thus, they lack the credibility associated with measures derived from actual observations of purchase behavior. Therefore, measures of behavioral customer value use observations of actual past consumer behavior as a basis for estimating value.

Choice models. Choice models use past behavior (often along with associated attribute ratings) to infer or estimate the value (or utilities) of product characteristics that might best explain or predict actual behavior.

Although marketers can ask people about what they claim they would do, actual purchase behavior, when appropriately analyzed with choice models, can provide even greater insight into the true drivers of behavior—the customer values we seek to measure herein. In recent years, the increasing availability of retail scanner data, Internet transaction data, and other customer purchase databases have provided new opportunities to use choice models to infer customer values.

A good way to understand choice models is to contrast them with survey-based perceived measures of value. Standard survey methods try to infer value (measured with importance weights) through direct questioning (as in the color carpeting example). However, as we discussed previously, the direct measurement approach might not represent true, underlying value. With choice models, firms can observe choices and infer the value (again, measured as importance weights) that best explains those choices. Therefore, the output of a choice model is an estimate of importance weights, along with the purchase probabilities of each market alternative for each customer.

A simple and powerful choice model, the multinomial logit model states that a customer's purchase probability for brand A equals the (weighted) utility of A divided by the sum of the customer's utilities for alternative brands:

$$\text{Purchase probability (A)} = \text{Utility of A/Sum of utilities of all alternatives.}$$

To obtain the utility of product option A (and its alternatives), the equation uses various drivers (e.g., evaluations of product attributes) of customer value for product A, as well as a random component that accounts for unknown factors that may influence utility and, therefore, choice. Within some general conditions, the logit model thus provides the revealed importance weights of the attributes, and we interpret these weights just as we interpret regression coefficients.

EXAMPLE

To illustrate these concepts, we use data from the ABB Electric case. ABB Electric (brand A), a manufacturer of transformers and power conditioning units, had three major competitors: General Electric (brand B), Westinghouse (brand C), and McGraw Edison (brand D). From each of its customers, ABB collected information about the brand they had bought last, as well as their perceptions of ABB and its three competitors using key attributes such as price, energy loss, and maintenance. The data describing four such customers appear in Exhibit 2.3, and Exhibit 2.4 displays the output of the logit model estimation, with importance weights. Issues such as price and warranty achieve the highest t-statistics (greater than $|3|$), which indicates they are most important in driving choice. In contrast, the brand image variables represented by the variables const1, const2, and const3 have low t-statistics. Therefore, the selected attributes do a good job of capturing the choice drivers in this market; if not, some "preference drivers" would remain, and the brand image variables would have higher t-statistics. In chapter 3, we describe how such a model could be used for segmentation.

EXHIBIT 2.3

Choice-based segmentation data for an ABB-type analysis. Thus, for example, Customer 1 has an annual purchase volume of $761,000, resides in district 1, bought brand B last, and rates price levels as 6, 6, 6, and 5 (on a seven-point scale) for brands A, B, C, and D, respectively.

Customer Attitude and Choice Data (Basis)

Brand	Cust ID	Purch Vol	District	Choice	Price	Energy Loss	Maint	Warranty	Spare Parts	Ease Install	Prob Solv	Quality
A	1	$761	1	0	6	6	7	6	6	5	7	5
B				1	6	6	6	7	9	9	7	5
C				0	6	5	7	5	3	4	7	6
D				0	5	5	6	7	8	2	6	5
A	2	$627	1	0	3	4	5	4	4	5	6	4
B				0	3	4	5	4	7	3	5	5
C				0	4	5	5	5	5	7	6	4
D				1	4	5	6	5	4	5	5	6
A	3	$643	2	1	6	6	7	7	6	7	7	6
B				0	5	6	7	7	5	6	8	6
C				0	5	6	7	5	5	8	6	5
D				0	6	5	5	4	2	8	6	5
A	4	$562	3	0	6	6	5	5	4	5	5	5
B				0	5	5	6	5	4	6	7	5
C				0	4	4	5	4	6	7	5	3
D				1	4	4	6	7	7	8	7	5

Logit models take advantage of actual customer choices to infer what customers value. They follow reasonable assumptions about the nature of the choice process, recognize and measure error, and try to explain as much behavior as possible. A wide variety of software (including that available on our website) can run such models. In addition, logit models provide explicit diagnostic measures (e.g., weights) that help marketers understand the factors that contribute to customer value.

Estimated Parameters - Logit Model

	Coefficient	Standard Error	T-statistic
Price	2.1806	0.5866	3.7175
Energy Loss	2.6556	0.6737	3.9418
Maintenance	0.5937	0.4370	1.3585
Warranty	1.1407	0.3310	3.4463
Spare Parts	-0.1326	0.2176	-0.6096
Ease of Install	0.5200	0.1729	3.0081
Problem Solver	2.0322	0.5497	3.6971
Quality	2.6394	0.6877	3.8378
Const-1	-0.1238	0.6785	-0.1824
Const-2	-0.6712	0.7194	-0.9330
Const-3	-0.6872	0.7150	-0.9611
Baseline	0.0000	NA	NA

EXHIBIT 2.4
Output of logit choice model, showing (according to the t-statistics) that the most important drivers of choice are price, energy loss, warranty, ease of installation, problem solving, and quality; maintenance and availability of spare parts are not as important.

However, logit choice models suffer the disadvantage of statistical difficulty in terms of estimating a model separately for each person. Consequently, many applications pool data from respondents to obtain sufficient data to obtain reliable estimates of importance weights. Modelers often must pre-segment customers into groups that likely have similar weights, even if their perceptions of brand alternatives differ, to develop groups of sufficient size for estimation. This a priori segmentation may be based on factors such as the strength of consumers' preferences for suppliers, consumers' knowledge base, type of choice situation, the nature of the underlying customer need, or, more frequently, simply company size and industry type. (There are also latent class choice models, where the software simultaneously determines the number of market segments, the membership in those segments and the importance weights for attributes in each segment—see a description of our software at decisionpro.biz.)

Data mining. Many organizations keep extensive records of customer purchases in a form that lends itself to statistical analysis. Sometimes these data can be cross-matched with other data pertaining to customer characteristics that come from commercial sources, channel partners, or information provided when the customer opened an account with the organization. By updating these data periodically, organizations can analyze the information to determine segments according to customer profitability, amount spent, lifetime value, the range of products and services acquired, and so forth. This type of customer analysis usually goes under the name of data mining. Companies like American Express find that segmenting their customer databases provides a better understanding of customer purchase patterns and often highlights opportunities for cross-selling, up-selling, and other marketing initiatives.

Analyzing current customers, however, provides only a partial picture of a market structure. This approach ignores non-customers who may differ systematically from customers but also may represent a significant source of potential growth. These non-customers can provide useful insights into shortcomings of the organization's products, services, and marketing. In addition, many customers buy a portfolio of products and services from competing suppliers, so an organization's internal database may not capture complete purchase histories. Finally, data mining indicates what has happened but rarely can explain why or suggest what to do about it. Given the limited picture that internal data provide about market segments, data mining best serves as an exploratory or supplementary customer value analysis method.

EXHIBIT 2.5

Comparison of various customer value assessment approaches.

Criterion	Objective Value Measures	Behavioral Value Measures	Perceived Value Measures	
			Constrained	Uncon- strained
Amount of customer information needed	High	Low	Medium	Low
Cost	Very high per respondent	Medium	High	Low
Insight	Very High	Medium	High	Low
Predictive of behavior	High	Moderate	Moderate	Low
Analysis timeframe	Long	Medium	Long/ Medium	Short
Number of customers	Low	High	Medium*	Any
Availability of past purchase data	Not necessary	Needed	Not necessary	Not necessary
Good in dynamic/ changing markets	Yes	No	Partly*	Partly*
Appropriate for lead users	Yes	No	Yes	No

* If it is possible to measure future customer behavior reliably on the basis of stated perceptions, preferences, or intent.

Comparison of Customer Value Measurement Approaches

Exhibit 2.5 compares the three approaches to customer value measurement on the basis of the criteria necessary for segmenting markets. Objective value measures require more customer information than do the other measures, whereas behavioral and unconstrained measures require far less customer information. These less information-intensive measures are cheaper to administer, but they provide less customer insight. In general, you get what you pay for in terms of the ability to predict customer behavior, so objective measures tend to produce the most accurate estimates of value. Measures of actual behavior are moderately effective in predicting future behavior (at least when the future marketplace is not too different from current conditions) because the predictions are based on actual behavior and not perceptions or preferences. Constrained perceived value measures also provide moderately effective predictions because of the trade-offs customers make in the process of providing such data.

The insights obtained from behavior- and preference-based value assessment methods differ substantially. Behavior-based methods implicitly embed several unknown or unknowable constraints that influence customer choice (e.g., what else was available? Who else was present? How urgent was the need?), and such constraints may not exist in the future. In contrast, perception-based approaches provide insights into choices that consumers are likely to make in an ideal situation. For example, if a customer buys a blue car, choice-based methods would assign a higher inferred weight to the color blue than to silver. However, the customer may actually prefer silver and only settled on a blue car because there were no silver cars on the dealer's lot.

The time needed to collect and analyze data from these value measures also varies considerably, such that objective measures take longer than unconstrained measures. Due to their modeling requirements, constrained approaches also demand considerable analytical time to understand and interpret the results.

Relative to the others, objective value measures need fewer customers for an analysis, whereas choice models (behavioral measures) require more customer respondents. Perceived measures vary in terms of the number of customers required, depending on the problem at hand and how well customers reliably report how they will ultimately behave. Behavioral measures are the only ones that are based on historical purchase data.

Objective value measures are particularly valuable in dynamic markets; they put the firm in direct contact with critical customers who provide current measures of value-in-use. In such markets, behavioral measures are much less valuable because they depend on historical data, which may not extend accurately to the future. Perceived value measures can be useful in dynamic markets if the measurement approaches prompt customers to respond in such a way that what they say they will do corresponds with their actual future behaviors. Appropriate measurement approaches thus might include incentives to align customers' stated intentions with actual behavior and should provide adequate descriptions of future conditions, developed from, for example, a scenario analysis (see Chapter 5).

Finally, measures vary according to their appropriateness for lead users, or those customers whose needs appear in advance of those of the rest of the market and whose behaviors therefore can forecast moves in the marketplace. These customers—trendsetters of a sort—often find their own solutions to problems and are especially important in markets in which most customers simply cannot articulate their needs and problems. Therefore, measures based on VIU and constrained approaches are most appropriate for lead users, whereas behavioral measures, which are based on historical data, are not particularly useful, and unconstrained measures fail to reveal the important trade-offs necessary for good value estimates.

Our review of the various measurement approaches thus suggests that no single measure of customer value works best in every circumstance. Good measurement practice requires marketers to employ several of the measurement procedures discussed and then evaluate them for potential convergence.

VALUING CUSTOMERS AND CUSTOMER LIFETIME VALUE

The lifetime value of a customer generally equals the total profit a firm can expect to earn from that customer during the time the firm continues to maintain an ongoing relationship with the customer. These profits include both transactions between the customer and the firm and referrals and other indirect sources of profit that can be attributed to a specific customer. The growing emphasis on building long-term customer relationships, especially in industries such as financial services, airlines, telecommunications, and B2B markets, indicates an ever-increasing need for firms to understand the overall value of customers, not just the revenue or profit derived from them in specific transactions.

The growing availability of CRM (customer relationship management) systems and other customer databases permits marketers to track and record the behaviors of individual customers in far more detail than ever before. The resulting data enable firms to discriminate among customer types and determine their relative lifetime value. Although this capability has been called a variety of names, such as customer equity and customer profitability analysis, it is most commonly referred to as a customer lifetime value (CLV) assessment. In this section, we sketch several key ideas behind CLV at the individual customer level and extend them to the concept of the customer portfolio.

Because CLV aims to assess the net profit or loss of a specific customer over that customer's lifetime, it must assess cash flows (usually positive) based on what the customer buys (and the gross profitability of those purchases), less the costs of acquiring, selling to, and servicing that customer. To compute these cash flow measurements accurately, firms need information about the specific times at which they invested in the customer (e.g., promotional offers), the timing of the customer's response (e.g., purchase), and the uncertainty or volatility of that response. Such information is critical for establishing the links between marketing actions and customer responses.

Blattberg and Deighton (1996, p. 137–38) give the following prescription:

First, measure each customer's expected contribution toward offsetting the company's fixed costs over the expected life of that customer. Then discount the expected contribution to a net present value at the company's target rate of return for marketing investments.

In other words, this basic prescription says:

$$CLV = (R_1 - C_1) + (R_2 - C_2) \times d + \ldots + (R_n - C_n) \times d^{n-1},$$

where:
- R_1 is the revenue from this customer in period 1,
- C_1 is the cost to acquire or serve this customer in period 1, and
- $d = 1/(1 + r)$, where r is the discount rate and n is the anticipated lifetime of the customer.

Although simple to explain, this formula makes several assumptions that can limit its direct applicability. Consider Exhibit 2.6, which highlights a limitation and important extension of this formula. Specifically, it identifies the crucial role that customer loyalty plays in the CLV calculation. Marketing investments (e.g., in communications, directly in the form of loyalty programs) can lower the cost to serve a customer, because more loyal customers require fewer marketing investments to retain their business. Even more crucially, the exhibit suggests that more loyal customers provide less variable revenue flows.

EXHIBIT 2.6

Links between the economic value of a customer and customer loyalty. Loyalty typically increases the volume of purchases and decreases the volatility associated with those purchases.

Economic Lifetime Value Calculation

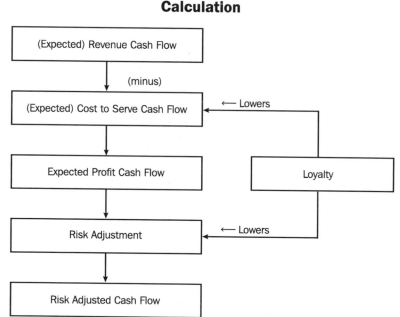

Just as financial markets place less value on more risky investments by discounting their future expected returns, and just as lower rated or junk bonds require higher premiums (or interest rates), revenues from more risky customers should be discounted at a higher discount rate than those from steadier, more loyal customers. Thus, an appropriate application of the preceding formula requires that customers be classified into different loyalty groups, with lower discount rates applied to the more loyal or stable customers. Varying the discount rate enables firms to determine the value they receive from a more loyal customer, not only in the form of higher (expected) sales but also in terms of lower sales volatility.

Customers and prospects vary in many other ways that make the application of the simple formula challenging. For example, the formula implies that all customers buy with the same frequency, but customers actually buy at their own discretion; some buy much more frequently (or in higher quantities) than others. Therefore, this formula should be considered customer or segment specific and, similar to customer- and segment-specific discount rates, be applied differently to different customer groups.

Let us elaborate. Suppose that a customer buys in period 1, and gross revenue from that customer equals R_1. Assume R_2 is the amount the customer will buy in period 2, given marketing expenditure C_2 AND that the customer bought R_1 in period 1. Further, suppose that we can assess the value p_2, or the likelihood of retaining this customer in period 2, given sales of R_1 in period 1 and marketing expenditures of C_2, C_1, and all previous expenditures. Then, the formula expands to:

$$CLV = (p_1 \times R_1 - C_1) + (p_2 \times R_2 - C_2) \times d + \ldots \\ + (p_n \times R_n - C_n) \times d^{n-1}.$$

Much research has focused on the determinants and calculation of the likelihoods, p_1, p_2, ..., p_n. For example, marketing expenditures, C_1, C_2, ..., C_n, are incurred to both acquire and retain customers, and the p's represent loyalty or retention, factors influenced by consumer experience with the product, competitor actions, special considerations offered that customer (e.g., membership in loyalty programs), and so forth. If buyers are grouped by frequency (frequent versus occasional buyers), the formula works similarly, but the time interval has a different interpretation for each group.

As another example, consider a rough calculation based on specific assumptions (Ofek 2002). Suppose R and C are constant across periods and that there is an initial acquisition cost, A, associated with inducing a customer to buy for the first time. If we assume a long (infinite) economic life, the formula reduces to:

$$CLV = (R - C)/(1 - p + r) - A.$$

Thus, if it costs \$17.50 to acquire a customer (A) and \$6.00 to support and service that customer in each period (C), the gross profit revenue stream from the customer is \$20 in each period (R), and the discount rate of 10% (r = .10) and retention rate of

$A = 17.50$

$R = 20$
$C = 6$
$r = 0.10$
$p = 0.75$

75% (p = .75) indicates that the lifetime value of this customer is $22.50.

To see how the process plays out over time, let's assume for simplicity that customers can be in one of two categories or states: active or inactive. If customers are active, they have a 75% chance of remaining active in the next period, and a 25% chance of becoming inactive. If the customers are inactive, they will have a 100% chance of remaining so. This information can be summarized by a simple *transition* matrix (Exhibit 2.7):

EXHIBIT 2.7

Example of simple two state transition matrix for customers.

	Active	**Inactive**
Active	75%	25%
Inactive	0%	100%

The inactive category means that once customers enter this state, they never leave it.

When we compute the evolution of the customer base over 15 periods, we obtain the following:

1. In period 1 all customers are active (100%), all generating $14 ($20-$6) in profit margin on average. The discount rate is $(1/(1+.1))=.91$. Hence, $14 in that period is worth $12.70 today (period 0).
2. In period 2, 25% of the customers become inactive, and the discount rate is equal to $(1/(1+.1))^2=.83$. There are 25% fewer customers, and they generate $8.70 each in today's dollars.
3. Etc.

After many periods, customers will not generate any additional value: most of them will be inactive (98% after 15 periods), and the value generated by the few customers still active will be heavily discounted ($1 by period 15 will only be worth $0.24 in today's dollars). The cumulative value of a customer will evolve toward $40 (see Exhibit 2.8). After subtracting the customer acquisition costs, we get the $22.50 figure from above.

The formula $(CLV = (R - C)/(1 - p + r) - A)$ is a special case of a more general CLV model:

1. The number of active customers in period 1 is known in advance, and is equal to 100%. This assumption may only be valid in a contractual setting (like a cell phone contract), where the number of paying customers can be foreseen

based on the number of contracts signed. In a transactional setting, e.g., a department store, where the firm does not know in advance how many customers will buy next period, the number of active customers in period 1 is usually estimated as number of current customers after a pass through the transition matrix. In the example above, it would begin at 75%.

2. The formula above summarizes a Markov process (where the likelihood of moving from one state to the next is known) with only two states: active and inactive. The model can be extended to more classes with different characteristics.

Period	1	2	3	4	5	6	7
Active	100%	75%	56%	42%	32%	24%	18%
Discount	0.91	0.83	0.75	0.68	0.62	0.56	0.51
Margin	$12.70	$8.70	$5.90	$4.00	$2.80	$1.90	$1.30
Cumulated	$12.70	$21.40	$27.30	$31.40	$34.10	$36.00	$37.30

Period	8	9	10	11	12	13	14	15
Active	13%	10%	8%	6%	4%	3%	2%	2%
Discount	0.47	0.42	0.39	0.35	0.32	0.29	0.26	0.24
Margin	$0.90	$0.60	$0.40	$0.30	$0.20	$0.10	$0.10	$0.10
Cumulated	$38.10	$38.70	$39.10	$39.40	$39.60	$39.70	$39.80	$39.90

EXHIBIT 2.8
The evolution of the value of customers over 15 periods using the transition matrix in Exhibit 2.7.

Consider a more general case where the firm classifies customers into four possible states: high-value customers (generating $20 of net margin, R - C, each period), low-value customers ($6 per period), inactive customers (no revenue, but with some probability of becoming active again in the future), and permanently inactive customers (no revenue).

Assume the associated transition matrix is as in Exhibit 2.9. In that exhibit, a high-value customer has a 60% chance of remaining in the same state, 20% of becoming a low-value customer, and 20% of becoming inactive. Note that each row sums up to 100%.

Based on these figures, and assuming a *transactional setting*, what is the CLV of a customer currently classified as a high-value customer (and assuming no acquisition cost)?

Note that in period 1, a high-value customer has a 60% chance or remaining high-value, and generate $20; has a 20% chance of becoming low-value, and generate $6; and has a 20% of generating no revenue whatsoever. The expected margin from that customer is ($20 × .60) + ($6 × .20) = $13.20, which translates into $12 of today's dollars (after applying a discount factor of 10%). As shown in Exhibit 2.10, that customer's CLV will evolve toward $44.20 in the long run and will be $43.40 after 15 periods.

EXHIBIT 2.9

An example of a four-state customer transition matrix.

	High value customer	Low value customer	Inactive customer	Permanently inactive
High value customer	60%	20%	20%	0%
Low value customer	30%	40%	30%	0%
Inactive customer	5%	15%	30%	50%
Permanently inactive	0%	0%	0%	100%

EXHIBIT 2.10

The evolution of the value of customers over 15 periods using the transition matrix in Exhibit 2.9.

Period	Now	1	2	3	4	5	6	7
High value	100%	60%	43%	34%	28%	23%	20%	17%
Low value		20%	23%	21%	19%	16%	14%	12%
Inactive		20%	24%	23%	20%	17%	15%	12%
Permanently inactive		0%	10%	22%	33%	43%	52%	59%
Discount		0.91	0.83	0.75	0.68	0.62	0.56	0.51
Margin		$12.00	$7.90	$5.70	$4.30	$3.30	$2.50	$1.90
Cumulated		$12.00	$19.90	$25.60	$29.90	$33.20	$35.80	$37.70

Period	8	9	10	11	12	13	14	15
High value	14%	12%	10%	9%	7%	6%	5%	4%
Low value	10%	8%	7%	6%	5%	4%	4%	3%
Inactive	11%	9%	8%	6%	5%	5%	4%	3%
Permanently inactive	66%	71%	75%	79%	82%	85%	87%	89%
Discount	0.47	0.42	0.39	0.35	0.32	0.29	0.26	0.24
Margin	$1.50	$1.20	$0.90	$0.70	$0.50	$0.40	$0.30	$0.20
Cumulated	$39.20	$40.40	$41.30	$41.90	$42.50	$42.90	$43.20	$43.40

For the above calculations, we assume that the transition matrix will remain constant over time. That assumption normally gives a pretty good approximation to what happens in many markets but can also be badly violated, leading to misleading results under circumstances like the following:

- Aggressive marketing campaigns (by the firm or competitors) in the past lead to atypical transition rates.
- The mix of customers changes over time, leading to customers switching to different segments.
- New competitors, products, prices, technologies, induce changing dynamics in the marketplace.

Marketing managers go to great lengths to influence the transition probabilities. For example, they might attempt to reduce churn or attrition rates (decrease the likelihood a customer will become inactive), or to transition customers toward higher-value states or segments. For an example, see Tirenni et al. (2007) for a description of a customer lifetime management program that IBM implemented at Finnair.

Various extensions of the basic CLV model address the variability of purchase intervals and purchase quantities across customers and groups, as well as drivers of acquisition and retention rates. Regardless of the exact formula used, a CLV analysis sorts current customers and prospects according to their lifetime value. In most cases, firms find that the 80–20 rule applies to their customer database, such that 20% of the customers contribute to 80% of the total lifetime value of the entire customer database. In such situations, companies often can do a much better job of allocating marketing resources by ignoring conventional wisdom, such as recommendations to (1) treat all customers equally, (2) spend more marketing resources on more valuable customers, or (3) focus on customers who are easier to reach. After a CLV analysis, a firm may develop guidelines for determining:

- Which customers to "fire" because they are generally unprofitable over time, which means it is best to allocate no marketing effort to them.
- How to reward customers, possibly by raising p (the retention likelihood) by incurring higher costs (C) or foregoing some revenue (R).
- Which win-back campaigns to run to regain customers who are not irretrievably lost, and whether the firm is better off targeting new prospects or attempting to win back prior customers.

- How to induce up- or cross-selling by encouraging a customer to purchase more of the focal product or buy other related products.

The discussion thus far has focused on the direct, long-term economic value of a customer or a set of customers, which implies the critical assumption that it is possible to draw an economic boundary around a customer. However, satisfied customers recommend the firm to others, which leads to increased sales, and dissatisfied customers actively dissuade others and thereby diminish sales. In this sense, the boundary is flexible, because customers offer a variety of indirect sources of value.

EXAMPLE

Consider NEUROMetrix (www.neurometrix.com), a developer of software and hardware used to support medical diagnostic testing. The company wants to grow its business by applying the CLV concept to its customer and prospect base (namely, physicians, including general practitioners, internists, orthopedic surgeons, and neurologists). After it prioritizes its customers on the basis of their computed CLV, the firm discovers it might need to "fire" some of the accounts that the marketing staff finds very valuable. However, NEUROMetrix staff identifies several indirect values:

- *Reference accounts:* These prestige, high-credibility accounts represent thought leaders in the medical field and provide the firm with credibility, which makes sales to other physicians easier.
- *Referral accounts:* These accounts provide high-quality leads because of their favorable prior experience with the product. When a prospect asks a salesperson for a reference, the firm can be confident these accounts will offer a strong recommendation, which again makes the sales process easier.
- *Learning accounts:* These accounts are willing to act as guinea pigs or beta testers for new offerings, testing them out and giving valuable feedback and suggestions prior to full market launches.
- *Innovation accounts:* Mostly university-based physicians, these accounts help the firm create and define new offerings and thus act almost like an external R&D team.

For NEUROMetrix, a direct CLV calculation might return negative economic values for any of these types of accounts, but because of their other values, which go beyond direct transactions, the firm should consider investing in them and reaping indirect benefits.

Although formal methods to assess noneconomic customer and relationship values are beyond the scope of our discussion, we summarize the core ideas in Exhibit 2.11. The idea is simple: Customers or customer segments offer two types of values to a firm—direct economic value (standard CLV) and a more difficult to quantify relationship value, which consists of the benefits derived from the type of accounts described in the NEUROMetrix example.

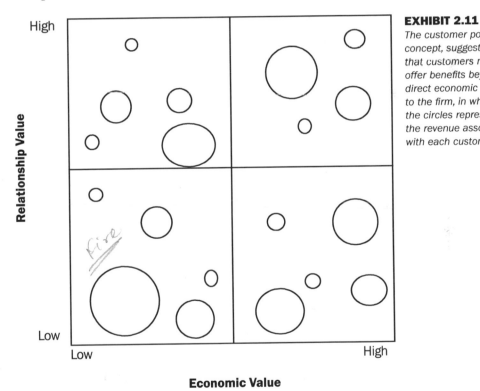

EXHIBIT 2.11
The customer portfolio concept, suggesting that customers may offer benefits beyond a direct economic benefit to the firm, in which the circles represent the revenue associated with each customer.

According to this view of the portfolio of customers, a firm should
- Nurture customers with high economic value and either high or low relationship value (high CLV customers).
- Assess the costs and benefits of those customers with low or negative economic value but high relationship value.

- Consider firing those customers with low economic and low relationship value.

In practice, a firm rarely finds many customers who score high on both relationship and economic values; if found, these customers may be the most valuable assets that a firm could have and should be treated accordingly.

The CLV concept has been extended to include customer referral value (CRV), customer influence value (CIV), and customer knowledge value (CKV). It is generally good to start with economic value as a foundation and then build upon that foundation to construct a more complete picture of the total value that a customer brings to the organization in both the short and the long run (Kumar 2008).

SUMMARY

In this chapter, we define customer value as what a customer exchanges for an offering to satisfy a particular need. We then explain that value is driven by customer needs, which influence the purchase decision process, which in turn provides motivation to move through the various states of need fulfillment. Marketing instruments, such as price, quality, communication, and positioning, can also influence the purchase process. Because our view of value is defined at the individual level, we require measures of individual customer value to identify segments of consumers that allow for a more focused marketing strategy.

We also discuss three primary measures of customer value that parallel the conceptual process of how needs are identified and satisfied: objective value, perceived value, and behavioral value. Our overview of various value measurement approaches includes four popular procedures used in practice: value-in-use analysis, conjoint analysis, choice models and Markov chain analysis. One or more of these customer value assessment procedures should be the vital ingredient in any Marketing Engineering process.

Finally, this chapter introduces the concept of customer lifetime value and extends it to include a number of benefits that extend beyond the revenues derived directly from that customer. We urge firms to consider using both direct financial measures as well as indirect measures of value when considering their portfolio of customers and prospects.

CHAPTER 3

Segmentation and Targeting[1]

Markets are heterogeneous. Customers differ in their values, needs, wants, constraints, beliefs, and incentives to act. Products (or more generally, offerings) compete to satisfy the needs and wants of customers. By segmenting their markets, firms can better understand their customers and target their marketing efforts efficiently and effectively. Through segmentation, a firm aims for a happy middle ground, where it does not rely on a common marketing program for all customers, nor does it incur the high costs of developing a unique program for each customer. Segmentation thus provides the foundation needed to address a core strategic issue facing all companies: Which markets or customer groups should we serve?

Two definitions are critical to the concept of segmentation: *market segment* and *market segmentation*.

Customers within a market segment are all looking for the offering to provide the same types of benefits or solutions to their problems, or they respond in a similar way to a company's marketing communications.

Market segmentation is a business process that enables a firm to evaluate the attractiveness of each group (segment) and select those segments that it is able to serve effectively and profitably.

Three fundamental factors provide the conditions that create the opportunity for a firm to segment a market successfully. First, and most crucial, is the heterogeneity of customer needs and

Market segment: *A group of actual or potential customers who can be expected to respond in a similar way to a product or service offering.*

Market segmentation: *The business process of finding groups of customers who are similar on some specific criterion of relevance to the firm's strategic context, such as needs, how they value an offering, behaviors, age, sex, or income, and differ from customers in different groups on those criteria.*

---

[1] *We are indebted to Grahame Dowling and Robert Thomas for their contributions to this chapter.*

wants. When customers are heterogeneous, some actively seek and pay a premium for products and services that better meet their needs and wants. Second, though customers may be heterogeneous, they must cluster into specific groups within which members' needs are more similar to those of other customers in that group than they are to the needs of customers in other groups. Third, the overall costs of serving customers in a segment must be equal to or less than the prices they are willing to pay, even if those costs are higher than the costs of serving an average customer. When customer needs differ or the costs of serving different types of customers vary substantially, a firm that does not segment its market presents its competitors with an excellent opportunity to enter its markets.

At one extreme, a firm could think of each customer as a unique market segment, or a segment of one. The business and production processes of most companies make it too costly to serve such small segments, and so companies strike a balance between the cost of serving a segment and the value that customers get from their offerings. Products and services designed to fit the needs of particular customers provide more customer value than do products that fit average needs. Because the seller provides this extra customer value, it may be able to charge a higher price for the more customized products; it also may reduce competitive pressures by making it more difficult for other manufacturers to tailor better offerings to meet the segment's needs.

THE SEGMENTATION, TARGETING, AND POSITIONING APPROACH

Segmentation is best viewed as the first step in the three-step process of segmentation, targeting, and positioning (STP). Segmentation groups customers with similar wants, needs, and responses; targeting determines which groups a firm should try to serve (and how); and positioning addresses how well the firm's offering competes with other offerings in the targeted segment. We address the first two steps in this chapter and describe positioning in the next.

The benefits of following the STP process are summarized in Exhibit 3.1 and include the following:

- By focusing marketing resources to better meet the needs of customers, a firm can profitably deliver more value to those customers.

- Customers who perceive and realize more value from a specific brand will develop a stronger preference for it than for competing brands.
- As a firm continues to provide good value to its customers, those customers become loyal to its brands and tend to repeat their purchases and communicate their favorable experiences to other potential customers.
- Strong brand loyalty can lead to increased market share and provide a barrier to competition.
- Strong brand loyalty requires fewer marketing resources over time to maintain market share.

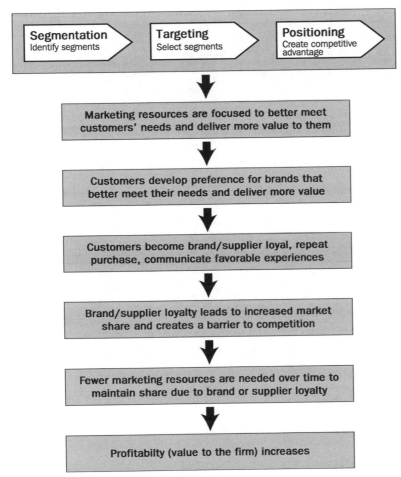

EXHIBIT 3.1
How STP adds value to a firm.

In essence, STP marketing offers the promise of a better fit between a company's offering to a customer and what the customer really values. Over the past couple of decades, General Motors has struggled to achieve a good fit between many of its cars and what U.S. customers want, causing it to lose substantial market share to Japanese brands. Without constant vigilance, such a lack of external fit is not uncommon. For example, a 25-year-old in a focus group highlighted the lack of her external fit with many financial services companies when she complained, "Why should I buy an investment product that can't be modified as my life changes?"

Firms use segmentation and the STP process to address a wide variety of strategic and tactical challenges (e.g., loss of market share, poor customer response to new product). In each case, they must first understand the potential responses of each market segment to proposed strategies (e.g., price changes, new product offerings, promotional plans) and apply them, possibly differently, to each segment.

EXAMPLE

Marks & Spencer has dominated the United Kingdom's retail landscape for decades. However, between 1999 and 2001, the company experienced substantial declines in its clothing sales (to the tune of about £1 billion) because it had not kept up with changing customer needs in women's clothing. To reverse its declining sales, the company began fine-tuning its stores on the basis of a segmentation study completed during 2001–02. The company had a rich and extensive customer database, which, in combination with external data sources (census, demographic, and national panel data), provided it with the information needed to undertake a major segmentation study using cluster and discriminant analysis. Using the results of this study, the company identified 11 core customer segments and applied this information effectively in its corporate branding, product launches, store merchandising, marketing and communication activities, and operational decisions. The segmentation strategy paid off. Marks & Spencer reported increased market share in women's clothing in 2002, and its launch of the Per Una fashion line helped revive its sales. Segmentation continues to be a key strategy for the company. For 2005–06, its women's wear market share increased from 9.4% to 10.5% as a result of the company's continuing refinement of its branding and segmentation strategies and has seen continued growth since, to 11.7% in 2011.
Source: Company website and annual report; SAS Institute.

Often, technology-based companies develop new capabilities and try to determine if segments of customers have needs that match those capabilities. This approach to product development (sometimes referred to as "tossing it over the wall to marketing") can be viewed as TSP rather than STP: The needs that the product or technology might satisfy have been preselected, so the second step in the process is to find one or more segments with such needs. Although we develop our discussion here in STP terms, bear in mind the more general nature of the concept as well.

Some management problems, both strategic and tactical, addressed by segmentation studies include the following:

- Which new product concepts evoke the highest respondent interest, and how do evaluations of these concepts differ according to segments, such as heavy versus light users of the product or users versus nonusers of the company's brand?

- In terms of target markets for a product, how do heavy and light users differ in their demographic and socioeconomic characteristics, attitudes, and product use characteristics?

- Would it be beneficial to segment the potential customers of new products on the basis of their price sensitivity (or other benefits sought)? What concept evaluations, attitudes, or product use, demographic, and other background characteristics do the various price-sensitive segments hold?

SEGMENTATION ANALYSIS

To answer management questions such as the above, we propose a Marketing Engineering segmentation model. The market segments identified by the model ideally satisfy three conditions: *homogeneity/heterogeneity*, *parsimony*, and *accessibility*.

Although the goal of any segmentation is to understand the heterogeneity of the market, no segmentation is perfect. Therefore, members of different segments frequently show considerable overlap in their responses to marketing variables. In fact, segmentation analyses will rarely result in a unique solution.

For a segmentation study to be useful, it should result in a manageable number of target segments (often between three and eight), each of a substantial size. It is difficult for most companies to manage more than a few distinct segments. United Airlines, for example, has identified five segments of current customers with different needs on the basis of the miles they travel on United— 1K, Premier Platinum, Premier Gold, Premium Silver, and all others—and created separate programs (e.g., upgrade eligibility, preferential access to seats) for each. Although companies might be able to identify further microsegments within each seg-

Homogeneity: A measure of the degree to which the potential customers in a segment have similar responses to some marketing variable of interest and differ from other groups of customers.

Parsimony: A measure of the degree to which the segmentation would make every potential customer a unique target.

Accessibility: The degree to which marketers can reach segments separately using observable characteristics of the segments (descriptor variables).

ment (e.g., United could microsegment the all others category on the basis of their geographic location), developing and delivering unique services to each microsegment rapidly becomes too costly to justify relative to its benefits.

Finally, descriptor variables characterize segments; such variables for online customers might include pages viewed, files downloaded, referrer page, new versus returning visitor, and screen resolution.

A segmentation model requires a dependent variable, usually called a segmentation *basis*, and independent variables, or segment *descriptors*. The segmentation basis should describe why customers respond differently (e.g., differences in their valuations of offerings, needs, or wants), whereas segment descriptors (e.g., age, income, use of media) help marketers deliver different offerings to various customer segments. In practice, the distinction between bases and descriptors depends on the reasons for conducting the segmentation study. Analytical methods such as regression or discriminant analysis can relate segment membership to descriptors; the equation that results from such analyses (e.g., discriminant function, classification tree) indicates whether a potential customer who was not part of the segmentation study would belong to a specific segment. For example, American Express had 94 million card members worldwide as of June 2011. If it takes a random sample of 1,000 or so customers to perform a detailed segmentation study that identifies distinct segments along the criterion of interest (basis), it can use readily available descriptors about all its members to assign them to the identified segments. Such classification according to descriptors is a key benefit of segmentation analysis.

In practice, many segmentation approaches focus on descriptors as a means to segment customers. For example, one online marketer classifies the non-shoppers at its website as "Fearful Browsers," "Shopping Avoiders," "Technology Muddlers," and "Fun Seekers." Or, sometimes, firms segment their customers based on frequency of purchase (e.g., Heavy Buyers, Light Buyers, or Non-Buyers).

The main problem with segmentation schemes based on demographics is that they are based on the needs of the company, and not the needs of the customers, and are, therefore, unlikely to result in products or marketing programs that best appeal to customers. Ideally, to be most effective, firms should identify segments using basis variables, particularly the observed or likely actions of customers. Sophisticated approaches blend both basis and descriptor variables to develop a segmentation model. The management problem at hand, combined with the cost of compiling the data should point to the best approach. There is no single best segmentation approach, as we note in Exhibit 3.2. The marketing problem, timing, availability of relevant data, and similar considerations should dictate the appropriate approach.

For General Understanding of a Market
    Benefits sought (in industrial markets the criterion used is purchase decision)
    Product-purchase and product-use patterns
    Needs
    Brand-loyalty and brand-switching patterns
    A hybrid of the variables above

For Positioning Studies
    Product use
    Product preference
    Benefits sought
    A hybrid of the variables above

For New-Product Concepts (and New-Product Introduction)
    Reaction to new concepts (intention to buy, preference over current brand, etc.)
    Benefits sought

For Pricing Decisions
    Price sensitivity
    Deal proneness
    Price sensitivity by purchase/use patterns

For Advertising Decisions
    Benefits sought
    Media use
    Psychographic/life style
    A hybrid (of the variables above and/or purchase/use patterns)

For Distribution Decisions
    Store loyalty and patronage
    Benefits sought in store selection

EXHIBIT 3.2
The most appropriate segmentation bases depend on the managerial uses of the segmentation. Source: Wind 1978, p. 320.

The STP Approach

Segmentation consists of two phases:

- *Phase 1:* Segment the market using basis variables (e.g., customer needs, wants, benefits sought, problem solutions desired, preferences, values, usage situations).

- *Phase 2:* Describe the market segments identified using variables that help the firm understand how to serve those customers (e.g., shopping patterns, geographic location, clothing size, family size), how to talk to these customers (e.g., media preferences and use, attitudes, activities, interests, opinions), and buyer switching costs (costs associated with changing products or suppliers).

Targeting consists of three phases:

- *Phase 3:* Evaluate the attractiveness of each segment using variables that quantify the demand levels and opportunities associated with each segment (e.g., growth rate), the costs of serving each segment (e.g., distribution costs), the costs of producing the offerings the customers want (e.g., production and product differentiation costs), and the fit between the firm's core competencies and the target market opportunity.

- *Phase 4*: Select one or more target segments to serve on the basis of their profit potential and fit with the firm's corporate strategy; determine the level of resources to allocate to those segments.

- *Phase 5*: Find and reach targeted customers and prospects within targeted segments in a variety of ways, including direct mail contact, advertising in selected media vehicles, targeted sales force presentations, and the like.

Following these phases, the firm must identify a positioning concept for its products and services that attracts target customers and enhances its desired corporate image.

We address the positioning issue in Chapter 4. Here, we elaborate on the first five phases.

Segmenting markets (Phase 1)

There are many approaches for segmenting markets, and there are many segmentation methods associated with each approach. Sophisticated methods require specialized knowledge of statistics and related areas, but anyone willing to learn a few basic concepts and tools can conduct an effective initial segmentation study. There are three types of segmentation methods.

A priori segmentation. Using either industry knowledge or marketing research, firms can directly segment customers according to their observable characteristics, assuming such criteria are related to differences in their underlying needs. For example, many firms segment car buyers by gender, assuming men and women have potentially different needs. Pharmaceutical companies segment physicians on the basis of their specialties, such as dermatologists and allergists, because these doctors cater to different types of patients and therefore have different prescription needs. The following example describes an a priori segmentation of computer users into Mac and PC users. While the results are interesting, it is not clear how they could be leveraged for strategic decision making.

EXAMPLE

Who really are the PC and Mac users?

In April 2011, Hunch.com did a study of the differences between Mac and PC users. Of the 388,000 Hunch users who responded to a question about computer loyalty, 52% identified themselves as PC people and 25% said they were Mac devotees. Hunch then cross-referenced those responses with answers to other questions to highlight cultural distinctions between Mac and PC user camps.

The study described the differences between Mac and PC users with regard to demographics, personality, fashion, taste and aesthetics, food & drink choices, technology interests, and media habits. Mac users were found to be bolder and more creative (or elitist and more pretentious?). 67% of Mac users had a college or advanced degree compared to 54% of PC users. Mac loyalists were 80% more likely than PC users to be vegetarians, and were more likely to ride a Vespa scooter than a Harley motorbike. PC users' tastes tended towards casual clothes, tuna fish sandwiches, white wine, stronger aptitude for mathematical concepts, Hollywood movies, USA Today, and Pepsi. Mac users were more likely to prefer designer or retro styles, hummus, red wine, indie films, Moby Dick, The New York Times, and San Pellegrino Limonata! (Brandon Griggs, CNN, April 22, 2011, and http://blog.hunch.com/?p=45344).

Traditional segmentation methods. This most widely employed approach is easy to understand conceptually and relatively simple to apply compared with the latent class methods (described next). Traditional segmentation approaches employ analytic methods to segment customers on the basis of a single composite measure developed from a set of observable characteristics. For example, two distinct segments of customers might exist because the first segment prefers moderately priced domestic sedans with good gas mileage, whereas the second prefers sporty domestic cars that are inexpensive but has no strong preference regarding gas mileage. Through further analysis of these two segments, a car company might find that the first segment consists of older customers with moderate incomes living in the suburbs, and the second consists of younger and less affluent customers living in cities. The company might label the first segment "value seekers" and target them with traditional sedans, then attempt to sell sporty cars to the second segment, labeled "thrill seekers." Generally, it is best to segment on the basis of characteristics related to underlying customer needs in a product category.

Latent class segmentation. The idea behind the more technically sophisticated latent class segmentation approach is that customers belong to groups that differ in ways that cannot be described just in terms of observable mean differences between segments. For example, an unobserved characteristic influencing prescription behavior may be whether the physician focuses more on patients or on scientific research. Patient-focused physicians may prescribe a treatment plan that accounts for all of the patient's medical and nonmedical characteristics, whereas research-oriented physicians likely prescribe a treatment plan that corresponds to the latest scientific findings. A pharmaceutical firm therefore may want to find observable correlates of these unobserved underlying characteristics, such as the age of the physician, the type of medical school he or she attended, and whether the practice is in a rural or urban area. Typically, latent class methods require much larger sample sizes than do traditional methods.

Of the many possible ways to segment markets, we recommend traditional segmentation methods (at least as a first step) that incorporate customers' needs and the situations in which they use the product. We can also start with an a priori segmentation using easy-to-identify characteristics of customers and see if the resulting customer groups have different needs. Many technology-driven B2B firms that first develop offerings and then seek to find markets for them use this reactive form of segmentation. However, when possible, firms should be proactive rather than reactive in segmenting their market; that is, they should actively identify differences in customers' needs, wants, and preferences and then determine if they can design offerings and corresponding marketing strategies to serve these different needs profitably. We recommend a five-step approach.

In **Step 1,** the firm explicitly outlines the role of market segmentation in its strategy. What objective does segmenting the market meet? How will it help the firm establish a competitive advantage, and what other actions might the firm take to achieve its objectives? What resources and constraints apply to the segmentation program (e.g., would it be effective to train the current sales force to reach multiple segments with different messages?)? How would segmentation improve the firm's ability to deploy its scarce resources? For example, the firm's abilities to develop truly new products or business processes represent strategic factors that may influence the way it segments its markets. The cost disadvantage associated with the potential loss of scale economies associated with serving smaller rather than larger segments is another factor that should be considered. A firm should not segment its market without first considering its overall strategic intent and core competencies.

Step 2 requires selecting a set of segmentation variables. These variables should be based on some aspect of potential customers' needs or wants and reflect differences between customers. To make this selection, the firm needs intimate knowledge of the factors that drive demand for its products and services. Geodemographic segmentation (often used in direct marketing) focuses on the location, income, gender, marital status, and other such characteristics of target customers. In many consumer markets, segmentation variables reflect customer differences on perceptual dimensions (see Chapter 4) or pertain to geodemographic, psychographic and socioeconomic characteristics. In B2B markets, the benefits the customers seek depend less on the psychological and socioeconomic characteristics of the person making the purchase decision and more on the use of the product in the buying firm's operations and the profitability the product generates. In the end, the chosen segmentation variables should isolate groups of customers whose needs are similar within a group but differ from the needs of other groups.

In **Step 3,** the company chooses the mathematical and statistical procedures to aggregate individual customers into homogeneous groups or segments. This aggregation entails an implicit strategic decision: Should customer segments be discrete (each customer constitutes only one segment), overlapping (a customer can appear in two or more groups), or fuzzy (each customer is assigned proportional membership in each segment)? Assigning each customer to a single segment is easier to understand and apply, but doing so may sacrifice some relevant information. Overlapping or fuzzy segments are intuitively more appealing, more realistic, and theoretically more accurate, but developing such a segmentation strategy is much more complex, because the firm needs to position identical products differently to appeal to the different overlapping segments.

In **Steps 4 and 5,** the firm must make two crucial decisions: Specify the maximum number of segments to construct according to the segmentation variables and search across those segments to determine how many to target. No theory dictates the correct number of segments; it is more art than science and depends on the resources and constraints facing the firm, as well as the opportunities afforded by the segmented market.

Therefore, firms must decide on the number of segments to target using both statistical criteria and managerial judgment. In most cases, firms split the (potential) market into two groups, then three groups, four groups, and so on, up to the maximum number of segments they have decided to consider. They examine each of these segment structures using various managerial and statistical criteria to eliminate any segments that are statistically (e.g., no statistical differences between segments) or managerially unsuitable. Robertson and Barich (1992) find that in B2B markets, at a broad strategic level, they could break customers down into three groups: first-time prospects, novices, and sophisticates. First-time prospects are new to the market and have just begun to evaluate vendors. Novices have purchased the product already but remain uncertain about its usefulness and appropriateness. Sophisticates have purchased and used the product and are knowledgeable about it (Exhibit 3.3). Although Robertson and Barich's approach is simple and limited, it illustrates a basic form of segmentation that relies on knowledge-based needs, independent of the idiosyncratic nature of the individual market. According to them, B2B markets generally exhibit such knowledge-based segments.

EXHIBIT 3.3

Classification of three generic segments in industrial markets and what they value. Source: Robertson and Barich 1992.

First-Time Prospects	Novices	Sophisticates
Dominant Theme: "Take care of me"	**Dominant Theme:** "Help me make it work"	**Dominant Theme:** "Talk technology to me"
Benefits Sought: • Knowledge of my business • Honest sales representative • Vendor who has experience • Sales representative who can communicate in an understandable manner	**Benefits Sought:** • Easy-to-read manuals • Technical support hotlines • A high level of training • Sales representative knowledgeable about products and services	**Benefits Sought:** • Compatibility with systems • Customization • Track record of vendor • Sales support and technical assistance
What's Less Important: • Sales representative's knowledge about products and services	**What's Less Important:** • Honest sales representative • Knowledge of my business	**What's Less Important:** • Sales representative who can communicate in an understandable manner • Training • Trial • Easy-to-read manuals

Describing market segments (Phase 2)

After isolating various segments in a market, firms need effective descriptions of them. The variables that describe the market segments should highlight the profit potential (e.g., price sensitivity and size) of each segment and how the company can serve these segments. Two general types of variables are available for this purpose: those that outline broad market characteristics and those that provide insight into serving one or more segments.

For both consumer and B2B markets, broadly similar variables describe the various segments (Exhibit 3.4). These variables categorize the segments in the market and thereby reveal actual and potential customers, clarify their purchase motivations, and indicate how firms should communicate with them.

	Consumer	B2B
Segmentation Bases	Needs, wants, benefits, solutions to problems, usage situation, usage rate.	Needs, wants, benefits, solutions to problems, usage situation, usage rate, size*, industry*.
Descriptors:		
• Demographics/ Firmographics	Age, income, marital status, family type and size, gender, social class, etc.	Industry, size, location, current supplier(s), technology utilization, etc.
• Psychographics	Lifestyle, values, and personality characteristics.	Personality characteristics of decision makers.
• Behavior	Use occasions, usage level, complementary and substitute products used, brand loyalty, etc.	Use occasions, usage level, complementary and substitute products used, brand loyalty, order size, applications, etc.
• Decision making	Individual or group (family) choice, low or high involvement purchase, attitudes and knowledge about product class, price sensitivity, etc.	Formalization of purchasing procedures, size and characteristics of decision making group, use of outside consultants, purchasing criteria, (de)centralized buying, price sensitivity, switching costs, budget cycle, etc.
• Media patterns	Level of use, types of media used, times of use, etc.	Level of use, types of media used, times of use, patronage at trade shows, receptivity to salespeople, etc.

EXHIBIT 3.4
Common bases and descriptors used to segment and describe markets, in terms of both consumer and B2B variables.

*These are "macro-segmentation"—or first stage—bases.

Many combinations of variables can be used to describe a market (Exhibit 3.5). In determining strategy, firms should select variables that help:

- Measure the size and purchasing power of the segments.
- Determine the degree to which they can effectively reach and serve the segments.
- Develop effective programs to attract customers.

Criterion	Examples of Considerations
I. Size and Growth	
1. Size	• Market potential, current market penetration
2. Growth	• Growth forecasts of adopting new technologies
II. Structural Characteristics	
3. Competition	• Barriers to entry, barriers to exit, position of competitors, ability to retaliate
4. Segment saturation	• Gaps in the market
5. Protectability	• Patentability of products, barriers to entry
6. Environmental risk	• Economic, political, and technological change
III. Product-Market Fit	
7. Fit	• Coherence with company's strengths and image
8. Relationships with other segments	• Synergy, cost interactions, image transfers, cannibalization
9. Profitability	• Entry costs, margin levels, return on investment

Properly implemented, this approach leads to readily distinguishable segments.

Evaluating segment attractiveness (Phase 3)

In the next phase, firms choose one or more markets to serve. Many firms have found it helpful to start with nine measures grouped into three broad factors, to evaluate the attractiveness of a segment of customers (Exhibit 3.5). One factor (criteria 1 and 2) pertains to the size of the segment and its growth potential. Although bigger, faster growing segments may seem intuitively appealing, the right size and growth potential for a company depend completely on its individual resources and capabilities. Many firms that pursue a large market opportunity find that large market segments attract many aggressive competitors, leading to tougher competition (and lower prices and lower profitability) than in smaller, niche markets.

The second factor relates to the structural characteristics of the segment and includes four criteria (criteria 3–6): competition, segment saturation, protectability, and environmental risk.

The third factor, product–market fit, includes criteria 7–9. A company should ask at least three types of screening questions:

1. Does serving a particular segment fit the company's strengths and desired corporate image?
2. Can the company gain any synergy from serving this segment?
3. Can the company sustain the costs of entering this segment, and can it price its products and services to achieve the desired margins and returns on investment (ROI)?

Many companies have tried to grow but failed by pursuing a market segment that offers high ROI but a poor fit with the firm's current capabilities.

Selecting target segments and allocating resources to segments (Phase 4)

After developing the criteria to evaluate the attractiveness of various market segments, the firm selects the segments it will serve. They have five basic options:

1. Concentrate on a single segment.
2. Select segments in which to specialize.
3. Provide a range of offerings to a specific segment.
4. Provide one offering to many segments.
5. Cover the whole market (all offerings to all segments).

Which option should the firm choose? A small company with limited resources probably cannot serve the full market. Despite their abilities to serve the entire market, big companies should also make strategic choices. Most firms use a simple heuristic; for example, they select only those segments that rate highest on the attractiveness criteria described in the previous section. This type of analysis, originally developed by General Electric, relies on a fairly common form of portfolio matrix.

A procedure to implement this process uses the following six steps:

1. *Specify drivers of each dimension.* The firm may start with the dimensions suggested in Exhibit 3.5 but should carefully determine those factors that are most important to its own specific, overall strategy.
2. *Weight drivers.* The firm should assign relative importance weights to the drivers. Some form of consensus-building process usually is required to agree on a set of weights, such as the Delphi method (see Chapter 5).
3. *Rate segments on each driver.* Similar to the process used to develop weights, this scoring step requires some form of consensus.
4. *Multiply weights by ratings for each segment.* A simple arithmetic operation.
5. *View resulting group.* A graph can clarify the results of the analysis (Exhibit 3.6).
6. *Review/sensitivity analysis.* The process should be repeated with other weights (there may be no consensus) and ratings.

EXHIBIT 3.6

Selecting segments to serve. Segments A–E become more attractive as they move horizontally to the right and more aligned with the firms' competencies as they move vertically upward, suggesting that segment E is likely to be the highest in overall attractiveness and segment A the lowest.

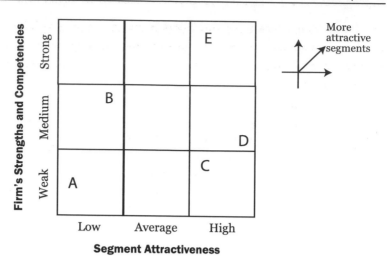

When a company targets only its most attractive segment, it concentrates all its resources on serving a single group of customers. This focus should enable the firm to understand and serve the needs of this segment effectively. However, such concentration also entails a price: The company has exposed itself to high risk by putting all its eggs in one basket.

EXAMPLE

McDonald's originally focused on lunchtime and dinnertime hamburger customers. But how could it make its existing business grow? It targeted the fast-food breakfast eater, opening earlier and adding such items as Egg McMuffins to the menu. It also targeted other tastes (beyond hamburgers) by adding chicken products (McNuggets). McDonald's even tested pizza varieties in several locations with mixed results. The firm continues to balance the benefits of targeting multiple segments against the costs of serving those new segments, which may make it less attractive to its traditional and loyal (hamburger) customers.

To reduce the risk associated with serving only a single segment, a company may instead decide to serve two or more segments. The choice of multiple segments progresses through two steps. First, which segments pass the attractiveness criteria previously outlined? Second, which of these acceptable segments offers the best combination of risk and return to the company, given its risk tolerance?

Another alternative involves a simple variant of the single-segment strategy. Using market specialization, the company identifies a particular segment and offers a broad range of products and services to meet its needs. For example, the explosives divisions of both DuPont and ICI target all open-cut and underground mines with a range of different explosives (e.g., wet hole, dry hole) and blasting control systems.

Or a company may engage in product-line specialization. In this case, the company makes one product or a limited range of products and sells them to any customer who can pay for them. For example, Boeing makes aircraft, Intel makes computer chips, and MGM makes movies, and each sells to anyone with the resources to buy their products. If you were to think of a particular product category, such as cola or rental cars, product-line specialists (Coke or Pepsi, Hertz or Avis) probably would come to mind.

Some firms choose to provide a little something for everyone. But trying to serve multiple types of customers simultaneously can be costly, so most companies alter their offerings for different market segments by varying the physical product or non-product attributes such as price, packaging, warranty, distribution, and image-based advertising. Most changes combine product and non-product attributes. However, if firms can achieve substantial economies of scale in production, they may just change the brand name, packaging, advertising, and price for reaching different segments.

EXAMPLE

Marriott Corporation has created a number of hotel brands each catering to a different segment by offering a completely different product, price point, and services. The flagship brand Marriott is typically designed for business groups and conventions, has ballrooms, meeting rooms, and other large-hotel amenities. Courtyard by Marriott was designed specifically as a moderately-priced hotel for road-warrior business travelers. Springfield Suites was designed for extended-stay travelers such as contractors, lawyers, and people who are re-locating to a new location. Fairfield Inns are located mainly near convenient highway access points for budget and business travelers traveling by car.

Differentiated offerings targeted to different market segments typically create greater sales than a single product targeted to an average customer. However, differentiated marketing almost always increases the costs of doing business through product modification, production, administrative, inventory, and promotion costs.

Finding targeted customers (Phase 5)

Firms may seek customers who are price insensitive or quality conscious, but unfortunately, customers do not tend to walk around with identifying tags that provide such information. The only "tags" they actually display are those associated with their demographic or firmographic (industry, size, location) profile, or their past behaviors. But demographics and firmographics are notoriously poor identifiers of customer value segments. Hence the crux of the problem: That which is easy to observe is often a poor predictor of what motivates behavior. Many segmentation studies identify segments with clearly different needs but cannot recommend a simple way to identify and selectively reach customers in those different segments. For example, there may be two distinct segments who prefer Tylenol in either large or small package sizes. However, both segments may shop in the same stores, watch similar TV programs, and have similar demographic characteristics, making it difficult to reach each segment selectively.

Three strategies have proven successful for identifying specific customers whose values and needs do not correlate well with easy-to-gather identifiers.

Customer self-selection. In this case, the customer and the company reverse roles. The company offers a range of products and services that fit the needs of different target segments, and customers sort through this assortment to choose the offering that best fits their needs. This approach is common in retail settings like supermarkets, which stock a wide variety of breakfast cereals from the same manufacturers on shelves from which customers choose the best one for them. If customers are price sensitive, they choose a brand with a coupon and take the trouble to redeem it. The less price-sensitive customers forget about the coupon and pay full price for the cereal they prefer.

Branding and packaging the same product in different ways can achieve the same result, as can the use of different distribution channels to deliver the same product or service. These approaches are most suitable when customers are many but the dollar volume associated with each is small.

Another way to help customers self-select into the correct customer value segment is to advertise by showing customers the range of offerings from which they may choose. Companies selling financial services often use this approach; in a brochure or website introducing financial investments, they include a section that asks prospective customers to determine their income and expense flows, risk profile, wealth situation, income needs, and so forth. On the basis of this self-analysis, the firms direct the customers to the financial service offerings that best suit their needs.

The online environment provides a convenient platform for customers to self-select into the appropriate segments, if those segments fall into clearly identifiable groups with distinct needs. For example, visitors to the DecisionPro website, decisionpro.biz (the developers of Marketing Engineering), can self select into one of three segments, students, instructors, and professionals, and then access the products and services most likely to meet their needs.

Scoring/classification methods. Typically, a segmentation study includes many more descriptive items than are needed to profile each segment reliably. Major segmentation studies can employ several hundred descriptor variables. To narrow the focus, discriminant analysis or CART (Classification and Regression Trees) analysis identifies a small subset of variables that can be used to assign customers to segments. These methods generate rules for scoring each customer on the basis of observable, discriminating characteristics; the resultant scores help assign customers to segments. The scoring mechanism can also generate questions for customers (or identify information to retrieve from a database), so that new customers may be scored and assigned easily to appropriate segments.

Discriminant analysis typically requires at least 5–10 questions to assign a customer to a segment. Salespeople can ask these questions when prospecting for new customers or visiting existing ones. These questions also can constitute part of the customer profiling process used by a call center or website—and be used to segment existing customer databases. For example, the firm can mail or e-mail a questionnaire to its current customers or contact them using customer service representatives. In other words, in just a short period of time, a company can overlay an entirely new segmentation scheme onto an existing customer database.

Segmentation Research: Designing and Collecting Data

Although there are many ways to segment markets, as well as many data sources internal and external to the firm, we focus on a typical formal segmentation research study that collects primary source data. Such a study consists of four key steps:

1. *Develop the measurement instrument*: What information needs to be collected, and how should it be collected (e.g., survey form)?
2. *Select a sample*: Who (which respondents? where? in what households or organizations?) needs to be studied?
3. *Select and aggregate respondents*: How do different responses from several individuals in a household or organization combine to predict how the household or organization will behave?
4. *Analyze the data and segment the market*: What statistical procedures will segment (potential) customers and describe aspects of their characteristics or behavior that are crucial to serving their needs?

These topics are covered in much more detail in marketing research texts; we simply outline the key issues and illustrate the important points. (Note: When you deal with data from a secondary source—that is, already collected data—you can bypass steps 1 and 2 but still must follow steps 3 and 4.)

Developing the measurement instrument

Measurement instruments for segmentation studies usually attempt to collect several types of data:

- *Demographic descriptors*, such as age, income, marital status, and education (consumer side) and industry classification, size (number of employees or sales), and job responsibilities (B2B side).
- *Psychological descriptors*, such as hobbies, interests, and lifestyle.
- *Demand*, including historical purchases or consumption and anticipated future purchases.
- *Needs*, whether stated, or in terms of customer value, as described in Chapter 2.
- *Attitudes*, pertaining to products, suppliers, purchase risk, or the product adoption process.
- *Media and distribution channel use*, such as the types and amount of media used and where products and services are typically bought.

Data collected in a segmentation study usually are structured into a data matrix, in which the columns correspond to the variables measured, and each row contains the responses of one respondent. Exhibit 3.7 shows part of a data matrix from a needs study pertaining to the organizational use of personal computers.

Comp-any	Job title	SIC code	# PCs	# employ-ees	Office use	LAN	Color	Mem. needs	Speed needs	Storage needs	Wide connect	Periph.
#1	design eng.	361	6	8	3	4	5	6	6	6	1	3
	purch agent.	361	6	8	3	4	4	4	4	5	1	2
#2	design eng.	363	4	5	3	4	6	5	5	5	2	4
	purch agent.	363	4	5	3	4	4	3	3	4	1	1
#3	design eng.	871	75	82	2	5	5	6	6	5	2	3
	purch agent.	871	75	82	2	4	4	5	5	3	1	2
#4	design eng.	871	52	57	2	5	5	6	6	5	1	3
	purch agent.	871	52	57	2	5	3	4	4	4	1	2
#5		602	90	100	6	4	2	3	3	5	7	2

EXHIBIT 3.7
Portion of a data matrix from PC needs study. Note that different decision makers in the same organization have different needs.

Even when a particular study does not organize data in this way, it offers a useful way to think about segmentation data. The goal of collecting such data and constructing a data matrix is the ability to address several key issues:

Q1: Who are the respondents, and how will they be identified in the data matrix (columns 1 and 2)? As Exhibit 3.7 shows, different respondents in the same household or, more critically, in the same organization may give quite different responses.

Q2: What are the characteristics of the gathered data? Nominal data, such as yes–no answers, or industry classification data are not as easy to use as basis variables as are data obtained from rating scales.

Q3: Are the measurement scales the same? If the scales differ (e.g., agree or disagree on a seven-point scale versus estimated demand on a 1–10,000 unit scale), some form of data standardization may be needed.

Q4: Are the variables correlated? Different variables often measure different aspects of the same thing. For example, if "quality of service" and "on-time arrival" means the same thing to airline customers, perceptions and importance ratings for these items should be combined in some way to avoid double counting.

Q5: What is the procedure for handling outliers, that is, unusual respondents? Some outliers represent incorrect data, and others may represent unique situations that are better discarded. But still other outliers may represent new, emerging segments that the firm cannot afford to ignore!

Updating and refreshing the database

Segmentation data age quickly, and a segmentation research program is not complete if it lacks a plan for monitoring and refreshing the database. Segmentation is an ongoing process, not an individual, one-time study, and regular market monitoring and updating are essential for the success of this process.

Forming and profiling segments

We have suggested that meaningful segmentation should satisfy three managerial criteria: (1) the market should be heterogeneous, (2) segments should be accessible (i.e., customers in selected segments can be reached through a marketing program), and (3) the segmentation should be cost effective to implement. Our suggested segmentation approach attempts to satisfy these three criteria on the basis of three related technical criteria: homogeneity, identifiability, and parsimony.

Homogeneity measures the degree to which potential customers within a segment have similar needs and values; in contrast, *heterogeneity* measures the degree to which groups of customers differ. Our segmentation methods seek homogeneity within segments and heterogeneity between segments.

Identifiability is the degree to which marketers, using observable characteristics (descriptors) of the segments, can identify (and reach) segment members; thus, it is a measure of accessibility.

Parsimony is a measure of how well the segmentation scheme derived from the data about (potential) customers trades off the amount of within-group homogeneity against the amount of between-group heterogeneity in a cost-effective way.

These criteria are crucial for an evaluation of the quality of any segmentation analyses.

TRADITIONAL SEGMENTATION[2]

As we have stressed already, there is no single best segmentation scheme, nor is there a single best segmentation method. Even the methods we outline here may not agree in terms of the number and composition of segments. Therefore, it is critical to use multiple approaches and cross-validate any findings; strong segments emerge regardless of the method and analytical choices, whereas weaker or perhaps unexpected relationships will appear only with specific methods. Cross-validation with different methods helps managers determine which relationships and segments are most substantive. Ideally, management should agree on the segment development and evaluation criteria before beginning the analysis to ensure that the process is the most effective and actionable for the organization.

Five steps pertain to applying traditional segmentation methods:

---

[2] *Readers not interested in the "how" of segmentation should skip this section.*

1. Reduce the data.
2. Develop measures of association.
3. Identify and remove outliers.
4. Form segments.
5. Profile segments and interpret results.

For a direct segmentation task, the customer data must be assembled in two data matrices, in which each row represents information about a particular customer. One data matrix contains the variables that create the basis for the segmentation, whereas the other contains descriptor variables. The basis variable data matrix applies to steps 1–4; the descriptor data matrix functions for step 5.

Reducing the Data with Factor Analysis

Many segmentation studies collect data about a wide variety of demand and need-based items, often by measuring similar or interrelated constructs. In subsequent analyses, this overlap may lead to misleading conclusions, because some data are overweighted and others are underweighted. Therefore, researchers must remove irrelevant variables from any study, because including even a couple of irrelevant variables can prevent detection of the segment structure in the data.

Factor analysis reduces a large set of segmentation variables to a smaller set of independent indicator constructs by analyzing the interrelationships among a large number of segmentation basis variables and then representing them in terms of common, underlying dimensions (factors).

Developing Measures of Association

Cluster analysis routines require the analyst to define a measure of similarity for every pair of respondents. Similarity measures fall into two categories, depending on the type of available data: Scaled data (e.g., how much do you agree or disagree with the following statement ...?) use distance-type measures, whereas nominal data (e.g., is feature X required/not required?) use matching-type measures. That is, the question implicit in the latter measure asks how many times, out of all possible matches, any two respondents agree on features that are required or not.

Identifying and Removing Outliers

In most data collection exercises, a few respondents' answers differ notably from those of all others. Such data outliers occur for two general reasons. The first is associated with data errors. The respondent may have misunderstood a question or put an answer in the wrong place. Coding or transcription errors also may have occurred. Regardless of the reason, the data are simply incorrect, and the response should either be corrected or the observation removed from the data set.

The second reason for an outlier is that a respondent really has needs that are quite different from those of the rest of the sample. These respondents fall into two categories: those that represent an uninteresting, unique set of needs and those whose needs indicate an emerging new segment. Both sets of responses should disappear from the data set, but the latter group may represent lead users, who can provide strong early indications of where other segments may be going in the near future. It is best to search for outliers and remove them early in the analysis process; retaining them leads to unstable and unreliable segmentation results.

Forming Segments

Cluster Analysis: A set of statistical techniques used to discover structure within data.

Cluster analysis uses a set of mathematical techniques to discover a structure (groupings) within a complex body of data, such as the segmentation-based data matrix. To understand the process of segmentation, think about a deck of cards. Each card differs from the other cards along three dimensions (variables): suit, color, and number. To partition a pack of cards into two distinct groups, you might sort them into red and black or numbered and picture cards. If you must sort them into three groups, it is not intuitively obvious what the segmentation criteria might be. But a four-group solution is again easy—just sort them into suits.

Although you might partition a pack of cards intuitively, partitioning a large number of items into groups can be very complex, especially if those items vary along many different dimensions. Consider partitioning 25 items (or respondents) into two groups, with at least one item in a group. There are $2^{24} - 1$ (= 16,777,215) possible partitions (market segments). In partitioning 25 items into five groups, the number of possibilities grows to 2,436,684,974,110,751 (2.43×10^{15}). Clearly, only a systematic and feasible method can find the best partition. Cluster analysis (also known as numerical taxonomy or partitioning) represents a set of statistical techniques developed to address this problem.

The input to cluster analysis is the set of distances or measures of association discussed previously. There are two basic classes of clustering methods:

- *Hierarchical methods:* Build up or break down the data row by row.
- *Partitioning methods:* Break the data into a prespecified number of groups and then reallocate or swap data to improve some statistical measure of fit (i.e., the ratio of within-group to between-group variation).

Hierarchical methods themselves fall into two categories: build up (agglomerative) and split down (divisive) methods. Each type produces a tree similar to that shown in Exhibit 3.8—called a dendogram—to help identify the clusters or segments.

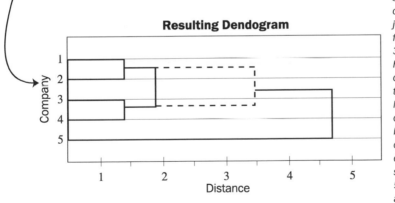

Distance Matrix

	Co#1	Co#2	Co#3	Co#4	Co#5
Company #1	0.00				
Company #2	1.49	0.00			
Company #3	3.42	2.29	0.00		
Company #4	1.81	1.99	1.48	0.00	
Company #5	5.05	4.82	4.94	4.83	0.00

Resulting Dendogram

EXHIBIT 3.8

A distance matrix yielding one dendogram for single linkage clustering (solid line) and another for complete linkage clustering (dotted line). The cluster or segments formed by companies 1 and 2 join with the segment formed by companies 3 and 4 at a much higher level in the complete linkage than in the single linkage. In both cases, company 5 appears to be different from the other companies—an outlier. A two-cluster solution results in A = 5, B = {1, 2, 3, 4}, and a three-cluster solution provides A = 5, B = {1, 2}, and C = {3, 4}.

Agglomerative methods generally follow a four-step process:

1. At the beginning, each item is its own cluster.
2. Join the two items that are closest on some chosen measure of distance.
3. Next join the next two closest objects, either by joining two items to form another group or by attaching an item to an existing cluster.
4. Repeat step 3 until all items are clustered.

Agglomerative methods also differ in how they join clusters.

- *Single linkage clustering* (also called the nearest neighbor method): The distance between clusters equals the distance between the two closest items in those clusters; used most often to identify outliers.
- *Complete linkage clustering* (also called the furthest neighbor method): The distance between two clusters equals the distance between the pair of items in those clusters that are farthest apart, so that all items in the new cluster formed by joining them are no farther apart than some maximal distance.
- *Average linkage clustering:* The distance between two clusters A and B equals the average distance between all pairs of items in the clusters, in which one of the items in the pair is from cluster A and the other is from cluster B.
- *Centroid clustering:* The distance between two clusters is typically the Euclidean distance between their centroids (or means).
- *Ward's method:* Clusters form on the basis of the least change in the error sum of squares associated with joining any pair of clusters.

In contrast, partitioning methods are most applicable when an analyst faces a big data set. These methods are computationally efficient, and their output is much easier to interpret when many items (e.g., 50 or more customers) are being clustered. Unlike hierarchical methods, they do not require the irrevocable allocation of a respondent to a cluster; that is, the routine reallocates a respondent if doing so improves the statistical fit of the solution. These methods also do not develop a tree-like structure; rather, they start with cluster centers and assign the respondents closest to each cluster center to that cluster.

The most commonly used partitioning method is K-means clustering, which works as follows:

1. The analyst specifies the number of clusters (n).
2. The routine begins with n (analyst-specified) clusters and allocates every respondent to its nearest cluster center.
3. It then reallocates respondents, one at a time, to reduce the sum of internal cluster variability until it has minimized the fit criterion (sum of the within-cluster sums of squares) for n clusters.
4. After completing step 3, the process may begin again for a different number of clusters. Managerial judgment and

defined segmentation goals will indicate the appropriate number of segments.

Profiling Segments and Interpreting Results

After forming segments by following one of these methods, the results must be interpreted and linked to managerial actions. This critical activity acknowledges that targeting and positioning decisions depend on the segment schemes chosen. This choice requires the consideration of at least the following issues:

- Are there really any distinct clusters?
- How many clusters should be retained?
- How good (interpretable) and robust (stable) are the clusters?
- How should the clusters be profiled?

What if there are no meaningful clusters?

Don't overlook this possibility. If only one or two basis variables show meaningful differences between respondents, it is possible that no distinct segments exist in the market, possibly because of a poor selection of segmentation bases or because customer needs in the sample really do not differ much.

If the revealed segment structure is weak, exploratory research methods can provide a better picture of targetable customers by profiling them according to the descriptor variables.

How many clusters (segments) should be retained?

This decision involves both art (the purpose of the study) and science (statistical criteria). It is useful to generate multiple potential segmentation schemes and, using statistical criteria, identify the best two or three of these. Managers or users of the resulting segmentation scheme can help decide which of these remaining schemes will be most useful.

How good are the clusters?

That is, how well do the clusters obtained from this particular sample of customers generalize to the market as a whole? Too few segmentation studies try to answer this question. Even if the sample is representative, measurement problems may still exist, or the analyst may have made some poor choices. Good cluster solutions are usually robust—that is, generally stable across segmentation methods and association measures. A good way to determine the robustness of the clusters is by using different methods (or different association measures) and then conducting a cross-tabulation to find how many respondents appear in the same groups according to the different methods. The higher the percentage, the better is the outcome of the analysis. Another way to test robustness is to split the data randomly into two groups, run the segmentation analysis separately on each half of the data, and compare results. Again, the higher the level of agreement, the better the solution. If an approach assigns fewer than 70% or so of cases to the correct clusters, that segmentation structure should be viewed with caution.

A second aspect of segmentation quality relates to managerial usefulness: Do the users (salespeople, call center personnel, advertising managers) find the results valuable? One way to understand managerial usefulness is to determine if managers can invent intuitively appealing names for the segments. Normally, cluster means—the average values of the basis and descriptor variables for each segment—should characterize segment members. For example, active investors need much more timely information about their portfolios than do investors in "the invest-and-forget" segment. They probably are also the most receptive to electronic trading schemes.

The idea behind *cluster profiling* is to prepare a picture of the revealed clusters based on both the variables used for clustering (segmentation bases) and those used to identify and target the segments (descriptors). The most direct approach to profiling compares the average values of the bases and the descriptor variables in each cluster.

EXHIBIT 3.9

Segment profiles (snake chart) for two segments of PC users.

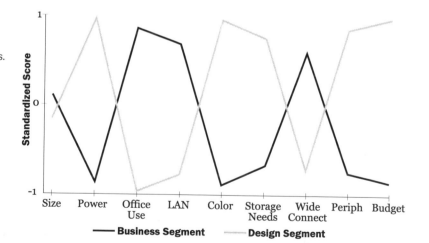

Exhibit 3.9 represents a snake chart based on the data in Exhibit 3.7. One PC-buying segment has a high relative need for power, color, storage, and peripherals and is not price sensitive

(budget), so we label them the *design segment.* The other segment, the *business segment,* is more interested in office use, local area networks (LAN), and wide area connectivity and has much higher price sensitivities. Profiles of the other (descriptor) variables show that the design segment includes primarily design engineers from smaller firms.

A more formal approach to profiling involves a technique called *discriminant analysis,* which seeks combinations of descriptor variables that best separate the clusters or segments. Other techniques, such as CART analysis, also can be used for this purpose.

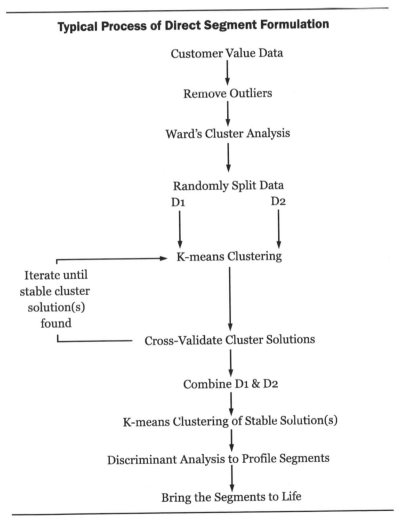

Typical Process of Direct Segment Formulation

Customer Value Data

Remove Outliers

Ward's Cluster Analysis

Randomly Split Data

D1   D2

K-means Clustering

Iterate until stable cluster solution(s) found

Cross-Validate Cluster Solutions

Combine D1 & D2

K-means Clustering of Stable Solution(s)

Discriminant Analysis to Profile Segments

Bring the Segments to Life

EXHIBIT 3.10
Typical process of direct segment formation.

Exhibit 3.10 depicts how the process we have outlined thus far might work. There may be many false starts, but this diagram should provide a good initial benchmark.

TARGETING INDIVIDUAL CUSTOMERS

We now consider some approaches used to target customers when rich data are available about each customer. With the increasing use of recording and tracking methods, especially transactions data (e.g., scanner, website data), many companies have detailed profiles and a rich set of behavioral data for each of their customers. For example, for each of its 15 million customers, Harrah's Entertainment possesses more than 200 customer-related variables. The company can use such data in many ways, including determining which offers to provide each customer. When a company decides that it wishes to target certain customers within its database with an offer of some sort (e.g., an e-mail solicitation), it usually can use one of three methods:

1. Demographic sorting.
2. RFM (recency, frequency, monetary value) modeling.
3. Choice modeling (Chapter 2).

Demographic sorting means that a firm arbitrarily selects a target list, using some customer characteristics like age, income, or the like, depending on the product category. Although far better than random/mass marketing in most cases, it still lags behind the two behavior-based approaches.

The RFM approach creates a score for each customer or prospect based not on demographics or firmographics but rather on related purchase behavior. The idea behind the RFM model is that, across a wide range of product categories,

- Customers who purchased recently are more likely to buy again (R);
- Customers who have purchased frequently are more likely to buy again (F); and
- Customers who have spent the most money in total (over some planning period) are more likely to buy again (M).

So, based on experience or some form of data analysis, the analyst assigns, for example, a recency score as follows:

Last purchased in the past 3 months	25 points
Last purchased in the past 3-6 months	20
Last purchased in the past 6-9 months	10
Last purchased in the past 12-18 months	5
Last purchased in the past 18 months	0

and then must develop similar "scoring rules" for frequency and monetary value, add them together, and thus create a composite score for each customer.

With these scores, targets may be sorted from highest to lowest total score in deciles (top 10%, second 10%). On the basis of market test data or a past campaign, the firm can construct a "lift chart" such as the one shown in Exhibit 3.11, which indicates that targeting the top 30–40% of the list generates the most profit for the campaign.

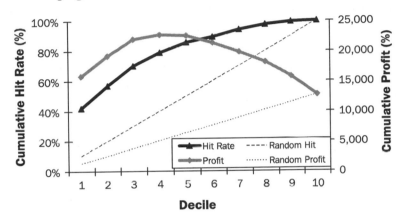

EXHIBIT 3.11

Hit rate and profit associated with RFM targeting rule, showing that targeting the top 30–40% of the list generates the most profit for the campaign.

Another powerful way to segment the market and target appropriately involves the choice models that we briefly described in Chapter 2. In this approach, we use actual customer behavior to understand customer value and develop a targeting strategy. Choice models are very powerful for segmentation and targeting because, at the individual customer level, they answer several questions, such as, "With marketing plan X, what is the likelihood that this customer will buy from us?" and "If this customer buys, how much will he or she purchase?"

In this case, marketing plan X might mean:

...if we send a direct mail piece,

...if we make an offer at price Y,

...if we include the customer within the set of "platinum" prospects (more customer visits), and so on.

Then, the targeting decision can be made on the basis of the following criterion: "On a customer-by-customer basis, if we take marketing action X, what are the short- and long-term returns we get from this customer after accounting for the cost of that action, relative to not taking that action?"

Note the elements of this statement: The firm must specify a marketing action (X), which may be appropriate for one set of customers but not for others. It must account for short- and long-term "returns" (sales? profit? customer loyalty? customer satisfaction?), as well as the costs associated with the marketing action dedicated to the individual customer or prospect.

This approach to joint segmentation (i.e., likelihood of purchase and expected return) and targeting (choosing which marketing programs to execute with which customers) requires some sophisticated statistical analysis to execute efficiently. However, the significance of this approach rests at the conceptual level: You must think about how marketing programs affect the likelihood of individual customers making brand choice and purchase quantity decisions and be able to calculate the financial returns from such programs.

Direct marketing applications make broad use of such approaches; a direct marketer often chooses a sample from a large database and sends out the offer to a test sample. By observing who purchases (and how much), the marketer can integrate that new information with other information available about customers to assess the likely response of other similar customers. The firm uses probability of purchase information to calculate expected customer profitability and directs its marketing campaign to those customer segments whose expected profitability exceeds the cost of reaching them.

EXHIBIT 3.12

Choice-based segmentation example for database marketing: Target customers whose (expected) profitability exceeds the cost of reaching them by comparing column D with the cost to reach that customer.

Customer	A Purchase Probability	B Average Purchase Volume	C Margin	D Customer Profitability = A x B x C
1	30%	$31.00	0.70	$6.51
2	2%	$143.00	0.60	$1.72
3	10%	$54.00	0.67	$3.62
4	5%	$88.00	0.62	$2.73
5	60%	$20.00	0.58	$6.96
6	22%	$60.00	0.47	$6.20
7	11%	$77.00	0.38	$3.22
8	13%	$39.00	0.66	$3.35
9	1%	$184.00	0.56	$1.03
10	4%	$72.00	0.65	$1.87

Average Expected Profit = $3.72

EXAMPLE

Exhibit 3.12 shows part of a direct marketing database after the firm has completed the choice modeling step. Choice modeling provides the data in column A—the purchase probability. Which customers should the firm target? Suppose that the total cost of reaching one of these customers is $3.50. What should the firm do? Firms commonly use several approaches to answer this question. First, if it looks at the average expected profit, it may decide to target all 10 groups and make a small profit ($10 \times (\$3.72 - \$3.50)$ = $2.20). Alternatively, it may target customers 1, 3, 5, and 6 and make $6.51 + $3.62 + $6.96 + $6.20 - (4 \times \$3.50)$ = $9.29. Simply by using choice-based modeling, the firm can target customers that enable it to improve its profitability by over 400%. In contrast, using a more traditional segmentation that relies on average purchase volume, the firm would target, say, 30%, or the three largest customers in this case—2, 4, and 9—and lose $5.02 per customer!

In practice, firms target customers who exceed some threshold (a profitability measure) or fall into the most profitable percentage of the customer database. Choice-based segmentation also can be used in various ways.

EXAMPLE

In its third year of existence, ABB Electric of Wisconsin faced a 50% drop in total industry sales. The company sold medium-sized power transformers, breakers, switchgear, relays, and the like to electric utilities in the North American market. As a new firm in an industry dominated by General Electric, Westinghouse, and McGraw-Edison, ABB had to find a way to win customers from these major competitors, or it would go out of business. ABB engaged a consultant, Dennis Gensch, to upgrade its information and help it gain insight into its customers. Gensch used customer research and consumer-choice models to comprehend the preferences and decision-making processes of ABB's customers. He then helped ABB use choice-based segmentation to segment its market and design new products and a service program to better fit the needs of the customers it targeted. At the heart of ABB's success was the insight it gained into its customers, as well as its greater understanding of how to segment the market to which it targeted its products and services. Gensch and ABB first isolated the 8–10 attributes customers used to select among alternative suppliers. Using these characteristics, they could predict choice behavior and form customer segments that valued different combinations of these attributes differently. Gensch thus estimated the choice probability of every customer for every major brand in the market. He then tested for significant differences in those choice probabilities and used the differences to assign customers to one of four segments:

1. *ABB loyal*: Customers for whom the probability of choosing ABB was significantly higher than for any other competitor.
2. *Competitive*: Customers whose probability of choosing ABB was highest but not by a statistically significant amount relative to the probability for the next-best alternative.
3. *Switchable*: Customers who preferred a competitor to ABB but for whom ABB was a close (not statistically significantly different) second choice.
4. *Competitor loyal*: Customers who preferred a competitor to ABB by a statistically significant amount.

ABB used this segmentation scheme to focus its marketing efforts, resulting in substantial gains over its "business as usual" and no incremental increases in marketing spending (Gensch, Aversa, and Moore 1990). Exhibit 3.13 shows the output from such choice modeling using data from Exhibit 2.3 as input.

EXHIBIT 3.13

Output of ABB choice model, with both probability of purchase and switchability indicators for each customer.

Customer	Annual Purchase Volume ($K)	District	Firm Chosen	Estimated Purchase Probabilities				Type
				A(BB)	Firm B	Firm C	Firm D	
1	$761	1	B	13.9%	83.8%	2.3%	0.0%	lost
2	$625	1	D	0.0%	0.0%	2.2%	97.8%	lost
3	$643	2	A	54.3%	45.7%	0.0%	0.0%	competitive
4	$562	3	D	39.4%	49.2%	0.0%	11.4%	switchable

Real-time targeting of online customers

The STP concept and the underlying principles apply to both online and offline customers. However, segmentation and targeting in the online world introduces some different implementation approaches. For example, pure online businesses (e.g., eBay, Amazon, Expedia) may randomly select Web visitors and ask them (either with or without incentives) to participate in a needs survey (i.e., these are the basis variables for segmentation). At the same time, profile variables can be accessed which include the following:

- Referral source for the respondent's visit to the website (e.g., referring site, whether the visit was direct or was it re-directed from another site such as a search engine or an affiliate site, referral from paid search versus non-paid search, keywords associated with the visit).

- Geographical location of respondent (e.g., country and region from IP address, Geo location from mobile device).
- Time of day of visit.
- Whether respondent is registered at the site.
- Whether respondent is a repeat visitor.
- Device used to access website (e.g., browser, screen resolution).
- Behaviors (e.g., time spent at site, page-view history, purchases made).

After segmenting the visitors using the survey data, the average values of the needs variables in each segment provide insights for developing the appropriate content and offerings for that segment. The profile variables can be used to target future visitors to the website by automatically identifying the closest segment to which they belong, and directing them to the most relevant content (perhaps through alternative landing pages) for the segment to which a visitor is assigned. For example, according to a December 2010 WK Roper poll (www.slideshare.net/sapient/sapientnitro-gfk-roper-ho), more than 30% of smart phone users use their mobile devices while they shop at a store to find more information about the product they are interested in, look for consumer reviews and to compare prices. Savvy retailers are providing the relevant information, including customized promotions via focused mobile landing pages combined with short mobile URLs.

SUMMARY

Segmenting a market means dividing it into distinct subsets of customers, such that each subset (which could be as small as an individual customer) reacts to messages and product offerings differently—in other words, has different needs. Marketing opportunities increase when a firm recognizes these differences and measures them. Market segmentation as a theory helps illuminate and explain these differences; as a strategy, our focus here, it helps firms exploit the differences as well through the STP approach.

Segmentation requires defining a market, ideally on the basis of shared customer needs rather than product similarities. Sound segmentation demands that analysts specify the objectives for the study, define a sample, collect relevant data, analyze them, and interpret the results. People use a number of techniques to address segmentation problems, including cluster analysis, discriminant analysis, cross-classification analysis, regression, and choice models.

When a firm has completed a segmentation analysis and targets one or more segments, it must implement its segmentation scheme, which consists of two related tasks: (1) allocating resources and developing a specific marketing program for each segment, including appropriate and appealing product features, price, distribution channels, and ad messages, and (2) identifying current or potential customers to determine their segment membership.

Customers described according to the same descriptor variables used to develop the targeting scheme can be assigned, using discriminant function(s), to membership in the appropriate segment. By following these two steps, firms can identify the target segment to which any current or potential customer belongs and thus direct the appropriate marketing program to those customers.

CHAPTER 4

Positioning

Think of a safe car. Did Volvo pop into your head? Now think about a cold medicine to take at night; did you bring forth an image of Nyquil? If you are looking for healthy frozen food, you probably think of Healthy Choice. These products (or more generally, offerings) have well-defined positions in the minds of customers and are differentiated from the other offerings in the market on one or more dimensions of importance to customers. Not long ago, the mention of photography would conjure up Kodak. However, today, when one thinks of "digital photography" Kodak is not the top brand that comes to mind, even though Kodak pioneered digital photography. Interestingly, Volvo did not pioneer many of the safety features for which its cars are known – GM was the first company to perform barrier crash tests in 1934; Saab was the first to produce cars with a safety cage in 1949; and Ford was the first to equip its fleet with airbags in 1971. But, Volvo was the first to adopt a corporate mindset of "safety first" by establishing a system of "safety engineering" to engineer its cars on the "safety" dimension, and communicating this position consistently to the markets.

"Positioning" in the minds of customers typically results when an organization follows deliberate strategies to design products with characteristics distinct from those of its competitors and then communicates these differences to the targeted customers. Thus, a differentiation strategy makes a firm's product superior in

Positioning: A deliberate strategy to differentiate a product according to its unique characteristics and communicate the differences to customers.

some way, whereas a positioning strategy finds a superior position in the minds of customers.

We use the term "positioning" to denote a management process that leads to a "position," but firms can only garner positions that customers in the targeted segment are willing to grant them. Some marketers argue that in today's information-rich and customer-centric markets, positioning is an archaic and unworkable strategy. Others suggest today's markets require firms to undertake a more flexible marketing approach that uses customized messages in different media to target different segments. Simon (1971, p. 40-41) expresses our view well: "A wealth of information creates a poverty of attention." That is, more than ever before, firms need well-conceived positioning and branding strategies that align with the limited-attention economy. Firms must seek a focused marketing approach that ensures customers remember the brand, associate a compelling benefit with it, and have favorable experiences with the product or service that reinforce the brand name and its benefits. A well-executed positioning strategy represents an essential ingredient for achieving these ends.

Other examples of clearly positioned products include Apple's exhortation to "Think different," Red Bull's conceptualization as an energy drink, Subway's association with healthy sandwiches, and *Forbes* as a capitalist tool. Advertising provides a common way to convey a product's position. Recall some of the classic advertising campaigns that have effectively conveyed positioning strategies, such as Avis's "We try harder" and United Airlines' "Fly the friendly skies."

But these are remarkable examples. How can other firms follow their lead and determine the most appropriate positioning strategy for their brands?

POSITIONING THROUGH BRAND LINKAGES

Positioning requires an understanding of three types of brand linkages: (1) to the product category, (2) to the customer segment, and (3) to the relevant purchase or usage occasion. For well-established brands or those with descriptive names (e.g., Travelers Insurance), the first link occurs automatically, but with a new brand, the firm must manage its positioning to tell people what it represents. Conversely, the customer segment link, though perhaps the most important of the three connections, rarely occurs explicitly through either the brand name or its advertising message. Sometimes the targeted customer segment is obvious; Motel 6 clearly targets budget travelers with its positioning claim that it offers a "comfortable night's stay at the lowest price of any national chain." Other times, the positioning and advertising fail to resonate with customers in the target segment, who then ignore any claims. For example, GM tried to reposition its Oldsmobile cars for a younger segment through improved styling and a creative ad campaign that called its offering, "Not your father's Oldsmobile." Yet, this approach never played well with the target segment.

In terms of its relative performance within the market, a brand's positioning can reflect a battle for the customer's mind. From an understanding of such battles, several generic positioning approaches have emerged. Most brands follow either a central or differentiation positioning strategy. A central positioning strategy appeals particularly to brands in a monopolistic or dominant position within their target segments. BMW's "The ultimate driving machine" and Coke's "It's the real thing" represent two statements of a central brand, and Intel's "Intel inside" or "the computer inside" taglines position the ingredient brand centrally. Similarly, a "me-too" or mimicking brand can employ a variation on central positioning by inhabiting a clone position, as long as the new copycat brand

- Delivers the same benefits as the market leader,
- Makes the benefits easy for the customer to determine objectively, and
- Offers a product at a *significantly* lower price than the leader.

For example, in the 1980s, clones of IBM personal computers flooded the market. Experienced users could evaluate the performance of these machines, so this segment of customers considered the clones a better value than the high-priced market leader IBM. Many low-involvement private-label retailer brands use a similar positioning strategy.

If a central positioning is not available, the firm can choose a differentiation or edge strategy. The most difficult differentiation or edge positioning to execute is in creating a new product category; more common and easier strategies involve using attributes not employed by the market leader, linking the product directly to a segment (e.g., "the Pepsi Generation"), or linking it to a specific customer benefit.

Although many positioning options are available, the management challenge is trying to understand current and possible future positioning options and communicating the selected option clearly. Perceptual and preference mapping techniques help develop and communicate the optimal positioning strategies.

POSITIONING USING PERCEPTUAL MAPS

To position products in increasingly crowded markets, managers must understand the dimensions along which target customers perceive products or services in a category, as well as their views of the firm's offering relative to competitive offerings. To understand the competitive structure of their markets, managers should ask the following questions:

- How do our customers (current or potential) view our brand?
- Which brands do these customers perceive to be our closest competitors?
- What product and company attributes are most responsible for these perceived differences?

Perceptual mapping methods provide systematic, structured approaches to answer these questions.

Perceptual Map: A two or three dimensional display of customer perceptions of competing alternatives in a market.

Perceptual maps use graphical displays with the following characteristics: (1) The distances between products indicate similarities in the minds of customers, such that the shorter the distance, the more similarly the products are perceived by consumers; (2) a vector on the map (shown by a line with an arrow) indicates both magnitude and direction, usually to denote product attributes; and (3) the map axes, a special set of vectors, which suggest the broad underlying dimensions that best characterize how customers differentiate among alternatives. Maps usually incorporate straight lines (axes) at right angles to represent dimensions, but these axes also can be rigidly rotated to aid interpretation. For example, in a two-dimensional map, horizontal and vertical axes often characterize the two dimensions, but they also can be rotated so that, for example, one axis moves from the lower left (southwest) to the upper right (northeast) quadrant, and the other refers to the shift from the lower right (southeast) to the upper left (northwest).

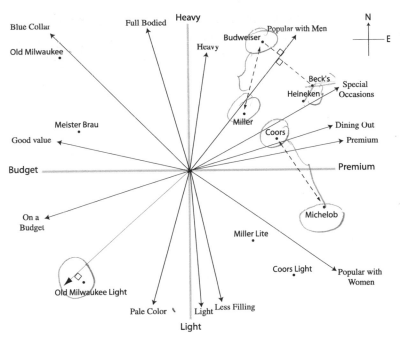

EXHIBIT 4.1

A perceptual map of the beer market, showing (among other things) that Budweiser is the most popular beer with men, whereas Old Milwaukee Light is the least popular. The map summarizes customer evaluations of beer according to 13 attributes into two dimensions: (1) budget–premium and (2) light–heavy. Source: Moore and Pessemier 1993, p. 145.

EXAMPLE

Consider the perceptual map in Exhibit 4.1, which summarizes how a customer segment views the beer market. The perceived distance between Budweiser and Miller is approximately the same as that between Coors and Michelob, and Beck's and Heineken are perceived as the closest pair among this set of brands. Moving in a northeast direction from the origin, the vectors show that these beers increase in popularity among men. That is, Budweiser is the most popular with men, and Old Milwaukee Light is the least popular. Budweiser (and then Beck's) appears the farthest along the northeast direction. If we drop perpendicular lines from the Budweiser and Beck's points to the vector denoted "popular with men," this connection becomes obvious. Similarly, a perpendicular line from Old Milwaukee Light to the popular with men vector, extended in the southwest direction, clearly demonstrates its lack of popularity. Customer perceptions of these beers, according to each of their attributes, can be interpreted in the same manner.

Note also that the horizontal axis (east direction) associates most closely with the attributes "premium," "dining out," and "special occasions." In the west direction, the horizontal axis is affiliated with the attributes "on a budget" and "good value." Thus, the horizontal axis (west to east or left to right) indicates an underlying dimension of "budget–premium," along which customers seem to characterize their perceptions of the differences between these beers. This map therefore captures significant factors that define the competitive structure of the beer market. In turn, beer manufacturers can draw several other conclusions from this map:

- The clusters of beers, such as Beck's and Heineken, identify (sub)categories that the market may perceive differently than the way brand managers define their competitors.

- Michelob is located between the heavy and light beers. If its advertising positions it as a "mid-strength" beer, it obtains a differentiated position; otherwise, the market likely regards it simply as a "nothing" beer.

- Old Milwaukee Light has very little direct competition (as indicated by the lack of other brands near its location), which indicates a potential opportunity for a new beer positioned in this quadrant (if, of course, there is a large enough segment of customers). To be positioned in this quadrant, a beer needs to be pale in color and low priced. Experienced beer drinkers probably do not consider this combination of attributes appealing, but novice beer drinkers may appreciate it. Thus, a new brand targeted toward new beer drinkers could choose a name that clearly communicates these benefits for this segment of consumers.

- Whether a beer is popular with women does not indicate anything about whether it will be popular with men (because these two attributes are perpendicular to each other). Thus, whereas Beck's and Budweiser are equally popular with men, among women, Beck's is more popular.

Despite the potential valuable insights it offers, the map in Exhibit 4.1 has a major weakness: It says nothing about the brand locations that are most attractive to customers. For example, do more customers prefer heavy premium beers or light budget beers? The map gives no indication, and without such insights, firms run the risk of investing in products differentiated along dimensions that are not aligned with increased customer preferences. To address this issue, preference maps incorporate such information and thus help determine the overall customer value of any location on a map.

COMBINING PERCEPTUAL AND PREFERENCE MAPPING

Scientists first developed perceptual mapping techniques to map psychological measurements of how people perceive objects that vary on multiple dimensions. Because both perceptions and preferences influence customer behavior, marketers have adapted multidimensional scaling (MDS) methods to represent customer perceptions and preferences for a set of entities (e.g., brands, company logos, department stores, presidential candidates) on a map or graph.

The MDS methods vary depending on the nature of the input data (e.g., similarities, perceptions, preferences) and the manipulations of these data used to derive the map. Exhibit 4.2 summarizes the mapping methods employed in a positioning analysis; we specifically discuss (1) perceptual maps derived from attribute-based data, (2) preference maps that rely on preference data (e.g., rank-orders of brands by customers, stimuli ratings based on customer preferences), and (3) joint-space maps that include both perceptions and preferences. We also briefly describe how to incorporate price as an attribute within perceptual and joint-space maps.

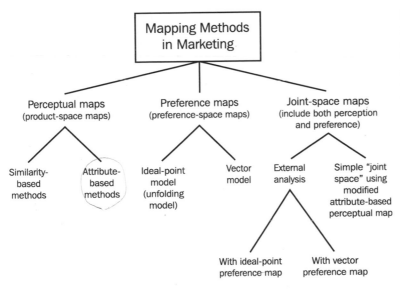

EXHIBIT 4.2

Mapping methods in marketing fall into three categories: perceptual, preference, and joint space. (The software available at www.decisionpro.biz supports all these types except similarity-based maps.)

Attribute-Based Perceptual Maps

Attribute-based methods can be used to derive perceptual maps from customer evaluations of competing products along pre-specified attributes. The evaluations are obtained from customers within a selected target segment of interest (Chapter 3). This process involves four major steps.

Step 1: Identify products and product attributes for evaluation

The attributes included in the analysis should depend on the objectives of the study. For strategic positioning studies (e.g., brand image), a broad set of competing alternatives and attributes (both tangible and intangible) work best, whereas tactical positioning studies (e.g., product design) focus on attributes that can be manipulated directly (e.g., roominess of car). In Exhibit 4.3, we summarize various generic attributes that may provide a useful starting point for selecting attributes.

FEATURES are characteristics that supplement a product's basic function (e.g., stereo system in a car).

PERFORMANCE refers to levels at which the product's primary characteristics operate.

DURABILITY is a measure of the product's expected operating life.

RELIABILITY is a measure of the probability that a product will malfunction or fail within a specified time period.

SERVICEABILITY is a measure of the ease of fixing a product that malfunctions or fails.

STYLE describes how well the product looks and feels to the customer.

PRODUCT IMAGE refers to attributes that convey the emotional aspects of the product - attributes that stir the heart as well as the mind of the customer. These include attributes such as the prestige or reputation associated with a product/company, the perceived lifestyle of the people who use the product, etc.

DELIVERY refers to all aspects of how the product or service is delivered to the customer. It includes the speed, accuracy, and the care attending the delivery process.

INSTALLATION refers to activities needed to be completed before the product becomes operational in its planned location.

TRAINING AND CONSULTING refer to the support services provided by the company to train the customer and its personnel in the use and maintenance of the product, and to help derive the maximum value from the use of the product.

REPAIR AND MAINTENANCE refers to convenience and quality of services provided by the company to prevent product failures, and to repair the product in the event it fails to conform to expected performance.

OTHER SERVICES include warranty, availability of "loaners," and services that add value to the customer's purchase or use of the product.

SERVICE IMAGE refers to a number of attributes that contribute to the overall perception of the service. It includes such attributes as competence, friendliness, and courteousness of service employees, the perception of being pampered with personalized attention, etc.

PERCEIVED QUALITY refers to the degree to which the product meets customers' expectations of what the product/service should be. It is closely associated with the other attributes such as features, performance, reliability, durability, etc. that are listed above (Garvin 1987).

Step 2: Obtain perception data from questionnaires given to defined target segments

Perception data should be organized into a matrix that represents customer perceptions of each alternative for each pre-specified attribute. Customers can rank or rate either all alternatives for one attribute at a time or one alternative at a time for all attributes. For example, airlines differ along many perceptual attributes, such as convenience, punctuality, overall service, and comfort. The following data matrix (constructed prior to the United–Continental merger), which summarizes the perceptions of just *one customer,* illustrates the nature of the data collected and the range of customer ratings, from 1 (worst) to 9 (best), for each attribute. Such data are usually averaged across customers to obtain average perceptions, which represent the perceptions of the target segment. This approach reflects a key assumption of perceptual maps, namely, that customers in a target segment share similar perceptions about the competing alternatives available to them. If that assumption is false, average perception data depict the segment's common beliefs inaccurately, and the firm should instead use sub-segments that actually do share similar perceptions.

	American	United	US Airways	Continental	Southwest
Convenience	5	8	3	3	8
Punctuality	6	5	5	4	8
Overall Service	8	7	5	4	6
Comfort	6	6	4	4	3

Step 3: Select a perceptual mapping method

Positioning studies often obtain customer evaluations of 10 or more attributes relevant to the set of alternatives. But all these attributes are unlikely to provide unique information about the perceptions customers have about these alternatives. Rather, subsets of attributes probably tap combined underlying themes, also known as factors, axes, or dimensions. Thus, in the airline example, perceived overall service and comfort might both be attributes that tap the more fundamental dimension of perceived quality.

Several statistical methods (e.g., factor analysis) help determine from the data whether attributes can be grouped or condensed into a smaller set of underlying constructs but still retain as much of the original information as possible.

Step 4: Plot the resulting map

The map that emerges from the previous steps should include the products and the relevant attributes, as illustrated in Exhibit 4.3. The output from Step 3 indicates the location of each product on each dimension. Two- or three-dimensional maps are most common, but the decision about the number of dimensions to use depends on how much extra information the third dimension provides compared with the two-dimensional map. As an example, we plot the airline perception data in a perceptual map in Exhibit 4.4.

EXHIBIT 4.4

Airline data perceptual map.

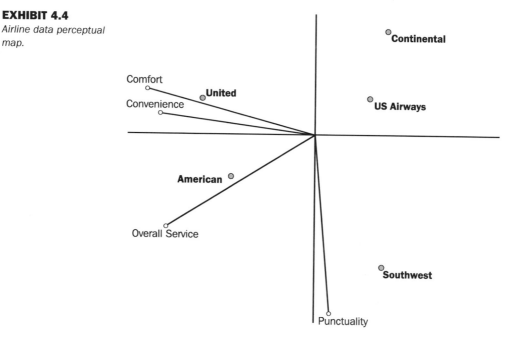

The perceptual map of the airline perception data shows that Southwest performs well on punctuality, American on overall service, and United on comfort and convenience.

Attribute methods plusses and minuses

Attribute-based methods thus provide a powerful set of tools for perceptual mapping. They are particularly useful when customers understand clearly how the various attributes differentiate the product alternatives. Furthermore, a perceptual map takes numerical data (which humans generally find hard to process) and translates it into a visual form, which the human brain processes much more readily.

However, perceptual maps cannot indicate which areas of the map are most desirable to the target segments of customers. In other words, the maps do not incorporate information about customer preferences. Two widely used mapping options incorporate such preference information: (1) preference mapping, which focuses just on mapping preferences, and (2) joint-space mapping, which incorporates both perceptions and preferences in the same map.

Preference Maps

Their preferences allow customers to choose among alternatives. Thus, preferences differ fundamentally from perceptions; whereas all customers may perceive Volvo as safe, some may place a high value on that safety while others may not. In addition, unlike perceptions, preferences do not necessarily change according to the magnitude of an attribute. That is, customers sometimes have an ideal level of an attribute (e.g., sweetness of a soft drink), above or below which the product becomes less preferable. However, in other cases, customers always prefer more of the attribute (e.g., quality of a TV image) or less of an attribute (e.g., waiting time before a car is repaired). Preference maps that incorporate the first scenario as inverted, U-shaped preferences are referred to as ideal-point (or unfolding) models, whereas those that employ linear preference functions are referred to as vector models. Exhibit 4.5 summarizes how these two types of preferences can be represented on maps.

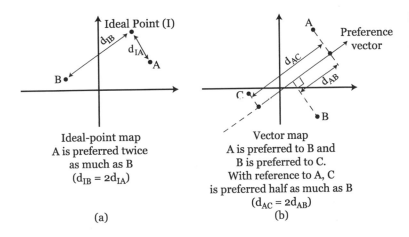

Ideal-point map
A is preferred twice
as much as B
$(d_{IB} = 2d_{IA})$

(a)

Vector map
A is preferred to B and
B is preferred to C.
With reference to A, C
is preferred half as much as B
$(d_{AC} = 2d_{AB})$

(b)

EXHIBIT 4.5

Two maps that represent preferences. In ideal-point maps, distances directly indicate preference, such that the greater the distance from the ideal point, the less preferred the brand is. In vector maps, product locations are projected onto a preference vector (dashed lines in b), and distances are measured along the preference vector.

In Exhibit 4.5a, a customer's preference appears as an ideal point (i.e., the location on the map where that customer's ideal product would be located). In the map, products located farther away from the ideal point are less desirable to that customer than are the closer ones. Therefore, for the customer in Exhibit 4.5, product offering B, which is twice as far from the ideal point as is product A, is preferred half as much as A.

If the customer questionnaire includes an attribute labeled "preference," and therefore permits the respondent to provide a preference rating for each alternative, the resulting map displays a vector that indicates the direction of increasing preference. The farther along the vector a product is positioned, the more that customer prefers the product. In Exhibit 4.5b, product A is farthest along the preference vector. If product B is half as far from A as C is from A along that vector, the customer prefers B twice as much as she prefers C—but not as much as A.

Although preference maps are useful, they also contain a crucial limitation: They cannot indicate which attributes should be changed to make a focal product more appealing to the target segment. That's where joint-space maps come into play.

Joint-Space Maps

Joint-space maps incorporate both perceptions and preferences into the same map. There are two simple methods for generating joint-space maps: Averaged Ideal-Point model and Averaged Vector model. More sophisticated methods employ external analysis, along with average perception data, to create joint-space maps.

Averaged ideal-point model

Generating an average ideal-point map requires a hypothetical *ideal brand* that appears among the set of alternatives customers can rate. That is, customers not only rate the available brands but also indicate where their ideal brand would fall, if it existed, in terms of the different attributes. The perceptual map thus includes these averaged perceptions of the ideal brand; the farther away an existing brand is from the ideal brand for the segment, the less it would be preferred by these customers.

Averaged vector model

As described previously, if a preference attribute appears in the set of attributes or if the market share of each brand is a surrogate for preference, the associated vector in the resulting perceptual map indicates the direction of increasing preference. Again, the farther a product appears along this vector, the more it is preferred, and other attributes closely aligned with this preference attribute can be interpreted as drivers of or explanations for customer preferences.

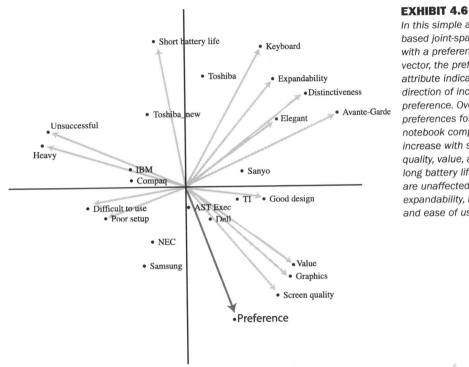

EXHIBIT 4.6

In this simple attribute-based joint-space map with a preference vector, the preference attribute indicates the direction of increasing preference. Overall preferences for notebook computers increase with screen quality, value, and long battery life but are unaffected by expandability, keyboard, and ease of use.

EXAMPLE

Exhibit 4.6 illustrates the preference vector approach for evaluating notebook computers. In it, the preference vector shows that customer preferences increase as screen quality and perceived value improves but decrease with lower levels of battery life. In this example, the two-dimensional map recovers, or explains, more than 80% of the variance in the preference attribute. However, in other cases, it could recover a much lower percentage, say less than 50%, which would make it unwise to use the map to interpret preference structures, even though it may still be useful for interpreting perceptual dimensions. When the variance recovery for the preference vector is poor, it may be worthwhile to drop some attributes from the analysis in an attempt to produce a joint-space map that is easier to interpret.

External analysis

External analysis refers to a mapping method that assumes respondents who have common perceptions about a set of product alternatives also have differing preferences for those alternatives. The model therefore overlays the preferences of each respondent onto a common perceptual map that has been developed externally. However, the external perceptual map normally derives from the same respondents and employs the previously described attribute-based approaches.

As an example, PREFMAP3 (Meulman, Heiser, and Carroll 1986) starts with a vector-based perceptual map that indicates the locations of the products. For each respondent, it then introduces either an ideal brand or a preference vector into the map that corresponds with the brand positions on the perceptual map. Each respondent has provided a unique ideal point or preference vector, as the case may be, so the model places each customer in a perceptual map in which the customer's preferences are closer to more preferred brands and farther from less preferred brands.

Thus, in addition to average preference data, a joint-space map also requires a data matrix that consists of preference ratings for a certain number of brands and respondents, such as in the table in Exhibit 4.6. This table indicates preference ratings for five airlines, which five customers rated using a 1–9 scale on which 1 is the most preferred and 9 the least preferred. An external analysis creates a preference vector for each customer, which it then superimposes on the prior perceptual map that corresponds to each customer's preferences.

	American	United	US Airways	Continental	Southwest
Customer 1	1	7	2	5	8
Customer 2	7	7	4	2	1
Customer 3	4	6	6	6	7
Customer 4	3	1	8	6	2
Customer 5	2	2	3	7	8

From the perceptual map in Exhibit 4.4, we know that this market segment perceives Southwest as the punctuality leader, American as best in overall service, and United as providing comfort and convenience; it also believes US Airways and Continental lag on all these dimensions. Now suppose American Airlines finds it is not doing well in this market segment and therefore considers repositioning itself as an airline that either arrives "On Time with Service to Spare" (Option A) to compete with Southwest or offers "Comfort on YOUR schedule" (Option B) to compete with United (the two potential gaps/opportunities in this market). But is there really a market for American in either gap? Recall that the map in Exhibit 4.4 only shows what customers perceive and nothing about what they prefer. To determine whether a market really exists in either gap, we also need data about customer preferences or choices.

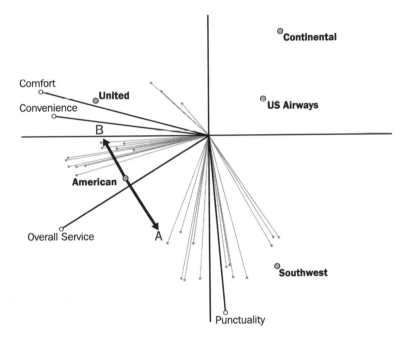

EXHIBIT 4.7

Airline map with individual customer preferences (narrow lines) and two possible new positions for American Airlines: A and B.

The map in Exhibit 4.7 is the same as that in Exhibit 4.4, except that preference information from 30 customers, including the five customers in the preceding table is overlaid on the map.

To read this map appropriately, remember that:

- A line on the map indicates the direction in which that attribute increases along that line and away from the origin (or decreases away from the origin in the opposite direction). Thus, airlines positioned in the upper left quadrant offer more comfort, whereas those positioned in the right quadrants offer less.

- The length of the line, measured from the origin, indicates the variance of that attribute that the map can explain. The longer this line, the greater explanatory power the attribute has for interpreting the map.

- Attributes that are both longer and closer to the horizontal (vertical) axis indicate the meaning of that axis.
- To position an airline on an attribute, we would draw an imaginary perpendicular line from the location of the airline onto the specific attribute (e.g., the dashed lines in Exhibit 4.1).

In the map in Exhibit 4.7, the narrow lines represent the direction of increasing preference for each individual customer. Thus, it identifies two segments of customers: one whose preferences increase in a westerly direction, generally toward United's current positioning, and another whose preferences increase in a southerly direction, toward Southwest's position.

TRANSLATING PREFERENCE TO CHOICE

We must caution at this point that higher preferences do not necessarily translate into more customer purchases. Customers might not be able to purchase the product offerings they prefer the most, especially if those offerings are expensive; people may prefer to stay at the Ritz-Carlton but end up choosing the Day's Inn. Alternatively, the product might not be available at the time of purchase or, if the customer seeks variety, he or she may prefer Coke to ginger ale but choose to purchase ginger ale on a particular day.

To ensure study results will reflect marketplace effects more accurately, several methods transform preferences into choices. Two commonly used choice rules are as follows:

- *First Choice Rule:* Customers always choose (or purchase) the product they prefer most, even if one or more other alternatives are also acceptable.

  The first choice rule typically applies well in product categories that are (1) infrequently purchased, (2) expensive, and (3) visible during use (e.g., clothing) and that (4) require high-involvement decision making on the part of customers. Automobiles, cosmetics, designer clothes, and digital cameras all represent product categories in which such a rule is appropriate.

- *Share of Preference Rule:* Customers distribute their purchases across different product offerings proportional to their relative preferences for each.

  This choice rule is applicable and useful for product categories that are (1) frequently purchased (e.g., soft drinks), (2) relatively inexpensive, and (3) not visible during use (e.g., blank CDs), as well as those (4) that do not require careful decision making or (5) for which customers seek variety from time to time. For example, the share of preference rule works well with the beer, wine, soft drink, and breakfast cereal categories.

In the airline example, under the first choice rule, American actually has achieved a rather poor position, because United "beats" it among customers whose preference vectors point west, and Southwest beats it among customers whose preferences point south. The map indicates that position B ("Comfort on YOUR schedule") would gain American significant market share, but a move to position A ("On Time with Service to Spare") would not.

REVERSE MAPPING (FROM MAP TO RAW DATA)

Traditional perceptual mapping transforms customer perceptions and preferences into maps to aid decision making. However, to more fully exploit the potential of perceptual mapping, it is useful to have a reverse transformation from the map to the data—a so-called "reverse map." For example, with such a reverse map, a manager could re-position the focal brand directly on the map and then assess the changes in perceptions that the firm would need to bring about in order to achieve the new position and calculate the forecasted market share at that new position. (See the Technical Note available at www.decisionpro.biz for more details and for an illustration of how a software implementation of reverse mapping allows users to go back and forth between the map and the data in order to explore alternative positioning strategies.) For the Airlines example above, Exhibit 4.8 summarizes the original perceptual data for American Airlines, and the reverse-mapped attribute values corresponding to the two new potential positions, **A** and **B**.

EXHIBIT 4.8

*Example of reverse mapping from the map to the attributes. The columns correspond to attribute values for various map positions for American Airlines. American Airlines would have to improve punctuality substantially even at the expense of lowering perceived comfort in order to move from its current position to position **A**.*

	Original perceptual data	Reverse-mapped data for position **A**	Reverse-mapped data for position **B**
Convenience	5	5.2	6.9
Punctuality	6	7.1	5.5
Overall Service	8	7.6	7.7
Comfort	6	4.9	6.2

INCORPORATING PRICE AS AN ATTRIBUTE

Perceptual maps can represent price in several ways. For example, in attribute-based perceptual maps, price appears simply as another attribute along which customers evaluate the products. Alternatively, actual prices of products can become additional attributes during map development, without questioning customers.

Another way to incorporate price divides the coordinates of each alternative by its price along each dimension of the map. Exhibit 4.9 provides an example: a map of the mouthwash category both with and without price. When price transforms the coordinates of each alternative, the underlying dimension becomes per-dollar coordinates. Without a "dollar-metric" transformation, it appears Signal should not survive in the market, because other brands dominate it along both dimensions (Exhibit 4.9a). For example, Listerine is perceived to taste better and have the same ability to fight bad breath. But the price-transformed coordinates (Exhibit 4.9b) clarify that its price-adjusted position makes Signal an attractive alternative that is not dominated by other alternatives on either dimension.

EXHIBIT 4.9

Perceptual maps with and without a "dollarmetric" modification, which show that Signal is dominated by the other brands on both attributes (a) unless price is considered (b). Source: Urban and Star 1991, pp. 138–139.

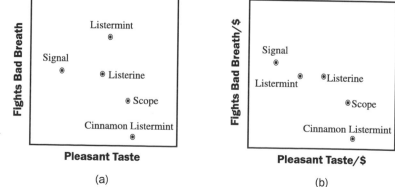

USES AND LIMITATIONS OF PERCEPTUAL AND PREFERENCE MAPS

The value of a perceptual map stems from the notion that perception is reality; that is, customer perceptions, in part, determine customer behavior. Perceptual mapping thus can provide insights into the market structure for a well-defined set of competing products. Because locations on a map result from the combined effects of various beliefs and perceptions, the map also suggests which product attributes the firm should modify to effect a desired change in its product's positioning. For example, the map in Exhibit 4.1 indicates the attributes Michelob's managers must change if they want to position their beer clearly as either a light premium beer or a heavy premium beer, instead of allowing it to continue occupying an intermediate mid-strength position. By making certain assumptions about how changes in the physical characteristics of a product will influence customer perceptions, managers can tentatively predict the sales or market shares associated with alternative positions on a map.

Furthermore, if a firm develops a clear positioning strategy on the basis of a perceptual map, it should be able to complete the following sentence succinctly: For [*target segment*], the [*offering*] is [*positioning claim*], because [*single most important support*].

EXAMPLE

"To the small business owner who wants to grow their business, SmallFuel is a marketing firm that provides products and services specifically designed to grow small businesses. Since we are a small business, and we work only with small businesses, we uniquely understand your needs and requirements. We guarantee that our products are the best way to grow your small business; if you aren't happy with the results, we'll give your money back."
Source: www.smallfuel.com April 2012.

EXAMPLE

The positioning statement for Microsoft.NET is as follows: "For companies whose employees and partners need timely information, Microsoft.NET is a new protocol and software system that enables unprecedented levels of software integration through XML Web services, because unlike Java, .NET is integrated into the Microsoft platform, providing the ability to quickly and reliably build, host, deploy, and utilize connected applications."

In addition to their effectiveness for general positioning decisions, perceptual maps are particularly useful in several specific areas of marketing.

1. *New product decisions:* During the stage in which the firm attempts to identify opportunities for new products according to existing market gaps, perceptual maps provide clear focus. During the concept-testing stage, they indicate the potential for the new concept in the context of other existing products and identify segments that would find the product appealing.

   In the early 1990s, General Motors used perceptual maps to evaluate the Buick Reatta, both as a concept and after test drives. These maps reassured GM management that the Reatta had a distinct new upscale image compared with other Buick models. (However, there was no real demand in this gap. The Buick Reatta sold only a few thousand cars before GM started discounting its price to reduce inventory.)

2. *A check on managers' views of competitive structure and positioning:* Marketing managers have their own perceptions of how customers and noncustomers perceive brands—perceptions that may or may not be consistent with various customer segments' actual views. Perceptual maps offer managers important insights into whether, how, and why their perceptions coincide with customer perceptions.

   For example, one manager, noting the contributions of a perceptual mapping study, acknowledged, "Some of the facts we learned from this study shocked us. We had focused on physical product benefits as a basis for competitive advantage. Instead, we found a market more interested in service issues."

3. *Identifying competitors:* Although marketers always want to differentiate their products from those of competitors, in some highly competitive markets, few gaps or opportunities for distinct positions exist. In such cases, firms can select a few specific competitors to target, on the basis of their weakest points. Perceptual maps highlight the attributes associated with close substitutes and which points of difference are least relevant in terms of customer pref-

erences. Thus, perceptual maps provide insights into the differences between competitive products that customers do not notice (which means the company has failed to communicate these differences to customers successfully), as well as those differences customers do notice but do not care about.

4. *Corporate image studies*: A complex, multidimensional concept, a corporate image summarizes what a firm stands for, according to its various stakeholders. A corporate image study attempts to both understand stakeholder perceptions of the firm and design an image consistent with the firm's strategic objectives. Just as they do for brands, perceptual maps can summarize the positioning of companies effectively.

In summary, the many strategic issues that positioning analysis can help resolve include:

- Finding unmet (or inadequately met) customer needs and wants (e.g., the American Airlines example).
- Identifying and leveraging product strengths that the market values.
- Determining how to overcome product weaknesses.
- Selecting competitors to compete against.
- Identifying market segments for which a particular new product or concept would be appealing.

Most important, these maps replace rhetoric and emotional arguments about alternative positioning strategies with a logical approach that asks, "What would happen if we did X?" Although perceptual and preference maps are hardly the whole answer to the gap in the market and market in the gap puzzles, they represent a big step forward for many organizations.

SUMMARY

In this chapter, we describe the methods available to produce perceptual and preference maps that help marketers position their products and services in the minds of their customers. Although many of the examples in this chapter refer to consumer products, maps are just as applicable to technical and industrial products and services aimed at business markets.

Mapping techniques enable managers to understand the competitive structure of their markets. Using this understanding, they can position their offerings to gain favorable responses from their target segments.

Although these techniques are powerful, they also contain several limitations. Perceptual mapping methods provide only a partial explanation of customer perceptions, preferences, and choices, as well as their relationships. Their insights are limited to the particular set of products and attributes included in a study, which means they only support positioning efforts within an existing framework. For example, in attribute-based perceptual maps, the set of attributes chosen limits the dimensions along which new positioning options might be considered. Therefore, users must constantly ask: Are the dimensions correct? What is missing?

Mapping techniques *represent* perceptions and preferences in a manner that aids decision making. They do not, however, explain *why* customers form certain perceptions or preferences. Although some methods exist to determine how well a map represents customer perceptions, any map can merely summarize (in a pictorial manner) a large volume of data, which means it must leave out much detail.

Despite these limitations, perceptual and preference maps offer major benefits: They help managers view the competitive structure of their markets through the eyes of their customers, they suggest a means to communicate about that structure, and they indicate what managers might do to take advantage of the market structure.

CHAPTER 5

Forecasting

Businesses must regularly make forecasts about market potential, product sales, and the like. Yet such forecasting tasks are notoriously difficult and challenging. Marketing strategy, with its focus on the long term, depends on forecasting the market's evolution and dynamics. Marketers are counseled to listen to customers. It is equally important for them to listen to, prepare for, and to shape the future of the marketplace. In this chapter, we outline several forecasting methods that marketers have used to successfully learn about the future for their products and companies.

Developing market forecasts requires the careful definition of the level of the market under study, for which forecasts are needed. We distinguish five levels (though coarser or finer grained classifications are possible):

- *The potential market* involves the potential sales associated with all customers who show interest in a product or service; survey methods can be used to determine its size.
- *The available market* defines those customers who not only have interest in but sufficient income to afford and access the product or service; to determine it, link the potential market to demographic and marketing channel data.
- *The qualified available market* pertains to customers who pass the availability criterion and are qualified (that is, are in a targeted market segment) to buy.

- *The served or target market* is the part of the qualified market that the company decides to pursue for whatever reason.
- *The penetrated market* refers to the customers who have already bought the product or service.

Business forecasting is not about getting the future right. Rather, its main purpose is to help companies manage uncertainties surrounding the future market acceptance of products and services. If forecasts convey an exaggerated sense of precision or certainty, their main purpose is defeated. On the other hand, if forecasts help companies develop strategies to capture future opportunities or minimize threats and uncertainties, they have served their role.

FORECASTING METHODS

Predicting the course of a company's or industry's market sales is essential if a company wants to plan and control its business operations. As markets fluctuate and become more unstable, prediction becomes an increasingly critical task for marketing management. Without some form of sales projection, firms would have no reasonable starting point for making strategic marketing decisions.

Vital as they are, forecasts are estimates at best. Some firms perform better than others, but no one has come up with a perfect method; rather, the best approach often relies on combining forecasts from more than one independent forecasting method, in the hope that they will converge to a more accurate forecast. Prominent forecasting techniques include judgmental and decompositional methods, market and survey analyses, time-series analyses, and causal analyses (Exhibit 5.1).

EXHIBIT 5.1

A classification of market forecasting approaches.

Judgmental	Market and Survey Analysis	Time Series	Causal Analyses
Sales force composite	Buyer intentions	Naive methods	Regression analysis
Jury of executive opinion	Product tests	Moving averages	Econometric models
Delphi methods	Chain ratio method	Exponential smoothing	Input-output models
Scenario analysis		Box-Jenkins method	Multivariate AutoRegressive Moving Average
		Decompositional methods	Neural networks

Thus, forecasting is as much about careful judgment as it is about data and science. As the following example illustrates, too much reliance on just data or just judgment can lead to disaster.

EXAMPLE

In June 2000, Nike introduced a highly touted automated forecasting system developed by i2 Technologies. Nine months later, the company had made very expensive forecasting errors and suffered a $200 million loss in sneaker sales. The reason for the failure? Employees accepted the system forecasts per se rather than as baselines they should judgmentally adjust to reflect the current market conditions they knew about but that were not reflected in the forecasting system data. However, judgments, even those of experts, can be way off the mark, as suggested by the following projections (Navasky and Cerf 1998):

"The wireless music box has no imaginable commercial value. Who would pay for a message sent to nobody in particular?"
—Associates of David Sarnoff, 1920s, talking about the radio.

"I think there's a world market for maybe five computers."
—Thomas Watson, chairman and founder of IBM, 1948.

"I predict the Internet ... will go spectacularly supernova and in 1996 catastrophically collapse."
—Bob Metcalfe, inventor and 3Com founder, 1995.

Judgmental Methods

There are four frequently used judgmental methods of market forecasting: (1) sales force composite estimates, (2) jury of executive opinion, (3) Delphi and related methods, and (4) chain ratio methods.

Sales force composite estimates

Many companies turn to members of the sales force for help when assembling forecasts about future sales. However, few companies use salesperson estimates without some adjustments. In the first place, sales representatives are biased observers. They may be characteristically pessimistic (if their quotas are related to their forecasts) or optimistic (if they want to expand their set of accounts), or they may go from one extreme to the other because of a recent sales setback or success (recency bias).

If these biasing tendencies can be countered, sales representatives often have more knowledge about and better insight into developing trends than any other single group. They are often especially knowledgeable when the product is fairly technical and subject to changing technology trends. And when they participate in the forecasting process, sales representatives may gain greater confidence in the derived sales quotas, which can increase their incentive to achieve those quotas.

Jury of executive opinion

A common judgmental approach combines the views of key stakeholders in the hope of gaining a more accurate forecast than can be achieved from a single person, even an expert. This combination may involve asking a group of stakeholders for forecasts and grouping them (e.g., taking the average or weighted average) to come up with a group forecast. Alternatively, the firm could host a meeting of stakeholders in which they come up with a consensus forecast. The participating stakeholders may be company executives but also could include dealers, distributors, suppliers, marketing consultants, and professional association members.

Using juries of executives entails several concerns, such as (1) the tendency of stakeholders to give too much weight to their own opinions, (2) the associated demands on executives' time, (3) a lack of incentives to ensure "truth telling," (4) the necessary decision regarding how to weight the individual forecasts to obtain a group estimate, and (5) the tendency of some stakeholders to dominate the discussions and create "groupthink" forecasts.

Delphi and related methods

The Delphi approach is similar to juries of executive opinion but also incorporates a structured process to minimize the undesirable aspects of group interactions (e.g., groupthink) and improve the reliability and accuracy of the consensus forecast. It therefore is most useful for forecasting events for which there is no reliable history or when marketers need to incorporate judgments. Early applications of the Delphi method enabled the U.S. military to forecast enemy actions (e.g., if the Soviet Union were to launch a nuclear missile, which locations in America would it target?). However, over time, many businesses have also realized great value from the application of this method.

The Delphi method assumes that forecasts developed by group consensus will be superior to forecasts developed by a single individual, because the total amount of information available to a group is likely greater than the amount of information available to a single person. Thus, the method is characterized by anonymity and structured feedback. Participants do not know which members of the group contributed particular opinions or forecasts, and any interactions take place anonymously through structured questions. Typically, participants provide both their forecasts and reasons in support of those forecasts. Once summarized, this information gets shared anonymously with all participants. Anonymity helps avoid the possibility that a participant will be influenced by the status or reputation of another participant, rather than by the strength of his or her arguments. The structured feedback process also allows participants to change their forecasts, or reasons, without anyone else knowing they have done so.

Group interactions also employ a structured sequence: Participants consider a set of questions, provide their responses, and then receive a summary of the responses of all participants. With the benefit of these group-level summaries, they answer the same questions again, and the two-step process repeats until the group converges in its estimates or decides their divergence is irresolvable. In marketing applications, we typically reach consensus within two or three rounds of feedback, and the consensus estimate becomes the best forecast by the group.

The accuracy of the Delphi method depends crucially on the information and expertise of the participants and the effectiveness of the consensus-building process. To develop market response models for resource allocation decisions, organizations use a particular form of the Delphi method, as we discuss in Chapter 7.

EXAMPLE

The University of Michigan's Office for the Study of Automotive Transportation conducted a Delphi study with 300 auto industry executives to forecast the sales of electric vehicles 10 years into the future. The consensus favored hybrids (electric-combustion engines), and if their estimates had been realized, 150,000 hybrid-drive vehicles would have appeared on the roads by 2004. The actual sales level for 2004 was approximately 83,000 units—a remarkably accurate forecast for 10 years into the future.

Chain ratio method

One of the simplest and most effective forecasting methods, the chain ratio approach is applicable when a firm lacks the time or resources needed to develop a detailed forecasting model. This method decomposes the overall forecasting problem into a sequence of smaller forecasting problems and often mixes managerial judgment with other inputs.

For example, consider the decomposition to forecast the market share of a brand:

Long run market share of brand =
  Number of customers in target market ×
  Proportion of customers aware of brand ×
  Proportion of aware customers who repeat purchase ×
  Average usage index,

where the usage index is the average number of units purchased by brand purchasers compared with the average units purchased by customers of all brands in the entire category.

The logic of the forecasting chain determines the most appropriate method for estimating the individual components of that chain. For example, the number of customers in a market may be available from archival data, the proportion of aware customers may be determined from the proposed advertising plan, and the proportion of customers who repeat purchase may be obtained through a judgmental estimation procedure (e.g., Delphi) or a survey of customers. As long as the overall decomposition logic is sound, this method provides forecasts of reasonable accuracy.

EXAMPLE

An assessment of the potential for online grocery sales by supermarkets might multiply together the following information:

- Number of households in the United States (Census Bureau).
- Grocery purchases per household per year (one visit per week × $120 spent per visit).
- Percentage of sales in supermarkets and grocery stores (from Progressive Grocer).
- Households with children (Census Bureau).
- Percentage of households with Internet access (Census Bureau).
- Whether household will order groceries online if available (survey results).
- Discount of survey intentions (judgmental estimate based on prior experience of managers).
- Online grocery shopping availability (judgmental estimate).

- Awareness, given availability (judgmental estimate based on current levels of advertising by online grocers).

Gathering these data, the online grocer emerges with the following equation:

$$105 \text{ million} \times \$5{,}300 \times 84\% \times 35\% \times 58\% \times 25\% \times 50\% \times 40\% \times 50\%.$$

Therefore, the estimated total market for online grocers equals $2,372 million.

In implementing the chain ratio method, it is important to define each stage of the chain to be "conditionally independent" of the previous stage so that the answer to one stage of the chain does not provide any information about the next stage. For example, in the above chain, we assume that knowing the number of households in the U.S. does not provide direct knowledge of the grocery purchases per household per year. To the extent feasible, the sequence of variables selected for specifying the chain should satisfy this criterion.

The chain ratio method has several key benefits: First, it forces the forecaster to think carefully about the major factors that may influence a forecast. Second, because it is normally not very expensive, it can be used to cross-check forecasts developed by other methods. Third, it enables the forecaster to identify components for which more data collection efforts would improve the forecasts significantly. Fourth, it allows forecasters to outsource (if needed) the different components to those sources that might have the best available information about particular components. Fifth, any errors in the component forecasts have the potential to cancel one another out, rather than get compounded, especially if different components rely on different methods. Sixth, the decomposition model, once developed, can be used again in the future. However, the chain ratio method also suffers from a major limitation: Sophisticated forecasting methods that rely on objective data often provide more accurate forecasts.

Market and Product Analysis Methods

Buying intentions

Marketing forecasting refers to the art and science of anticipating what buyers are likely to do in a given set of conditions.

This definition immediately suggests that the most useful source of information would be the buyers themselves. Ideally, a firm can draw on a probability sample of potential buyers and ask each buyer how much of the product he or she will buy in a future time period, given certain stated conditions. It would also ask buyers to state what proportion of their total projected purchases they will buy from a particular firm or at least which factors influence their choice of supplier. With this information, the firm seems to have an ideal basis for forecasting its sales.

Unfortunately, this method contains various limitations when used in practice, the most important of which are:

1. The weak relationship between stated intentions and actual behavior.
2. The potential for nonresponse bias (i.e., those who respond to the survey may be different in unknown ways from those who do not respond), which is particularly critical in B2B markets composed of just a few buyers.

The value of this method therefore depends on the extent to which the buyers have clearly formulated intentions and then carry them out.

To help resolve these issues, secondary source surveys can provide information about buyer intentions in both consumer and B2B markets. Two indices provide data related to consumer durable purchases and contain information about consumers' present and anticipated future financial positions, as well as their expectations about the economy: the Consumer Sentiment Measure from the Survey Research Center at the University of Michigan and the Consumer Confidence Index from The Conference Board. For industrial products, the best-known surveys are published by the U.S. Department of Commerce, the Opinion Research Corporation, and McGraw-Hill.

Market tests

The usefulness of opinions, whether those of buyers, sales representatives, or other experts, depends on their *cost, availability*, and *reliability*. When buyers typically do not plan their purchases carefully or are erratic in carrying out their intentions and when even the experts are not very good guessers, firms need a more direct market test of likely behavior. Unlike forecasts based on buying intentions, which rely on what people say they will do, forecasts based on market tests rely on what people actually do. A direct market test is especially desirable for forecasting the sales of a new product or the likely sales of an established product in a new distribution channel or territory. When a firm wants a short-run forecast of likely buyer response, a small-scale market test is usually a good solution. (We describe one example of this approach, ASSESSOR, in more detail subsequently in this chapter.)

Scenario analysis

A scenario is a plausible, coherent, rich story of how the future might evolve in a particular decision context. A scenario is not a forecast but merely represents a plausible future that enables the decision maker to comprehend the opportunities and challenges associated with that scenario. In that sense, scenario analysis represents a process for systematically developing and analyzing scenarios, which helps improve forecasting and decision making by prompting more complete considerations of various future outcomes and their implications. It also offers a way to identify and analyze uncontrollable or weakly controllable factors—such as customer behavior, competitive factors, the financial and economic environment, or regulatory concerns—associated with a particular future scenario.

EXAMPLE

The pharmaceutical industry might imagine the following scenario for 2004–2015: A global flu outbreak causes public outrage about the lack of investment in new antibiotics and vaccines. Governments assume a more active role in directing R&D priorities toward acute and then chronic diseases. Over time, elements of a Social Business Compact become clear, including government commitments to expanded access; sophisticated purchasers who negotiate price according to value-for-money calculations; higher rewards for innovation in exchange for more secure IPR agreements; patient agreements to healthy living packages as part of insurance and pension plans; and pharmaceutical company agreements to less aggressive pricing in exchange for volumes and rewards for true innovation.
Source: http://www.pharmafutures.org/.

The application of scenario analysis can be structured as a seven-step process.

1. *Identify major stakeholders,* those who will be important players in the future evolution of the focal industry, product, or company. These stakeholders may include customers, competitors, regulators, distributors, and strategic partners.

2. *Summarize core trends* relevant for the decision context, including technological, economic, and social aspects, within the time frame of interest.

3. *Specify main uncertainties surrounding future outcomes* (e.g., TV studio adoption of new recording methods; FDA approval of new drugs; customer willingness to discard the old product and install the new version). Typically, it is useful to separate knowable uncertainties from those that are unknowable. For example, a controlled experiment or analyses of similar situations can make certain questions potentially knowable, such as, "What might happen if we reduce the price of our new product by 20%?" Other questions, such as demographic shifts, may be predictable, whereas still others are simply unknowable or require significant speculation.

4. *Construct an initial set of scenarios*, eliminating those trends that are relatively straightforward and focusing on plausible paths related to important factors whose effects are unknown or unknowable. For example, eliminate combinations of factors or outcomes that are unlikely to coexist (e.g., low gas prices and strong pressure on automakers to develop hybrid cars), as well as those situations that conflict with the natural incentives driving key stakeholders (e.g., demanding customers quickly change well-established behaviors).

5. *Assess the consistency and plausibility of the scenarios*, if possible, by simplifying and combining scenarios. In this step, "themes" that combine some trends into meaningful composites (e.g., slow adoption of the new product until acceptable standards emerge in the industry, followed by rapid adoption) can be very valuable.

6. *Identify important unknown factors* to resolve through more research (e.g., likely prices of product components) and seek additional information to resolve those uncertainties. However, this step also requires the identification of important unknowable aspects that must be managed through strategic choices (e.g., hedging). Historical analogs can be helpful in finding and controlling for these uncertainties to lead to logical recommendations, as we discuss with regard to the Bass model later in this chapter.

7. *Explore current strategic choices* that will help realize the outcomes (forecasts) specified in a scenario. The strategic choices typically fall into three broad categories: (1) *Core*

strategies to implement regardless of which scenario plays out (e.g., apply for patents, set up an agreement to share IP across partners), (2) *Contingent strategies* to implement depending on which scenario seems to be developing (e.g., do a test market and proceed further if the test market is successful), and (3) *Hedging strategies*, to allow the company to experiment at low cost with multiple options so it can be prepared for whichever scenario might occur (e.g., buy rights to land at various locations where a factory could be built, invest in learning about alternative technologies).

Time-Series Methods

As an alternative (or complement) to surveys, opinion studies, and market tests, many firms prepare forecasts based on statistical analyses of historical data (past data arranged in temporal order are referred to as a "time series"). The logic of this approach is that past data incorporate enduring causal relationships that should carry forward into the future and can be uncovered through quantitative analysis. Thus, the forecasting task becomes in essence a careful study of the past combined with the assumption that the same relationships will hold in the future.

The many time-series analysis and forecasting methods differ mainly in the way they relate past observations to forecast values.

Naive methods

The simplest time-series forecasting procedure uses the most recently observed value as a forecast; that is, a naive forecast is equivalent to giving weights of 1 to the most recent observation and 0 to all others. Other naive methods may modify this procedure by adjusting for seasonal fluctuations. These methods therefore serve mainly as a basis for comparing alternative forecasting approaches.

Slightly more sophisticated naive methods include

- *Freehand projection*, a visual exploration of a plot of time-series observations. This method delivers a forecast quickly and cheaply and is easy to understand, but it offers poor accuracy, especially for nonlinear series, and two people may make very different projections.
- *Semiaverage projection*, in which the analyst divides a time series in half, calculates averages for each half, and draws a line connecting the average points to produce a forecast. This method has the same advantages and disadvantages as freehand projection.

Smoothing techniques

The notion underlying smoothing methods is that a pattern underlies the values of the forecast variables and appears in past observations, along with random fluctuations or noise. Using smoothing methods, the analyst tries to distinguish the underlying pattern from the random fluctuations by eliminating the latter.

One way to lessen the impact of randomness in individual short-range forecasts averages several prior values. The *moving-average approach,* one of the simplest procedures for doing so, weights the past N observations with a value of 1/N, where N is specified by the analyst and remains constant. As N grows larger, the smoothing effect becomes greater. If, for example, a year's worth of monthly data were available, the moving-average method would forecast the next period as 1/12 of the total for the past year. When new data become available, the newest observation replaces the oldest, which is why we refer to the average as moving. Moving averages are particularly effective for forecasting a single period in advance, but they do not adapt easily to pattern changes. Although this method produces a forecast quickly, at low cost, and with relatively few technical demands, it also is limited by poor accuracy and an arbitrary number of observations. Furthermore, simple moving averages are not very effective in the presence of complex data patterns, such as trend, seasonal, and cyclical patterns.

Another procedure, the *double moving average*, computes a set of single moving averages and then an overall moving average on the basis of the values of the first estimation.

Smoothing methods rely on the idea that a forecast can emerge from the weighted sum of prior observations. In the case of simple moving averages, the individual weights are 1/N, whereas for exponential smoothing, another popular method, the analyst must postulate a declining weighting factor. Adaptive filtering offers another approach to determine the most appropriate set of weights, based on an iterative process that determines those weights that minimize forecasting error.

Box-Jenkins method

The Box-Jenkins method entails an overall philosophy for forecasting problems. The most general of the short-term forecasting techniques, it is also one of the most powerful available today and provides an adequate model for almost any pattern of data. However, it is sufficiently complex that users must possess a relatively high level of expertise. Its originators, Box and Jenkins, propose three general classes of models that can describe any type of stationary process (i.e., the process remains in equilibrium around a constant mean level): (1) autoregressive (AR), (2) moving average (MA), and (3) mixed autoregressive and moving average (ARMA).

In contrast to the methods we describe next, time-series methods assume the analyst has no knowledge about the cause of the trends and that the future will look pretty much like the past. Therefore, time-series methods are most useful for short- or medium-term extrapolations (usually less than a year in the future). Causal methods relax that assumption.

Causal Methods

Causal models are useful not only for forecasting but also for facilitating a better understanding of a situation. For example, regression and econometric models specify the structure of the relationship between customer demand and its underlying causes.

EXAMPLE

In business-to-business (B2B) markets, firms often want to relate product demands to published data about the specific North American Standard Industrial Classification (NASIC) codes the company believes have high sales potential. In these analyses, the number of employees often provides a readily available surrogate for customer size. As Exhibit 5.2 shows, the Machinco Company, a maker of high-technology components, currently has 17 customers, whose number of employees and purchase volume differ.

If the number of employees is a rough predictor of sales potential, sales might relate to the number of employees via a linear equation:

$$Sales = a_0 + a_1 \text{ (number of employees).}$$

According to the linear regression, $a_0 = 8.52$ and $a_1 = 0.061$. The U.S. Census of Manufacturers reports that the organizations that represent prospective customers for Machinco's products have a total of 126,000 employees. Therefore,

$$Potential\ sales = 8.52 + (0.061 \times 126,000) = 7,695.$$

This value is nearly 10 times the current sales of Machinco (823), so Machinco could greatly expand its sales to other prospects. Now suppose that Machinco has two likely prospects: Company A has 1,600 employees, and company B has 500 employees. A good guess for the sales potential for company A therefore is 8.52 + (0.061 × 1600), or 106 units, and that for company B is potentially 39 units.

EXHIBIT 5.2

Machinco's customer data, including number of employees and current sales level, for input into a regression model of demand.

Customer Number	No. of Employees	Sales in $1000s*
1	110	9.8
2	141	21.2
3	204	14.7
4	377	22.8
5	395	48.1
6	502	42.3
7	612	27.8
8	618	40.7
9	707	59.8
10	721	44.5
11	736	77.1
12	856	59.2
13	902	52.3
14	926	77.1
15	1045	74.6
16	1105	81.8
17	1250	69.7
	Total =	823.0

*Regression of sales versus employees gives sales = 8.52 + 0.061 x no. of employees, $R^2 = 0.77$.

The Product Life Cycle

aAn important concept underlying most dynamic business planning models is the product life cycle. Because a product's sales position and profitability change over time, every firm needs to revise its product strategy periodically. Using the concept of the life cycle, the firm tries to recognize distinct phases in the sales history of the product and its market and thereby develop strategies appropriate to those various stages.

The life cycle concept emerges out of many sources. Biological life forms are born, grow, mature, and die. Many human enterprises (like the Roman Empire) experience a beginning, a heyday, and a decline or death. For products, the length of the life cycle varies from one to another—long for commodity items such as salt, peanut butter, and wine but shorter for more differentiated products such as California wine coolers and Darth Vader Halloween masks. Several factors affect the length and form of the product life cycle (PLC), including changing needs and wants, changes in technology that lead to close substitutes, and the speed with which the market adopts a new product.

The lesson of the life cycle concept is not that all products have a life cycle or even that life cycles have specific, distinct stages. Rather, the life cycle concept instructs firms how to anticipate the way sales might evolve so they can develop strategies to influence those sales. For example, in the introductory PLC stage, the firm should devote considerable resources to advertising to increase customer awareness of the new product; in the mature stage, it should devote its resources to differentiating and positioning its offering in contrast with those of competitors.

In most discussions of the PLC, the sales history of a typical product follows an S-shaped sales curve (Exhibit 5.3), typically divided into four stages: introduction, growth, maturity, and decline. The introduction is a period of slow growth as the product enters the market. As the profit curve in Exhibit 5.3 shows, profits are low or negative in this stage because of the heavy expenses associated with a product introduction. During the growth period, the product achieves rapid market acceptance, and the firm enjoys substantial profit improvements. Maturity refers to a period of slowing sales growth, because the product already has been accepted by most of its potential buyers. Profits peak in this period and then start to decline because of the increased marketing outlays needed to sustain the product's position in the face of increased competition. Finally, in the decline stage, sales show a strong downward drift, and profits erode toward zero.

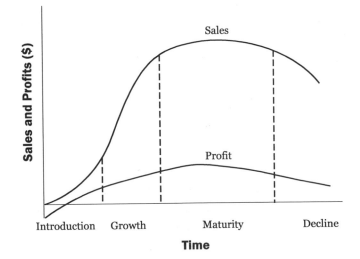

EXHIBIT 5.3

Typical stages in the sales and profit cycles, showing that profit typically lags behind sales growth.

We can understand this phenomenon more clearly by assuming that a human need or want (e.g., calculating power) exists and that a product (e.g., a calculator) satisfies that need. Exhibit 5.4a shows how different technologies can substitute for one another, which leads to a sequence of technology cycles within an overall demand cycle. Exhibit 5.4b breaks this process down further to show how successive product forms can replace one another within the context of a single technology cycle. Finally, Exhibit 5.4c illustrates the effect with actual data related to a specific product: random access memory chips.

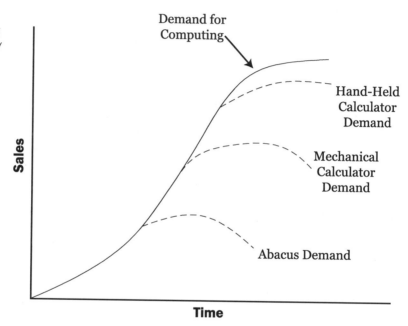

EXHIBIT 5.4(A)

Demand for computing is satisfied over time by different technologies that substitute for one another.

Growth rates are only one aspect of the PLC; elements such as market concentration, competitive structure, economic cycles, supply constraints, and replacement sales also affect the structure of the life cycle.

Research results get even further confounded by differences in the level of product aggregation and the difficulties associated with defining a new product. Three possible levels of aggregation exist: product class (e.g., cigarettes), product form (plain-filter cigarettes), and brand (Philip Morris, regular or nonfilter). The PLC concept applies differently in each case, in that product classes have the longest life histories, longer than particular product forms and certainly longer than most brands. The sales of many product classes continue in the mature stage for an indefinite duration because they are highly related to population trends (consider, for example, cars, perfume, refrigerators, and steel). Product forms tend to exhibit a standard PLC curve more faithfully, because they pass through a regular history of introduction, rapid growth, maturity, and decline (consider dial telephones for example). In contrast, a particular brand's sales history often is erratic, because changing competitive strategies and tactics produce substantial ups and downs in sales and market shares, even to the extent of causing a mature brand suddenly to exhibit a new period of rapid growth. Therefore, life cycle researchers must frequently tackle difficult forecasts of stage transitions and phase duration.

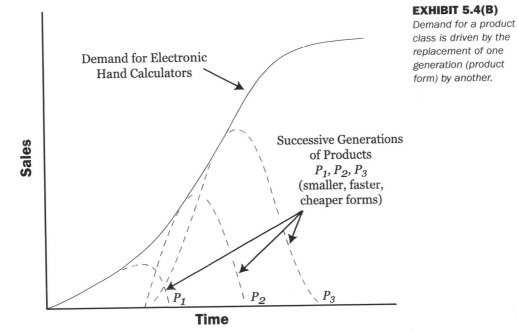

EXHIBIT 5.4(B)

Demand for a product class is driven by the replacement of one generation (product form) by another.

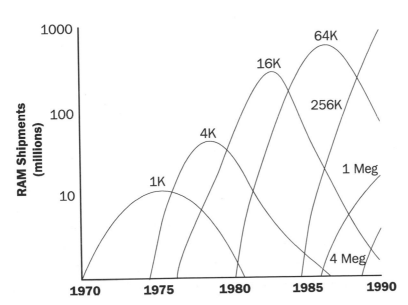

EXHIBIT 5.4(C)

Technological life cycles for random access memory chips, showing greater peaks and shorter cycle times (a pattern that has continued in this market). Source: Urban and Star 1991, p. 96.

Although forecasting methods have had some success in forecasting life cycles, they typically rely on data from one phase to forecast the timing and length of the next phase. Accurate long-range forecasting is quite difficult; little is known about the true length and sequence of life cycle phases (Day 1981). The challenges associated with forecasting phase changes and length have become even more difficult as life cycles grow shorter.

Two important trends currently influence the use of life cycle analyses. First, products generally exist in different life cycle stages in different countries, a crucial point to take into account when developing a global marketing strategy. Second, improvements in communications technology—the Internet in particular—have led to more rapid diffusion and are at least partially responsible for shortening PLCs.

What are we to make of these trends? A realistic view states that life cycle analysis remains only one important element in an overall analysis of marketing opportunities. The life cycle acts as a classification device and suggests conditions in which market growth, for example, may occur. During market growth, competitors can enter the market easily, and new opportunities for product offerings become available in selected market segments. Price and advertising elasticities change over the PLC as well, so though the discussion of definition and measurement is destined to continue, the PLC clearly is critical in determining appropriate marketing strategies.

NEW PRODUCT FORECASTING MODELS

Thus far, we have focused largely on the general problem of demand assessment and sales forecasting for established products. But when products or entire markets are new, the challenges differ somewhat—there are little or no historical data and limited experience on which to base the forecasts. New products can be classified into four categories, depending on whether the product is new to the company, new to the world, or both. Exhibit 5.5 summarizes the forecasting techniques that are most useful in each of these four categories.

Some people working in science and technology domains are reasonably good at predicting what technologies will emerge in the future (e.g., computers that can speak in many different languages, personalized medicine, low-energy consuming light bulbs), but are rarely good at predicting how such technologies will affect people, how customers would react to those technologies, and whether and when consumers will embrace products based on those technologies. In these situations, the past provides an imperfect, or even poor, indicator of the future.

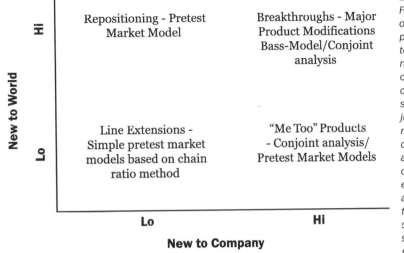

EXHIBIT 5.5
Forecasting sales of breakthrough products (i.e., new to the world and new to the company) often requires the combination of sophisticated modeling, judgment, and marketing research data. Products that are line extensions, in contrast, can leverage existing knowledge and experience, so forecasting combines simple models with solid marketing research data.

In this section, we outline two well-known approaches to addressing the sales forecasting problem for new products: the Bass model, applicable for new technologies and infrequently purchased durables, when the focus is customer trial as the form of adoption (e.g., first-time purchase of high-definition TV), and the ASSESSOR model, appropriate for more frequently purchased products, for which trial is just a step on the path to loyalty. In Chapter 6, we also describe a popular technique called conjoint analysis that provides another option for new product forecasting.

The Bass Model

Managers need forecasts for likely adoptions (first-time purchases) and sales of new offerings (i.e., products, services, technologies) that may take several years to realize, because critical early funding and production planning decisions depend on such forecasts.

The Bass model offers a good starting point for forecasting the long-term adoption pattern of new technologies and new durable products if the firm has either (1) recently introduced the product or technology and observed its sales for a few time periods or (2) not yet introduced the product or technology but recognizes some similarities between the product and existing products or technologies whose sales history is known. The model attempts to predict how many customers eventually will adopt the new product and when they will do so. This question of timing is crucial, because the answer guides the firm in terms of how to deploy its resources to market the new product.

Exhibit 5.6 shows the potential "sales" trajectories for various innovations, including innovative scientific articles. Some start with explosive growth, but their sales fall off almost from the start. Others exhibit a sleeper pattern (S-shaped), in which sales start out slow, then pick up momentum, and eventually decline. Surprisingly, the simple and elegant Bass (1969) model, with just three easily interpretable parameters, can represent all these patterns quite well.

EXHIBIT 5.6

The patterns of sales for several products and services in different product categories.

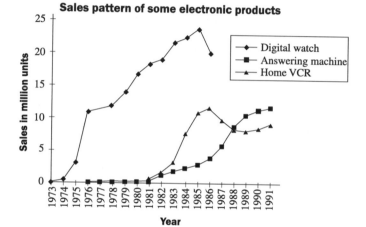

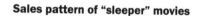

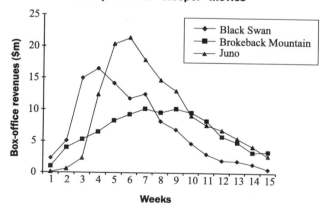

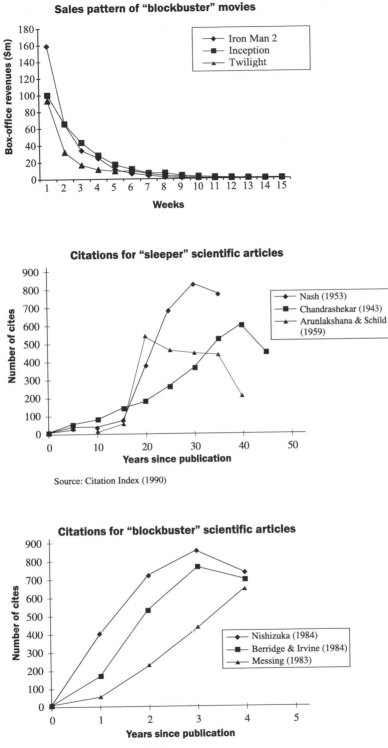

Sales pattern of "blockbuster" movies

Citations for "sleeper" scientific articles

Source: Citation Index (1990)

Citations for "blockbuster" scientific articles

Source: Citation Index (1990)

The Bass model makes the following assumptions:

- A customer either adopts in a specific period or waits to adopt, and all potential customers eventually adopt.
- There is fixed maximum potential number of buyers.
- No repeat or replacement purchases occur, only first-time purchases.
- The impact of word-of-mouth communication on product adoption is the same, regardless of when a customer adopts the product.

Following these assumptions, the Bass model can be represented as:

$$n(t) = p \times \text{Remaining Potential } (N - N(t)) \\ + q \times \text{Adopters } (N(t)) \times \\ (\text{Remaining Potential } (N - N(t)),$$

where the first component is the innovation effect or external influence, and the second component is the imitation effect or internal influence ("internal" to the social system in which word-of-mouth effects spread).

Specifically, we define these terms as follows:

N = market potential (eventual number of customers who will adopt the new product).

$n(t)$ = number of adopters at time t.

p = coefficient of innovation.

q = coefficient of imitation.

$N(t)$ = total adopters up to time t, such that $N(t) = n(0) + n(1) + n(2) + ... n(t)$.

Estimating the Bass model parameters

Several methods exist to estimate the parameters of the Bass model, and we classify them according to whether they rely on historical sales data or judgment for calibration. If historical sales data are available for the new product for at least a few periods, we can use linear and nonlinear regression. However, if we require judgmental methods, we can use analogs or surveys to determine customer purchase intentions.

The analog approach has proved very useful in practice. By identifying previous innovations that are analogous to the current product, the firm can determine p and q from the sales trajectories of those previous innovations. Combining these determinations with the N estimated for the current product (through customer surveys, managerial judgment, or the chain ratio method), the firm forecasts the sales pattern for the new product. Instead of simply guessing at the adoption and sales levels of a new product, this approach only requires managers to guess about the inputs to a well-established model, and the model takes care of the structure by which the inputs get incorporated into forecasts.

However, firms must take great care in choosing analogous products. Analogies based on similarities in expected market behavior work better than those based on product similarities. For example, in forecasting the sales path of digital cameras, it may be better to use CD-ROM drives as the analog rather than 35mm SLR cameras. Furthermore, especially in technological fields, firms should consider the increasing speed of customer adoption; though it took 27 years to sell 1 million telephones, the same number of TV sets sold in just 11 years, VCRs in 6 years, and CD players in 5 years. And Hewlett-Packard's OfficeJet all-in-one printer/fax/copier/ scanner needed only 2 years to reach the 1 million mark. Exhibit 5.7 provides a summary of parameter estimates reported for various innovations (we also include these estimates in the software version of the Bass model on www.decisionpro.biz to facilitate your selection of analogs).

The Bass model has seen extensive use because of its ability to indicate how successful innovations diffuse through the target population. However, when applying the Bass model, especially in forecasting contexts, it is important to recognize its limitations. Past data (from analogs) may describe how successful innovations previously have diffused, but they cannot account for the chances of a new product's success. That is, analog data of past successful products will predict favorable forecasts for any new product, which results in a clearly untenable success bias. To minimize such bias, the model must also include failure probabilities, but inherently, much less information about the sales patterns of failed innovations is available. In addition, though the Bass model provides good estimates of parameters based on several observations of actual sales data, by this point, the firm has already had to make critical investment decisions. Therefore, though analogs can help firms make forecasts before introducing an innovation into a market, the choice of a suitable analog is critical and requires careful judgment. In addition, this discussion points to the evident need for better ways to calibrate diffusion models before product launch, perhaps by using laboratory measurement methods.

EXHIBIT 5.7
This exhibit summarizes the estimated values of the p and q parameters of the Bass model for various product categories. For each product, the reported values here are the average values of these parameters obtained from an exhaustive search of the literature. (Compiled by Christophe Van den Bulte).

PRODUCT CATEGORY	p-Value	q-Value
Agricultural		
Artificial insemination	0.014	0.437
Bale hay	0.010	0.519
Corn	0.039	1.005
Hybrid corn	0.000	0.798
Tractor	0.007	0.118
Consumer Electronics		
Cable TV	0.021	0.270
Calculator	0.053	0.263
Camcorder	0.044	0.304
Cassette deck	0.013	0.227
CD player	0.028	0.368
Cell telephone	0.005	0.506
Cordless telephone	0.002	0.388
Digital watch	0.016	0.394
Diskdrive	0.021	0.995
Kodak instant camera	0.138	0.000
Polaroid instant camera	0.092	0.000
Radio	0.017	0.377
Recording media (records, cassettes, CDs)	0.009	0.328
Telephone	0.008	0.082
Telephone answering machine	0.016	0.423
Turntable	0.058	0.210
TV (Black & White)	0.065	0.335
TV (Color)	0.021	0.583
TV (Projection)	0.016	0.188
VCR	0.010	0.608
Videogames	0.020	0.307
Household Appliances		
Automatic coffee maker	0.011	0.226
Blender	0.005	0.381
Broiler	0.001	0.156
Can opener	0.019	0.290
Clothes dryer	0.017	0.389
Clothes washer	0.010	0.084
Coffee maker ADC (Automatic Drip Coffee)	0.077	1.106
Curling iron	0.060	0.454
Deep fryer	0.034	0.740
Dishwasher	0.013	0.185
Disposer	0.010	1.087
Electric coffee maker	0.022	0.203
Electric knife	0.115	0.275
Electric toothbrush	0.110	0.548
Fluorescent lamp	0.001	0.055
Fire extinguisher	0.069	0.160
Food processor	0.018	0.563
Fondue	0.166	0.440
Freezer	0.023	0.138
Frypan	0.222	0.000
Hair setter	0.131	0.350
Heating pad	0.027	0.222
Hot plates	0.076	0.072
Knife sharpener	0.066	0.500
Lawn mower	0.007	0.310
Microwave oven	0.018	0.337
Mixer	0.000	0.148
Power leaf blower (gas or electric)	0.013	0.315
Range	0.038	0.033
Range (built-in)	0.041	0.227
Refrigerator	0.012	0.297
Room AC	0.010	0.454
Shaver	0.000	0.234

PRODUCT CATEGORY	p-Value	q-Value
Household Appliances (cont.)		
Slow cooker	0.044	0.597
Steam iron	0.036	0.318
Styling dryer	0.078	0.253
Toaster	0.039	0.131
Trash compactor	0.075	0.292
Vacuum cleaner	0.021	0.209
Waffle iron	0.013	0.430
Water softener	0.018	0.297
Information Technology		
8-bit microprocessor	0.008	0.585
Mainframe computers (number of units installed)	0.059	0.384
Mainframe computers (units of computing performance)	0.028	0.723
Personal Computer (PC)	0.003	0.253
Static Random Access Memory (SRAM) chips	0.026	1.101
Supercomputer	0.071	0.175
Medical		
CT scanner for head only	0.041	1.090
CT scanner for whole body	0.034	1.390
CT scanners (all types for hospitals with 50-99 beds)	0.040	0.461
CT scanners (all types for hospitals with >100 beds)	0.035	0.261
Mammography	0.005	0.704
Population using fluorinated water (community adoption)	0.265	0.335
Ultrasound imaging (adoption by hospitals)	0.003	0.506
Antihypertensive	0.045	0.000
Beta Blockers	0.002	0.503
Diuretic	0.011	0.066
Transportation		
Diesel cars in Europe	0.006	0.140
ABS (Antilock Braking)	0.003	0.241
Electronic fuel injection	0.003	0.625
Other Products		
Bed cover	0.006	0.151
Blanket	0.003	0.260
Boat trailer	0.009	0.376
Diaper	0.024	0.268
Drillbit	0.110	0.415
Milkpack (containers for milk)	0.001	0.396
Nylon cord	0.004	0.234
Oxygen steel furnace (USA)	0.001	0.456
Plastic milk containers (1 gallon)	0.012	0.333
Plastic milk containers (half gallon)	0.011	0.301
Retail scanner equipment (POS Scanners)	0.004	1.174
Structural wood panel (plywood, waferboard)	0.017	0.035
Styling mousse	0.203	0.986
Toothbrush	0.083	0.130
Universal Product Code (UPC)	0.008	0.181
Services		
Accelerated program (educational innovation)	0.003	0.913
ATM machines (adoption by banks)	0.008	0.197
Foreign language (educational innovation)	0.003	0.619
HoJo (Number of restaurants)	0.021	0.258
McDonalds (Number of restaurants)	0.018	0.538
Motel	0.011	0.338
Phone Banking	0.014	0.884
Solar energy (BTU generated)	0.060	0.033
Average (across all products)	0.035	0.390

Pretest Market Forecasting and the ASSESSOR Model

According to a Nielsen Report[1], in 2008, there were 122,743 new products (UPC codes) sold through U.S. grocery, drug, and mass merchandiser channels. About 98% of these products were extensions of existing brands. Only 4,095 of these products (3.3%) generated sales of more than $1 million each, and only 15 new products generated sales of more than $50 million each. Thus, most new products will not achieve the objectives set for them and likely will be withdrawn within two years of introduction. The costs incurred to introduce these new products generally occur after they appear in the market, so minimizing costs requires methods that can forecast the sales of a new product before its introduction. Firms also need diagnostic information that allows them to identify potential problems with their new products and improve their chances of success before the introduction.

In the past 20 years, several successful pretest forecasting models have been developed, primarily in the packaged goods industry. Models such as NEWS, TRACKER, SPRINTER, BASES, ASSESSOR, and LTM are available commercially. Shocker and Hall (1986) provide an overview of several of these models and summarize their similarities and differences, so we focus specifically on the publicly available ASSESSOR model, which shares underlying concepts and features with the other models. The description of the model we use relies primarily on Silk and Urban (1978) and Urban (1993).

Pretest market forecasting and analysis occur only after the product and packaging are available (at least in trial quantities), the advertising copy is ready, and the firm has formulated a preliminary plan about marketing mix elements, such as the price, channels of distribution, and marketing budget. Given these inputs, ASSESSOR is designed to

1. Predict the new product's long-term market share and sales volume over time.
2. Estimate the sources of the new product's share—whether it draws market share from competitors' brands (draw) or from other products of the same firm (cannibalize).
3. Generate diagnostic information to improve the product, advertising copy, and other launch materials.
4. Permit rough evaluations of alternative marketing plans, including different prices, package designs, and so forth.

[1] http://blog.nielsen.com/nielsenwire/consumer/new-products-generate-21-billion-in-sales-in-2008/

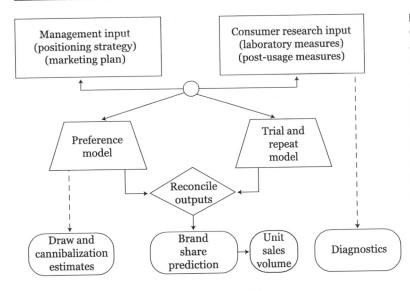

EXHIBIT 5.8
*Overview of ASSESSOR
modeling sequence.
The model uses
managerial judgment
and consumer research
data to make sales
forecasts (brand share,
sales volume) and
offer diagnostics (draw
and cannibalization
estimates, reasons
for purchase of new
product). Sources:
Silk and Urban 1978;
Urban and Katz 1983.*

Overview of the ASSESSOR model

Exhibits 5.8 and 5.9 summarize the overall structure of the ASSESSOR model, as well as the measurement approach for calibrating the model. The ASSESSOR model actually consists of two models: a preference model and a trial–repeat model. If these two elements provide similar forecasts, confidence in the forecast is high, but if they differ, the analyst needs to determine the sources of discrepancies to diagnose the issue.

EXHIBIT 5.9
*Overview of ASSESSOR
data-collection
procedure. Source: Silk
and Urban 1978, p.
174, Table 1.*

Design	Procedure	Measurement
O_1	Respondent screening and recruitment (personal interview)	Criteria for target-group identification (e.g., product-class usage)
O_2	Premeasurement for established brands (self-administered questionnaire)	Composition of "relevant set" of established brands, attribute weights and ratings, and preferences
X_1	Exposure to advertising for established brands and new brand	
$[O_3]$	Measurement of reactions to the advertising materials (self-administered questionnaire)	Optional, e.g., likability and believability ratings of advertising materials
X_3	Simulated shopping trip and exposure to display of new and established brands	
O_4	Purchased opportunity (choice recorded by research personnel)	Brand(s) purchased
X_3	Home use, or consumption of new brand	
O_5	Post-usage measurement (telephone interview)	New-brand usage rate, satisfaction ratings and repeat-purchase propensity; attribute ratings and preferences for "relevant set" of established brands plus the new brand

O = Measurement; X = Advertising or product exposure

The laboratory phase of the study literally occurs in a testing facility (e.g., a room in a mall, a specially equipped trailer) located in the immediate vicinity of a shopping center. Participants should include approximately 300 persons who have been screened as relevant for the study and representative of the target segment. The participants receive a small amount of money for participating.

Upon arriving at the testing facility, participants fill in a self-administered questionnaire to indicate their consideration set (i.e., brands they are aware of and would consider buying), brands that they have purchased in the category in the immediate past, and their preferences for competing brands within the consideration set. The participants then watch five or six commercials, one for each product and one of which introduces the new product. To avoid systematic position effects, the researchers must rotate the order in which participants view the commercials.

In a simulated store containing a shelf display of products in the test category along with representative prices for each product, participants then may purchase any product or combination of products. Participants also may choose not to buy anything and keep all the money they were given to participate. However, even those who do not choose to purchase the new product receive a quantity of it for free after the completion of all buying transactions. This procedure parallels market behavior: Some participants try a new product on their own after seeing an ad, whereas others will try it only if they get free samples. After allowing respondents time to use the new product in their homes, the researchers contact them by telephone for a post-usage survey, offer participants an opportunity to repurchase the new product (to be delivered by mail), and ask them to respond to the same questions (perception and preference measurements) they were asked in the laboratory setting. The laboratory measurements provide inputs for calibrating both the trial–repeat and preference models.

Trial–repeat model

The ASSESSOR model uses a standard chain ratio formula to generate the long-run market share of the new product according to the new product trial and repeat measures obtained from the laboratory experiment, as follows:

$$\text{Market Share Estimate} = t \times r \times w$$
$$= \text{Trial} \times \text{Repeat} \times \text{Usage rate,}$$

where,

t = cumulative proportion of the target segment who eventually will try the new product;

r = proportion of those trying the new product who will become long-run, repeat purchasers of the new product; and

w = relative usage rate, where w = 1 is the average usage rate in the market.

ASSESSOR estimates the trial rate (t) as follows:

$$t = \underbrace{FKD}_{\substack{\text{Those} \\ \text{who} \\ \text{try}}} + \underbrace{CU}_{\substack{\text{Those} \\ \text{given} \\ \text{samples}}} - \underbrace{(FKD)(CU)}_{\substack{\text{Adjustment} \\ \text{for double} \\ \text{counting}}},$$

where,

F = long-run probability of trial given unlimited distribution and total awareness of the new product in the target segment, equal to the proportion of the participants who purchased the product in the simulated store (O_4 in Exhibit 5.9);

K = long-run probability of awareness, estimated on the basis of managerial judgment and the projected advertising plan;

D = long-run probability that the product will be available where the target customers shop, according to managerial judgment and expectations of the proportion of outlets that eventually will carry the product;

C = probability that a customer in the target segment will receive a sample of the new product, estimated on the basis of the introduction plan for the new product; and

U = probability that a customer who receives a sample will use it, estimated on the basis of past experience and managerial judgment.

The first term, FKD, represents the proportion of customers who will be aware of the new product, have it available where they shop, and try it. The second term, CU, represents the proportion of customers who will obtain a trial sample, and the third term, (FKD)(CU), adjusts for double counting those persons who both purchase the new product and receive a sample. However, the trial–repeat model does not provide estimates of draw and cannibalization, which are important to a firm in developing its marketing plan for the new product.

Next, the model estimates the repeat rate (r) from the information in the postusage telephone survey (O_5 in Exhibit 5.9).

Preference model

In the second element of the ASSESSOR model, the preference model transforms the measured preferences of the participants (observations O_2 in Exhibit 5.9) into choice probabilities that indicate the likelihood that participants will purchase each product in their consideration sets. The ASSESSOR model uses the logit choice model for this task, in which one parameter links stated preference to choice, calibrated with preference data prior to the introduction of the new product.

"After use" preference data (O_5) for the new product is incorporated into the preference model for estimating the new product's potential market share if it is introduced into the market. The preference model also enables the estimation of the new product's draw (market share taken from competitor brands) and cannibalization (market share taken from the firm's brands).

As in the trial–repeat model, these estimates must account for awareness (so that the brand appears in the consideration set) and distribution to come up with a final market share estimate for the new product.

The trial–repeat and preference models provide independent estimates of the market share for the new product. When these two estimates are close, they increase managers' confidence in the forecasted market share of the new product.

Validity and value of the ASSESSOR model

Commercially available pretest market models all claim good success rates, but ASSESSOR is one of the few models whose validation studies appear in academic journals as well (e.g., Urban and Katz 1983). The success rate of new products that undertake an ASSESSOR evaluation is 66%—significantly higher than the success rate of 35% among products that do not undergo a formal pretest model analysis. Moreover, only 3.8% of products that would fail according to ASSESSOR and yet were then introduced in the market succeeded. In a study of 44 new products that had been subject to ASSESSOR analysis, the average forecasted market share was 7.77, and the actual achieved market share averaged 7.16, with a standard deviation of only 1.99. The correlation between the forecast and the actual market share was an astounding 0.95.

Urban and Katz (1983) also compare the average monetary gains of firms that use the ASSESSOR model and those that use no market-based testing to determine whether to introduce a new product. The average incremental gain associated with the use of ASSESSOR is $11.7 million, a substantial return compared with the required investment of $50,000 for the ASSESSOR model. Compared with those that use just a regular test market, firms that use ASSESSOR in addition still make an incremental gain of more than $300,000.

Pretest market models are particularly useful for forecasting and evaluating a new product that is about to enter a well-defined category. The preference model in ASSESSOR provides diagnostic information that the firm can use to design the marketing plan to guide the introduction of the new product. However, firms must also remain aware the preference model is accurate only in well-defined product categories in which (1) customers learn about new products rapidly enough that preferences stabilize quickly and (2) customers' usage rates for the product category do not change as a result of a new product.

WHICH FORECASTING METHOD TO CHOOSE?

In this chapter, we cover a broad and potentially confusing set of forecasting methods. Which should you or your firm choose? Armstrong (2001) provides a useful set of research-based guidelines for selecting a forecasting method:

1. *Use structured rather than unstructured methods.* Although you cannot avoid your own judgment, you should use it in the context of a structured model.

2. *Use quantitative rather than judgmental methods if enough data exist.* When sufficient data about the dependent and independent variables exist, quantitative methods are at least as accurate as judgmental methods—and often considerably more so. The key codicil to this guideline is that the forecaster must be reasonably competent in using the methods and the methods themselves should be relatively simple (see guideline 4).

3. *Use causal rather than extrapolation methods.* Extrapolation methods often work quite well and inexpensively, and they offer good short-term forecasts, especially if the situation has been and is likely to remain stable. However, when the historical or future environment exhibits significant changes, causal methods are best.

4. *Use simple methods unless substantial evidence shows complexity helps.* Simple methods usually are just as accu-

rate as more complex methods. For some reason, many
forecasters use overly complex methods, which may fit
historical data better but often harm forecast accuracy.

5. *Match the forecasting method to the situation.* The person with many clocks rarely knows the correct time; so it is
with forecasting methods.

Armstrong also provides sound evidence to support the
flowchart in Exhibit 5.10. For example, if a marketer possesses
sufficient objective historical data, good knowledge of the relationships among those data, and an expectation of significant market
changes, econometric methods would be most appropriate. If several methods seem equally effective for providing useful forecasts,
combine them! The website www.forecastingprinciples.com offers
a comprehensive overview of forecasting findings and references.

EXHIBIT 5.10

*Selection tree for
forecasting methods.
Source: Armstrong
2001, p. 376.*

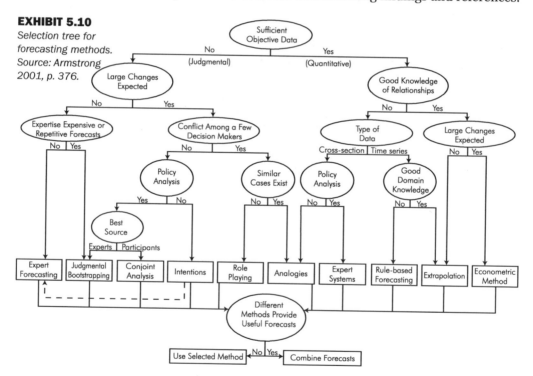

As President Eisenhower once said, "Plans are nothing. Planning is everything." In a similar way, "Forecasts are nothing. Forecasting is everything." A disciplined forecasting process can help
a firm anticipate and prepare for the future, even if the resulting
forecasts turn out to be imperfect. A well-structured forecasting
process enables firms to build up the right amount of flexibility so
they can handle unanticipated events.

EXAMPLE

On September 11, 2001, Walmart stores sold more than 100,000 U.S flags, compared with 6,400 on the same day the previous year. No forecasting system, whether judgmental or data-based, could ever have predicted the steep increase in sales for that day or the events that triggered those sales. However, because Walmart's forecasting system had access to all kinds of information about its vendors' production capacities and inventory levels at its various stores, the company was able to respond more effectively than its competitors to this surge in demand. Thus, the real value of forecasting comes not from the quantification of uncertainty but rather from the resulting ability to understand how the firm should be organized to respond to various unknown or unknowable marketplace events that fall within the realm of possibility.

SUMMARY

To devise a marketing strategy, firms must define a market appropriately and assess and forecast the demand for that market. We outline the most widely used methods for forecasting the sales of both new and established products. Those methods may be classified as judgmental, survey-based, time-series–based, and causal. We stress that though the wide range of forecasting methods vary in terms of their data needs, sophistication, and problem focus, almost all real forecasting problems require some level of judgment.

We also stress that despite our focus on a wide range of forecasting methods, forecasting remains a foundational process that provides input to marketing and business decisions and is not an end in itself.

CHAPTER 6

New Product and Service Design

For marketers, a product (or, more generally, an offering) refers to anything that can be offered in the market for attention,
acquisition, use, or consumption and that might satisfy a want or
a need. Most products people think of are physical, but products
also include services, such as concerts, overnight package delivery, management consulting, vacation tours, Web browsers, and
MBA programs. Even such entities as the American Red Cross can
be viewed as products, in the sense that when "consumers" trans-
act with the Red Cross, they feel positively toward the organization and fulfill their need to feel good about themselves because
they have acted charitably.

Marketing managers view products at three levels:

- *Core product:* That part of a product that satisfies the customer's central underlying need or want; the essence or
  fundamental aspect of a product. As Ted Levitt, a former
  Harvard professor, once noted, a customer buys a three-
  inch hole, not a three-inch drill-bit; as Charles Revson of
  Revlon put it: "In the factory, we make cosmetics; in the
  store, we sell hope."

- *Tangible product:* The transformed core product con-
  sisting of features, styling, quality level, brand name, and
  packaging that make the core product into something

that customers can buy. A vacation package at Club Med transforms customers' desires for adventure, excitement, romance, or escape into a tangible product they can conveniently purchase. A Visa credit card represents a transformation of customers' desire for secure, convenient, and quick access to credit into a tangible product.

- *Augmented product:* Enhancements to the tangible product in the form of additional services and features that make the product attractive, such as toll-free customer information, installation guides, delivery, warranty, or after-sale services. In recent years, the emphasis has grown on augmenting a physical product with services that enhance customers' overall experience, especially in B2B domains, because such enhancements help firms cement their relationships with their customers.

The product is the most important element of the marketing mix, around which all other aspects of the marketing program revolve. To develop and manage successful products, managers must make crucial, difficult decisions during the new product development (NPD) process while managing the portfolio of existing products. We focus primarily on the NPD process, which consists of several stages (Exhibit 6.1).

THE NEW PRODUCT DEVELOPMENT PROCESS

During the first stage of the NPD process, opportunity identification, firms generate ideas and articulate the market opportunities associated with those ideas. For example, R.J. Reynolds Tobacco Company came up with the idea of the "smokeless cigarette" to address the opportunity represented by increasing social objections to smoking. Gillette proposed a spring-mounted razor (Sensor) that would provide a closer and smoother shave than any other razor available in the market. Steve Jobs and his team at Apple saw an opportunity to redefine the digital music experience and therefore initiated iPod and iTunes offerings. The sources for new product ideas are as diverse as the products themselves and include customers, competitive products, and employees. For example, the idea for the iPod was first proposed by an independent consultant, Tony Fadell, who then joined Apple to bring the idea to fruition (Kahney 2006).

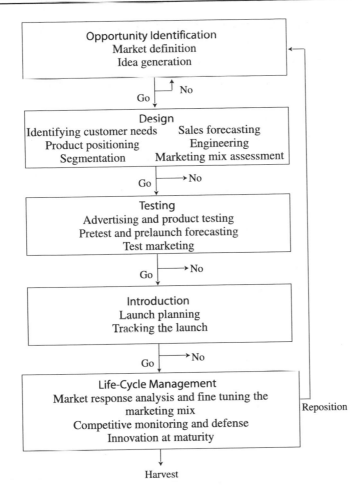

EXHIBIT 6.1
The various stages and decisions involved in the new product development process. Adapted from Urban and Hauser 1993, p. 38.

If a firm decides that a new idea is attractive, it proceeds to the second stage: design. In the design stage, the firm transforms the idea into a physical model, picture, or a verbal description to denote its form, features, and meaning. For example, the design of the smokeless cigarette mandated that it heat, instead of burn, the tobacco, which would reduce the "environmental" tobacco smoke in the air by 65-99% compared with a regular cigarette. But other design features were visual, such as the sleek packaging featuring thin, golden, diagonal lines on a white background to convey the image of a "cleaner cigarette" and the brand name "Premier" to indicate a superior product. In the case of the iPod, from the very first moment of the design stage, the product design included the capacity to hold and play a large number of songs (the first model allowed storage for 1,000), unlike traditional CD players that played one CD at a time or existing MP3 players that could store only a few songs. To enable customers to manage their playlists of 1,000 songs, Apple also created an award-winning, intuitive user interface. The iPod features numerous other elements and engineering innovations that emerged during the design phase to store, quickly retrieve, and play songs.

During the design stage, managers also seek a better understanding of the target market segments, explore alternative ways to position the product in those segments (Chapter 4), work with engineers to determine cost-benefit trade-offs for various product features, develop and evaluate product prototypes, create initial marketing plans, and generate sales forecasts for selected product designs.

The testing stage comes next, and managers use it to assess whether the product will gain market acceptance when it is introduced or meet the firm's profit and market share goals according to the proposed marketing plan. Testing also offers diagnostic information about which changes to the product or marketing program might improve its chances of success. If the various tests (e.g., taste, advertising copy, simulated shopping) indicate success, the firm proceeds to introduce the product.

In the case of Premier cigarettes, for example, test market results indicated that consumers did not value the social benefits enough to overlook negative perceptions: poor taste (it left a charcoal-like aftertaste), higher price, and "strangeness" (each package required special instructions on how to light the cigarette). Most test stores reported high trial rates but low repeat purchase rates. Therefore, R.J. Reynolds did not introduce Premier nationally.

The fourth stage, actually introducing the product into the market, calls for careful decisions about coordinating production and marketing plans, fine-tuning the product design for manufacturability, and managing the distribution pipeline. It also requires continuous market performance monitoring to refine the introductory strategy (e.g., price, advertising copy).

Finally, if the firm successfully introduces a new product, it institutes a life cycle management plan with the goal of maintaining the growth and profitability of the product. Successful products invite competition, so the firm needs both offensive and defensive strategies. Successful products also draw a disproportionate percentage of organizational resources, so the firm needs to undertake portfolio, not just individual product, management strategies to ensure the short-term and long-term profitability of its entire portfolio of products.

During each of the five stages, the firm makes a "go or no go" decision about moving to the next stage; R.J. Reynolds' Premier smokeless cigarette prompted "go" decisions through the third stage, but the decision prior to moving on to the introduction stage was "no go." However, this five-step process only represents an ideal example. Individual firms customize the process depending on their product requirements and specific capabilities. In some cases, a firm may skip a stage (e.g., testing) or reiterate several stages before moving forward.

The costs and risks associated with any new product are high. Most new products fail to achieve the objectives managers and firms set for them, and so they disappear from the market. Even 25 years ago, the average NPD costs ranged as high as $700,000 to identify opportunities, $4.1 million for design, $2.6 million for testing, and $5.9 million to introduce a product, according to Urban and Hauser (1993, p. 61). (The projects they analyze break down into 60% industrial, 20% consumer durables, and 20% consumer nondurables.) In other industries, the costs could be much higher (or lower). For example, the Tufts Center for the Study of Drug Development estimates that the average cost of bringing a new biotech product to the market today is approximately $1.2 billion. In some categories, short product cycles (e.g., a few weeks for new movies, a few months for notebook computers) demand that managers get the product right the first time rather than refining it after its introduction. Because of these high costs and high failure rates, firms continually seek ways to improve the efficiency of the NPD process.

Several research studies indicate that using a disciplined approach to developing new products improves the likelihood of success. For example, Hise et al. (1989) report that firms that use the full range of upfront activities associated with the five NPD stages in Exhibit 6.1 have a 73% success rate, compared with a 29% success rate for firms that use only a few stages.

In today's competitive markets, as companies scramble to develop new products that accomplish several objectives simultaneously, the NPD process is coming under even closer scrutiny. New products must not only be competitive in global markets but also offer good value to customers, be environmentally friendly, enhance the strategic position of the company, and enter the market at the right time. To meet these challenging objectives, companies use various approaches that can support or suggest changes in their NPD processes, including techniques such as quality function deployment and stage-gate reviews, measures such as cycle time, and organizational mechanisms such as cross-functional teams (e.g., Griffin 1993; Zangwill 1993). At the same time, more and more sophisticated analytics facilitate decision making at every stage of the NPD process (Rangaswamy and Lilien 1997). Therefore, in the rest of this chapter, we describe a few computer-supported modeling approaches that offer opportunities to enhance decision making associated with the early stages of the NPD process. We also note that the new product forecasting models we described in Chapter 5 represent additional tools firms can apply to support their NPD process.

MODELS FOR IDEA GENERATION AND EVALUATION

Many seemingly great ideas like Ford's Edsel car and Apple's Newton PDA do not evolve into great products. In other cases, simple serendipity leads to great success. Consider that the microwave oven and baldness remedy Rogaine evolved from accidental discoveries by astute and observant researchers. This type of seemingly random discovery process has led marketers to refer to the early part of the NPD process as the "fuzzy front end." Even acknowledging the often unpredictable nature of new products, marketers still desire more systematic approaches to the front end of the NPD process.

Creativity in NPD requires both divergent (lateral) and convergent thinking. Using divergent thinking techniques such as free association, brainstorming, and synectics, people can generate many ideas. In the synectics process, a facilitator stimulates new thoughts about familiar things, typically using analogies and metaphors (e.g., "How is music like water?"). Convergent thinking, in contrast, describes the process used to identify the most promising of the generated ideas, a step we call idea evaluation.

Creativity Software

Idea generation

Several commercial software packages offer support to the creative process, based on the premise that interactions between people and software enhance creativity. Software programs such as the Brainstorming Toolbox (www.infinn.com) and Idea Fisher (www.thoughtrod.com) help individual users expand their creative thinking. The Brainstorming Toolbox stimulates divergent thinking through various questions and triggers:

Q: What's the problem?

A: We want to increase the battery life of the iPod.

Q: What is the ideal solution?
A: Double the current battery life.
Q: What prevents you from reaching this solution?
A: The hard drive continues to spin even when a song is not playing.
Q: How might you resolve this problem?
A: Use a memory bank to store several songs that can be accessed with less battery power.

The Idea Fisher software program attempts to encourage divergent thinking by helping users make nonobvious connections through free association. The software combines two databases: one with 10 million words and cross-references between words, and another with a bank of over 10,000 questions (e.g., "How would a child solve this problem?") organized into categories. When the user enters a word or phrase, the software retrieves associated words and phrases. For example, the term "*new product*" retrieves such associated terms as "*marketing*," "*imagination*," and "*research experiments*," which each in turn triggers other connections (e.g., imaginary people and places). This process continues iteratively until the user stops it.

Software-supported models, such as Imaginatik (www.imaginatik.com), help large, decentralized companies facilitate and manage the idea generation process among their own employees. In the public domain, the website www.whynot.net offers anyone in the world the opportunity to share new product ideas and have them evaluated, while www.innocentive.com offers monetary incentives to its member network of millions of scientists and engineers worldwide to provide ideas and solutions for various R&D problems posted by member companies.

Idea evaluation

Software programs also can help evaluate new ideas, especially if there are so many that the task seems overwhelming. Using a spreadsheet to develop an overall score for each idea according to a specified set of managerially relevant criteria, commercially available software such as DecisionMill (www.gyronix.com) helps firms normalize the resulting scores, such that the best idea(s) gets scores of 100 and the worst one(s) earns 0 points. Regardless of the type of software used, the overall score should depend on at least two specific criteria, namely, how well the idea fits with the company's strategic objectives and how well it will appeal to customers in targeted segments. Widespread adoption of the Internet also makes it possible to invite customers to evaluate ideas, even if there are lots of them. For example, Toubia and Flores (2006) have developed an online model (www.branddelphi.com) in which each respondent evaluates only a few ideas, and those that appear to have been misclassified as either very good or very bad in the previous stage move forward for further evaluation.

GE/McKinsey Portfolio model

If the ideas to be evaluated are limited (e.g. 10 or fewer), the firm can use the GE/McKinsey Portfolio model (see Chapter 3) to evaluate selected ideas in a deeper way. The specific criteria incorporated in a GE/McKinsey model should reflect the strategic context surrounding the NPD process. For example, the following criteria might appear within a GE/McKinsey portfolio designed to evaluate new product ideas:

- Business Strength Dimensions
  - Fit with strategic focus of company.
  - Technical feasibility.
  - Resource requirements (finance, manufacturing, marketing).
  - Ability to protect intellectual property.
  - Organizational and channel support.
- Industry Attractiveness Dimensions
  - Size of potential market.
  - Growth rate of potential market.
  - Attractiveness of market (competitive superiority, profitability).
  - Regulatory compliance.

Company managers rate each new product idea on each criterion and combine them in the GE/McKinsey model framework to determine the idea's overall attractiveness and select the most attractive to take to the next NPD stage. In virtually every case, the size of the potential market provides a critical factor in determining an idea's attractiveness. To assess the size of a potential market associated with an idea (especially in the consumer packaged goods industry), marketers can use an intent-to-use or intent-to-purchase survey of a random sample of customers from the target segment. This approach requires the company to create descriptions of the product ideas or mock-ups of the products to show customers, who then respond to questions such as the following for each new product idea:

I would:

- Definitely buy the product.
- Probably buy the product.
- Probably not buy the product.
- Definitely not buy the product.

With these survey results, the analyst assigns a score to each product idea that equals the percentage of respondents who checked the "definitely would buy" box plus half the percentage of the respondents who checked the "probably would buy" box. In other words, this score represents the percentage of the target population who *eventually* will likely become customers of the product. Because these percentages result from a survey (i.e., not a setting that forces customers to make real purchase decisions), their initial scores are positively biased, so firms must deflate them to reflect the actual percentage of customers who will buy. From their extensive experience administering such intent-to-buy studies, many market research firms have developed proprietary deflation factors.

Even without the benefit of such extensive experience though, it is possible to derive appropriate deflation factors using one of two simple approaches: First, a real product already available in the market could appear in the survey as one of the ideas evaluated by respondents. In this case, the deflation factor would be as follows:

$$\text{Deflation Factor} = \frac{\text{Actual \% of people using the real product}}{\begin{array}{c}\text{\% of people using the real product}\\\text{as estimated from the survey}\end{array}}$$

Second, various deflation factors are available in the public domain. For example, Exhibit 6.2 provides the deflation factors for durables and frequently purchased products at each level of the intent-to-buy scale. As Exhibit 6.2 makes clear, some people who say they will definitely not buy eventually buy the product, and some who say they definitely will buy never actually do so.

If, after these various analyses, the idea still seems to offer potential for further development, the next phase entails translating the idea into a product with specific features that appeal maximally to customers in the target segment.

EXHIBIT 6.2

Deflation factors for intent-to-buy scales pertaining to consumer durables and nondurables. For example, only 13% of those who say they will definitely buy a durable actually purchase the product within six months (Jamieson and Bass 1989).

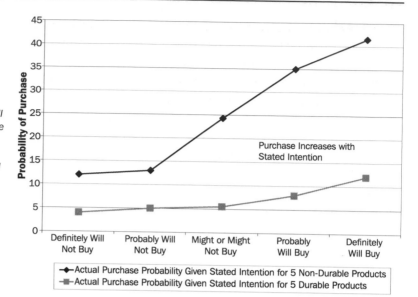

CONJOINT ANALYSIS FOR PRODUCT DESIGN

Conjoint analysis: A method for assessing customers' preferences that decomposes preferences for product bundles into preferences (value) for each product attribute option (partworths).

According to studies by Cooper (2001), when firms clearly define products during the early stages of the NPD process, those products are 3.3 times more likely to be successful; they also earn significantly higher market share and greater profitability than products that are not well defined. Conjoint analysis helps companies develop sharper product definitions by identifying those product features that will appeal to customers. This beneficial method can be applied in both the early and late stages of the NPD process.

For many products and services, it is helpful to view them as bundles of attributes. For example, a pizza represents a composite of several attributes, such as type of crust and topping and amount of cheese. An attribute can have many options or levels (e.g., the toppings can consist of pepperoni, veggie, cheese, and any variations thereof), and a bundle (i.e., a product) consists of one chosen option (or level) of each attribute.

Conjoint analysis uses data pertaining to customers' overall preferences for a selected number of product bundles and decomposes them into the utility values (partworths) that customers assign to each level of each attribute. The set of decomposed utility values thus represents the partworth function.

To collect data for conjoint analysis, the firm obtains respondents' preferences for a carefully selected set of product bundles, also known as profiles. The selected bundles typically do not include those that dominate the other bundles on all attributes of interest. Respondents rate or rank-order the bundles to indicate their degree of preference for each, which means they must trade off among attributes, because one product bundle may have their preferred level of one attribute (e.g., pepperoni topping) but contain less preferred levels of others (e.g., higher price and no vegetables). These preference data enable the firm to derive partworth functions, which it then uses to predict respondents' preferences for any product (i.e., any combination of attribute levels), even those not directly evaluated by respondents. In turn, managers can efficiently determine the value of a wide range of product design options, far more than the respondents could evaluate directly. Numeric partworth functions even allow managers to develop quantitative forecasts of the sales or market shares of alternative product concepts and price noneconomic attributes (e.g., delivery in three weeks versus four weeks is worth $X to the respondents).

EXAMPLE

To illustrate the basic concepts of conjoint analysis, imagine how a packaged foods firm might use it to design a new frozen pizza. Start by assuming that pizza can be described by combinations of specific attributes—type of crust, type of toppings, amount and type of cheese, and price. The firm considers three types of crusts (thin, thick, and pan), four types of toppings (veggie, pepperoni, sausage, and pineapple), three types of cheese (mozzarella, Romano, and mixed), three quantity levels for the cheese (two, four, or six ounces), and three prices ($7.99, $8.99, and $9.99). The pizzas are identical in all other respects, such as size, type of tomato sauce, and brand name. Even considering just this limited set of attribute levels, the company faces a choice among 324 (3 × 4 × 3 × 3 × 3) different types of pizzas. Which will be the most preferred by customers in a target segment? Using a conjoint study, the pizza maker presents potential customers in selected target segment(s) with several carefully chosen alternatives. It could describe the various pizza alternatives in words, with pictures, or, better still, with samples the respondents can taste. However, no respondent could taste all 324 possibilities, so the company limits the sample to 16 selected pizzas per person. It chooses 16 because only 16 (3 + 4 + 3 + 3 + 3) discrete attribute levels exist, so the model needs to estimate only 16 parameters. That is, technically, conjoint analysis can estimate the partworths a respondent associates with each attribute level from his or her evaluation of only 16 product bundles. With the information the firm obtains from this respondent's limited evaluation, it can assess how this customer will evaluate any of the 324 pizza combinations. Conjoint analysis provides (1) the (imputed) relative importance that each respondent attaches to each pizza attribute (e.g., type of topping is three times as important as amount of cheese), and (2) each respondent's partworth for each level of each attribute (e.g., on a scale of 0-30, a customer values the veggie topping at 10 points and the pepperoni topping at 30 points). Exhibit 6.3 depicts the summation of these partworths, which enables the company to compute any respondent's (or customer segment's) valuation of any possible pizza.

EXHIBIT 6.3

A conjoint analysis showing one customer's partworth function for frozen pizza. Numbers in parentheses are the partworths. For this customer, the topping attribute is worth 30 points (scale of 0–100), and the crust attribute is worth half as much. Within the topping attribute, going from a pineapple topping to a veggie topping is worth 10 points; going from veggie to sausage is worth an incremental 15 points.

Crust (15 points)	Amount of cheese (10 points)
Pan (0)	2 oz (0)
Thin (10)	4 oz (8)
Thick (15)	6 oz (10)

Topping (30 points)	Price (35 points)
Pineapple (0)	$9.99 (0)
Veggie (10)	$8.99 (20)
Sausage (25)	$7.99 (35)
Pepperoni (30)	

Types of cheese (10 points)
Romano (0)
Mixed cheese (3)
Mozzarella (10)

Ratings for three alternative pizzas for this customer based on the part-worth function

Aloha Special	Meat-Lover's Treat	Veggie Delite
Pan (0)	Thick (15)	Thin (10)
Pineapple (0)	Pepperoni (30)	Veggie (10)
Mozzarella (10)	Mixed cheese (3)	Romano (0)
4 oz (8)	6 oz (10)	2 oz (0)
$8.99 (20)	$9.99 (0)	$7.99 (35)
Utility = 38	Utility = 58	Utility = 55

Among these three pizzas, this customer prefers the Meat-Lover's Treat.

According to the partworths assigned by the respondent in Exhibit 6.3, the ideal pizza is a thick crust pizza with pepperoni topping and 6 ounces of mozzarella, priced at $7.99, which earns a utility score of 100. This respondent's lowest-rated pizza, a pan pizza with pineapple topping, 2 ounces of Romano cheese, and priced at $9.99, achieves a utility score of 0, and the other 322 possible pizzas score somewhere between 0 and 100. For example, the Aloha Special scores 38, the Veggie Delite 55, and the Meat Lover's Treat 58. This particular respondent prefers pepperoni (30) to veggies (10) by 20 points and prefers paying $8.99 to $9.99 by the same 20-point difference, which implies that pepperoni topping is worth an incremental $1 to this respondent compared with a veggie topping.

Although the firm could produce the pizza that earns a utility score of 100 for this customer, it is far from clear that doing so would be profitable. First, not all pizzas cost the same to produce, so the firm must balance customer preferences for various attributes, including price, with its costs to determine which pizza will generate the most profit. Second, the preferences in Exhibit 6.3 apply only to one customer; others will not have identical preferences. Even within a target segment, customers vary in their preferences. Most customers in the target segment may prefer to pay the lowest price and pepperoni topping but differ in their preferences for the type and amount of cheese and the type of crust. Thus, no single pizza can be the ideal choice for everyone in the target segment. The firm therefore might seek to develop several pizzas that are among the more preferred options for a large group of customers within a segment—a far more complicated problem than simply putting together a pizza with the highest average utility score among that target segment.

The preceding example suggests that conjoint analysis is particularly useful for designing products that maximize the measured utilities for customers in a target segment. That is, the firm can use the utilities (partworth) data from the study to modify existing products and services and develop new products that appeal maximally to customers. Although early conjoint applications certainly followed this expectation, firms increasingly also use conjoint analysis to make strategic decisions, such as selecting market segments for which a given product delivers high utility; plan their competitive strategy; and analyze pricing policies. In just the past few years, researchers have begun to explore whether Web capabilities can enhance the value of conjoint studies by enabling the firm to (1) recruit respondents in narrowly defined target segments, (2) use more flexible and adaptive designs customized to the specific attributes of interest to a particular respondent, and (3) provide richer product descriptions (e.g., pictures, working demos, audio) for customers to evaluate.

EXAMPLE

Polaroid decided to use conjoint analysis to develop an
updated version of its i-Zone instant camera in 2001. The
existing i-Zone camera printed mini-photos, was targeted at
teenagers, and was priced in the $17-25 range. Polaroid won-
dered: Should it add new features, which would increase the
price, or focus primarily on styling? The feature options the
firm considered adding included improved picture quality,
autofocus capability, and motorized picture ejection, as well
as styling aspects like unusual colors, interchangeable panels, and newer styles. To address this design problem, Polaroid implemented an online conjoint analysis study by asking
a sample of teen respondents to assemble their ideal i-Zone
camera. The participants viewed pictures of the camera that
showed both how the proposed features would work and how
the camera would look with the style changes. Each time a
respondent added or removed a feature, the website updated
the product's price.

As a result of this study, Polaroid uncovered the trade-offs its
customers would make among styling, features, and price:
Teenagers were not willing to pay very much for advanced
features but rather preferred catchy styling that enhanced
the camera's image as a fashion accessory. The study also revealed that the respondents attached great value to one styling option in particular: a changeable front panel that Polaroid's development team had not considered very important.
When Polaroid added changeable panels and launched the
new i-Zone in March 2001, it became an immediate success.
Revenue from the i-Zone brand increased by 35% and gross
margin by 42.3% from the year 2000 to 2001.

Source: Compiled from several sources, including Whiting (2001).

How to Conduct Conjoint Analysis

Conjoint analysis studies typically include three stages: design, data collection, and decision exploration (Exhibit 6.4).

Stage 1: Designing the conjoint study

Step 1.1. Select attributes relevant to the product or service
category by conducting a focus group study of target customers
(e.g., design engineers in an industrial marketing context); asking the NPD team which features and benefits it would consider;
or using secondary data, such as Consumer Reports, to identify
an appropriate set of attributes. Studies that include more than

six attributes may become unwieldy and require special expertise, though many conjoint studies have been conducted with far more attributes.

Stage 1 - Designing the conjoint study:
  Step 1.1: Select attributes relevant to the product or service category,
  Step 1.2: Select levels for each attribute,
  Step 1.3: Develop the product bundles to be evaluated.

Stage 2 - Obtaining data from a sample of respondents:
  Step 2.1: Design a data-collection procedure,
  Step 2.2: Select a computation method for obtaining partworth functions.

Stage 3 - Evaluating product design options:
  Step 3.1: Segment customers based on their partworth functions,
  Step 3.2: Design market simulations,
  Step 3.3: Select choice rule,
  Step 3.4: Adjust market shares to reflect support marketing programs.

EXHIBIT 6.4

Steps in designing and executing a conjoint study.

Step 1.2. Select the levels of each attribute to study. For example, an analyst might start by asking the NPD team what specific design options it is considering. In selecting the levels of attributes, several conflicting considerations come into play:

- To improve the realism of the conjoint study, the attribute levels should cover a range similar or broader to that actually observed in existing products, with both the highest prevalent attribute level (e.g., highest miles per gallon rating among the competing cars) and the lowest prevalent level (e.g., lowest tensile strength).

- Include as few attributes and attribute levels as possible to simplify the respondents' evaluation task. Typically, studies use between two and five levels for each attribute.

- To avoid biasing the estimated importance of any attribute, include roughly the same number of levels for each attribute; otherwise, some attributes receive higher importance rankings simply because respondents have more levels (options) of the attributes to evaluate. Equalizing the number of levels in attributes requires redefining attributes, combining two or more attributes, or breaking up an attribute into two or more attributes.

Overall, the range of attribute levels should be consistent with ranges observed in the marketplace, and each attribute should entail roughly the same number of levels, which both simplifies the evaluation task for the respondents and avoids misleading conclusions about the importance of the attributes.

Step 1.3. Develop the product bundles—the combinations of attribute levels to be evaluated. As in the frozen pizza example, it is unreasonable to expect respondents to evaluate every possible combination, so firms must choose the product bundles (or profiles) it presents to respondents carefully. Rather than full-factorial designs (which include all possible combinations of attribute levels), fractional-factorial designs (carefully selected subsets) reduce the number of products respondents must evaluate. Orthogonal combinations of attribute levels help lower the number of evaluated product bundles, yet still provide measures of the independent contributions of each attribute to the utility function. An experimental design is orthogonal if the levels of any attribute balance out (i.e., occur in roughly equal proportion) across the levels of the other attributes. Exhibit 6.5 presents a set of products that conform to an orthogonal design for the pizza example. If the firm also needs to incorporate the interactions among attributes, it could use more complex designs as well.

EXHIBIT 6.5

Sixteen product bundles that form an orthogonal design for the frozen pizza study.

Product bundle #	Crust	Topping	Type of cheese	Amount of cheese	Price	Example preference score
1	Pan	Pineapple	Romano	2 oz.	$9.99	0
2	Thin	Pineapple	Mixed	6 oz.	$8.99	43
3	Thick	Pineapple	Mozzarella	4 oz.	$8.99	53
4	Thin	Pineapple	Mixed	4 oz.	$7.99	56
5	Pan	Veggie	Mixed	4 oz.	$8.99	41
6	Thin	Veggie	Romano	4 oz.	$7.99	63
7	Thick	Veggie	Mixed	6 oz.	$9.99	38
8	Thin	Veggie	Mozzarella	2 oz.	$8.99	53
9	Thick	Pepperoni	Mozzarella	6 oz.	$7.99	68
10	Thin	Pepperoni	Mixed	2 oz.	$8.99	46
11	Pan	Pepperoni	Romano	4 oz.	$8.99	80
12	Thin	Pepperoni	Mixed	4 oz.	$9.99	58
13	Pan	Sausage	Mixed	4 oz.	$8.99	61
14	Thin	Sausage	Mozzarella	4 oz.	$9.99	57
15	Thick	Sausage	Mixed	2 oz.	$7.99	83
16	Thin	Sausage	Romano	6 oz.	$8.99	70

Notes:
Preference scores could be rank orders (1 to 16), relative preference ratings (on a scale of 1 to 100) or allocation of a constant sum (e.g., 100 points) across the 16 bundles.

We can compute the relative utility of an attribute level by averaging the preference scores for the bundles in which that level occurs. For example, to compute the preference score for pan crust, compute the average of the scores of bundles 1, 5, 11, and 13, which gives a value of 45.5. Likewise, the average preference score for thick crust is 60.5, and for thin crust is 55.5. Thus, the customer gets an incremental utility of 15 points from having thick crust instead of pan crust and five incremental utility points from thick crust instead of thin crust.

To minimize respondent fatigue, the evaluation should include a maximum of 25 product bundles and preferably 16 or fewer. Traditional assessment procedures mandate approximately twice the number of products for evaluation as there are parameters to be estimated by the model.

Stage 2: Obtaining data from a sample of respondents

Step 2.1. Design a data collection procedure. With a study design in hand, the firm next must obtain evaluations of the selected product bundles from a representative sample of respondents in the target segment(s). To present the bundles to respondents, the firm might use verbal, pictorial, or physical (using prototypes or samples) descriptions. Pictures have some advantages, in that they make the task more interesting and are superior to verbal descriptions for some products (e.g., a picture of a vacation property is better than a verbal description). And though physical prototypes are desirable, their expense prevents them from appearing too often in conjoint studies. After determining the presentation mode, the firm next must decide how to obtain data from customers:

- *Pairwise evaluations of product bundles:* The respondent considers two or more products at the same time and allocates 100 points among the options. This task is simple but forces the respondent to make many pairwise comparisons. For example, with 16 product bundles, the respondent must evaluate 120 pairs [(16 × 15)/2], a tedious and burdensome task. Exhibit 6.6 shows a pairwise comparison for two of the alternatives from Exhibit 6.5.

Product 1		Product 2
Pan pizza		Thin crust
Pineapple		Pepperoni
Romano	OR	Mixed cheese
2 oz. cheese		2 oz. cheese
$9.99		$8.99

Strongly Prefer Product 1   1—2—3—4—5—6—7—8—9   Strongly Prefer Product 2

EXHIBIT 6.6
Pairwise comparison for two products from Exhibit 6.5.

- *Rank-order product bundles:* The respondent ranks (or sorts) the products presented, assigning the most preferred option rank 1 and the least preferred a rank equal to the number of products presented. If necessary, the respondent can first sort the products into piles of similarly valued products, then sort within each pile, and finally sort the entire set.

- *Evaluate products on a rating scale:* The respondent evaluates each product on a rating scale (e.g., 0-100), with larger numbers indicating greater preference. Alternatively and more difficult, respondents could allocate a constant sum (say, 100 points) across the study. This approach assumes that respondents can indicate how much more they prefer one product bundle to others. Using ordinary least squares (OLS) in conjunction with such measures, analysts can compute partworth functions. The widespread availability of regression analysis packages makes this approach the most convenient for managers. The last column of Exhibit 6.5 lists sample ratings for a customer in the frozen pizza study.

Step 2.2. Select a computation method to obtain partworth functions. Regardless of which of the foregoing methods the firm chooses, respondents may find the evaluation task difficult if they have to evaluate many product bundles. To simplify the task, the firm can use several approaches:

- *Hybrid conjoint model:* With this method, one first obtains "self-explicated" preferences, and then combines them with a reduced set of data obtained through the traditional methods—a hybrid. In the self-explication phase, the customer evaluates the levels of each attribute separately on a desirability scale (say, 0-10). Next, he or she allocates points (say, 100) across the attributes to reflect their relative importance. The initial partworths for the attribute levels come from multiplying the importance weights and respective attribute-level desirability scores. That is, data obtained from each respondent in reference to a smaller set of complete product bundles augment the self-explicated data.

- *Adaptive conjoint analysis:* This approach uses a computer program to obtain data from respondents interactively. The respondent puts attributes in a rough order of importance (a simpler version of self-explication), then refines the trade-offs between the more important attributes using pairwise comparisons. The program selects the pairs of product bundles that will maximize the level of information provided by the responses, given the respondent's previous responses.

- *Bridging designs:* This method is based on using sophisticated questionnaire design to ask respondents to evaluate the product bundles only on a subset of attributes and "bridging" attributes common across several respondents. It thereby distributes the burden of evaluating a complete set of product bundles across several respondents.

Stage 3: Evaluating product design options

Step 3.1. Segment customers on the basis of their partworth functions. In the frozen pizza example, one segment of customers might prefer thin crust pizza, whereas another prefers pan pizza, but their preferences for the other attributes remain roughly similar. Imagine further that these two segments differ systematically in terms of their demographic characteristics (e.g., age) and media habits (e.g., watching MTV). Traditional cluster analysis, as we discussed in Chapter 3, provides a simple way to identify such segments, in that the partworths correspond to needs variables.

Step 3.2. Design market simulations. Once the partworths of a representative sample of respondents are available, conjoint analysis makes it easy to assess the likely success of a new product concept in various simulated market conditions. For example: What market share will a proposed new product achieve in a market with several existing competitors?

To answer this question, the firm first specifies all existing products in the market as their own combinations of the attribute levels under study. If more than one competing product has identical attribute levels, only one representative needs to appear in the simulation.

Step 3.3. Select a choice rule. Completing the simulation design requires specifying a choice rule that can transform partworths into the product choices customers are most likely to make. The three most common choice rules are maximum utility, share of utility, and logit. The maximum utility rule allocates all of a respondent's likely purchase volume to the alternative (i.e., the product bundle) with the highest utility, whereas the share of utility and logit rules allocate the total volume across all alternatives to reflect their relative utilities. Another option, the alpha rule, tries to scale the partworth functions so that the market shares predicted by a study that uses existing products match their actual market shares as closely as possible. The rescaled partworth functions then provide inputs for computing the new product's market share.

Step 3.4. Adjust market shares to reflect the marketing programs that support each product in the market. In a conjoint study, all participants are aware of the new product, and the analysis assumes that everyone who is aware of the new product will consider buying it and can find it when it comes time to purchase. But realistic predictions of market share must adjust the study results to reflect the marketing plan for both the new product and existing competitive products in the market, as illustrated in Exhibit 6.7. Even though the simulation suggests a market share of 10% for the new product, the levels of marketing support limit it to just 2.5% of the market.

EXHIBIT 6.7

Adjusted conjoint analysis market share results.

Products	Market Share from Conjoint Study (%) (a)	Indexed Awareness Level (maximum=1) (b)	Indexed Distribution Level (maximum=1) (c)	a x b x c (d)	Adjusted Market Share, or (d)/47.7
New product	10	0.2	0.6	1.2	0.025
Existing product 1	30	0.5	1.0	15.0	0.315
Existing product 2	40	1.0	0.7	28.0	0.587
Existing product 3	20	0.35	0.5	3.5	0.073
(Total)				47.7	

After determining the market shares for one or more new products, the firm must determine which product bundle it should introduce. Of course, it could maximize its market share by offering a product at an unprofitable price, but obviously, some profitability or revenue index rule needs to appear in a conjoint study to bridge the gap between expected market share or revenue and the firm's objectives and constraints.

Strengths and Limitations of Conjoint Analysis

Conjoint analysis is a sophisticated method and, like most sophisticated things, must be applied with care. The following checklist provides guidelines you can use to determine if conjoint analysis is suitable in a particular decision context:

1. In designing the product, you must make trade-offs among various attributes and benefits offered to customers.
2. You can decompose the product or service category into basic attributes that managers can act on and that are meaningful to customers.

3. The existing products are well described as combinations of attribute levels, and new product alternatives can be synthesized from those basic attribute levels.
4. You can describe the product bundles realistically, either verbally or pictorially. (If not, you should consider using actual product formulations for the evaluations.)

Furthermore, conjoint analysis has several limitations. For example, conjoint analysis equates a customer's overall utility for a product with the sum of his or her utilities for the component parts. Clearly, highly valued options can compensate for unattractive options on another attribute; a low price can compensate for lots of things, like when a pizza does not have pepperoni topping (Exhibit 6.3). In other situations however, customer choices are noncompensatory, so no matter how good the price on a new car, if you cannot drive a stick shift, you will not want it. In this case, "stick-shift" should be the only attribute level that should be included in the simulations involving target segments that want only stick shift cars. And no matter how many meat options may be available, if you are a vegetarian, you will reject all pizzas with meat. To the extent that a problem context includes noncompensatory processes, conjoint analysis may produce misleading conclusions.

In addition, the validity of any conjoint study depends on the completeness of the set of attributes, but including too many attributes increases respondent fatigue, which leads to inaccurate responses. Therefore, most commercial applications typically use a maximum of 16-25 product bundles, which means they can measure five or six attributes with three or four levels each.

Finally, we note that our discussion centers on a basic type of conjoint analysis. In recent years, more sophisticated approaches to gathering data for conjoint analysis, such as choice-based conjoint, adaptive conjoint analysis, menu-based conjoint and choice-based conjoint with hierarchical bayesian estimation have gained commercial acceptance. These alternatives should be considered as potential alternative methods when developing a conjoint study.

SUMMARY

The never-ending quest for new products is, quite simply, a strategic necessity for firms to survive and thrive. In this chapter, we outline the five major stages of new product development

(NPD), as well as some of the many decision models firms can use to improve their decisions. Emerging tools can aid both idea generation and evaluation processes, and conjoint analysis provides an important set of product design tools. Firms should use such tools in the early stages of their NPD process to help them make effective decisions about the most appropriate products to bring to market.

CHAPTER 7

The Marketing Mix

The marketing mix refers to the levers that marketing managers can pull to create and implement a marketing plan. These levers are often called the 4Ps: Product, Price, Place, and Promotion. In Chapter 6, we described the product lever, focusing specifically on product design. In this chapter, we explore issues related to pricing and managing the marketing communications mix, including decisions regarding:

- *Advertising:* Any paid form of nonpersonal presentation and promotion of ideas, goods, or services by an identified sponsor.
- *Direct marketing:* The use of mail, telephone, the Internet, and other non face-to-face contact tools to communicate with or solicit a response from specific customers and prospects.
- *Sales promotion:* Short-term incentives to encourage customers to try or purchase a product or service.
- *Personal selling:* Face-to-face interactions with one or more prospective customers for the purpose of making a sale.

The methods marketers use to influence customer demand involve complex processes that encompass interactions among the marketing levers (advertising, price, and promotions), delayed effects (spending now may affect demand in the future), competitive effects (current actions may cause or be driven by competitive actions), and product line, geographic, and channel considerations (many firms manage thousands, if not hundreds of thousands, of products in multiple channels across diverse geographies). In view of these complexities and dynamics, firms frequently must reevaluate, adjust, and fine-tune their marketing mix activities. For example, because of optimism about economic recovery, some companies are planning to invest more in advertising in 2012: Unilever plans to increase ads in digital and social media and to buy ad space from companies like Apple and Facebook (Elliott 2012).

We deal with each marketing mix element individually and ignore some complexities, particularly the interactions among elements, for several reasons. First, market reactions to single marketing mix elements are far easier to understand than are their interactions. Second, an improved understanding and the resultant ability to fine-tune individual marketing mix elements often represent "low-hanging fruit"—the profitable first step toward optimizing marketing spending across a wider range of marketing mix elements. Third, the optimization of the entire marketing mix may cross organizational boundaries and require sophisticated processes for managing them.

PRICING DECISIONS

Price is the only marketing variable that directly affects revenue. The profit function,

$$\text{Profit} = (\text{Unit price} - \text{Unit cost}) \times \text{Quantity sold},$$

clearly demonstrates that price is involved in all parts of the profit equation. Price affects margin (i.e., unit price less unit cost) in two ways: It is the first term (unit price) in the equation by definition, and it has an indirect effect on unit cost, which is often determined partly by the quantity sold. Because price affects the quantity sold (and hence unit cost indirectly), it represents a portion of all three components of the profit equation.

The Classical Economics Approach

For a classical economist, price is the driving force that allocates goods and services in the marketplace. For the customer, it represents the cost of a purchase in monetary terms. And for the producer or seller, price helps determine the level of supply and the allocation of economic resources on the production side.

A basic relationship in economic theory, known as the Law of Demand, states that the quantity demanded per period (or time rate of demand) is negatively related to price. This law is based on the postulate of a rational customer who has full knowledge of the available goods and their substitutes, a limited budget, and a singular drive to maximize his or her utility. For any given structure of relative prices, customers allocate their income across goods (including savings) to maximize their utility. If the price relations change, these customers substitute less expensive goods for more expensive goods to increase their utility in the new scenario.

Central to this model is the concept of price elasticity, the ratio of the percentage or fractional change in demand to the percentage or fractional change in price:

$$e_{qp} = \frac{\text{Fraction Change in Demand}}{\text{Fraction Change in Price}} = \frac{(Q_1 - Q_0)/Q_0}{(P_1 - P_0)/P_0}$$

where

e_{qp} = elasticity in the quantity demanded with respect to a change in price;

Q_1 = quantity demanded after a price change;

Q_0 = quantity demanded before a price change;

P_1 = new price; and

P_0 = old price.

Therefore, we cannot assess elasticities without specifying a model of how sales (quantity sold) respond to price changes. In most cases price elasticities are negative. A price elasticity of 1.0 means that demand rises (falls) by the same percentage that the price falls (rises). In such a case, total revenue remains unaffected. When the price elasticity is greater than 1, demand rises (falls) by more than the price drop (increase) in percentage terms, and total revenue therefore rises (falls). Finally, a price elasticity of less than 1 means that demand rises (falls) by less than the decrease (increase) in price in percentage terms, and total revenue therefore falls (rises).

If we know the demand function (i.e., price elasticity at every price level), we can determine whether the firm's price is too high or too low with greater precision. When we want to maximize revenue, we can determine that the price is too high if the demand elasticity at that price is less than 1. Whether this rule also holds true for maximizing profit depends on cost behavior.

EXAMPLE

The XYZ Corp. sells 1,000 units of a product at $10 per unit, which costs the company $5 to produce and market. Therefore, the gross profit is 1000 × ($10 − $5) = $5000. The XYZ Corp. is considering a price increase of $1 to $11 per unit, which would decrease demand to 950 units (a price elasticity of 0.5), for a resulting profit of 950 × ($11 − $5) = $5700, or a profit increase of $700. However, if the market were more price sensitive and demand dropped to 800 units (price elasticity of 2.0), the resulting profit would be 800 × ($11 − $5) = $4800, a decrease of $200. Thus, the lower the price elasticity, the more likely a company can justify a price increase.

The Law of Demand is not specific to any particular shape of the price–quantity relationship; the shape varies according to the product and the product class. However, two equation forms are particularly appropriate for representing this relationship: linear and constant-elasticity. One simple demand–price relationship depicts quantity going down linearly with price (i.e., a unit change in price leads to a constant change in demand, so a $1 price drop increases demand by 1,000 units). A more common curvilinear relationship occurs when a proportional decrease in price (say, 10%) leads to a constant, proportional increase in demand (say, 20%). This curvilinear relationship presupposes a constant elasticity of demand (in this example, elasticity is −2).

However, the classical model relies on several key assumptions that limit its applicability, including the following:

- The firm's objective in setting its price is maximizing the short-run profits it can realize from a particular product.
- The only outside parties to consider in setting the price are the firm's immediate customers.
- Price setting occurs independently of the levels set for other variables in the marketing mix.
- Demand and cost equations can be estimated with sufficient accuracy.
- The firm has true control over price; it is a price maker, not a price taker.
- Market responses to price changes are well understood.

Economic theory usually assumes near-perfect information about market prices and a downward-sloping demand curve. However, all customers will not interpret prices in the same way. A price reduction that would normally attract more customers may not be known to all of them. Furthermore, customers may interpret changes in prices as signifying that

- The product is about to be superseded by a newer model.
- The product has some faults and is not selling well.
- The firm is in financial trouble and may not stay in business to supply future parts.
- The price will come down further, so it pays to wait.
- Quality has decreased.

Conversely, a price increase that would normally deter or slow sales may carry a variety of different meanings to potential buyers:

- The product is hot and may soon be unobtainable.
- The product represents an unusually good value.
- The customer feels more price increases are ahead and it is better to buy now.

Thus, the influences on demand include not only the current price but also the information the price provides and customers' expectations about future prices.

Despite its conceptual elegance and intuitive appeal, the classical model just is not very useful for decision making. In practice, firms tend to base their pricing decisions on one of three key factors—cost, demand, or competition—and then rely on models that ignore the other two factors.

Cost-Oriented Pricing

Many firms set their prices largely or even wholly on the basis of their costs. Typically, they compute all costs, including allocations for overhead expenses, based on expected operating levels.

The most elementary examples of cost-oriented pricing are markup and cost-plus pricing. Both methods determine price by adding either a fixed amount or a fixed percentage to the unit cost. Does the use of a rigid, customary markup amount over cost make logical sense in pricing products? Generally, the answer is *no*. Any procedure that ignores the current elasticity of demand when setting prices probably will not lead, except by chance, to maximum profits, in either the long or the short run. As demand elasticity changes—as it virtually always does seasonally, cyclically, and over the product life cycle—the optimum markup should also change. If the markup remains a rigid percentage of cost, in ordinary conditions, it will not lead to maximum profits.

However, we must note that under special conditions, a rigid markup at the right level can lead to optimum profit, if (1) average (unit) costs are fairly constant for different points on the demand curve and (2) costs are constant over time. If a situation seems to correspond to these conditions, the firm can consider a constant markup over unit price and could derive optimal profits, as long as it ensures the markup is higher when elasticity is lower (in absolute value terms, closer to 1). Thus, the more inelastic the demand for the product is, the higher the markup over marginal cost should be. These special conditions—constant (marginal) costs and constant elasticity—characterize many retailing situations, which may explain why so many retailers use rigid markups and still remain consistent with optimal pricing requirements. However, durable consumer products and industrial products rarely meet the two special conditions.

Demand-Oriented Pricing

Whereas cost-oriented approaches to pricing center on the costs of producing and distributing the product, demand-oriented approaches are based on observing demand for the product at various price levels and thereby focus on customer value. As one of its central premises, demand-oriented pricing generally results in a higher price when demand is strong and a lower price when demand is weak, even if production costs remain the same.

EXAMPLE: THE GABOR-GRANGER METHOD (1964)

The Gabor-Granger method is a simple method to estimate customers' willingness to buy at different price points (and interpolate between those price points). It can be viewed as a simple alternative to conjoint analysis, except that it focuses only on price, keeping all other attributes constant.

The method works like this: A product is described to customers (attributes, features, sample, etc.) who are then asked to indicate their buying intention for that product at a number of different price levels (at least 3, usually more). Customers answer on a simple scale (usually a Likert 1-5 scale) ranging from "will never buy" to "will definitely buy." The trick is to transform these answers into probabilities of purchase. Customers normally overestimate their likelihood of buying a given product. As a consequence, unless there is situation-specific data or a benchmark database of stated-actual purchases in the category, it is common practice to interpret a "will definitely buy" as a 50% chance, a "will probably buy" as 20% chance, and everything else 0% chance.

Usually, there is not enough data to estimate a demand curve for each respondent so data of respondents are aggregated, and a response curve is estimated for the entire sample. That response curve is fitted to the average purchase likelihood, using a Logit specification (very much like Customer Choice models).

As an illustration, assume the 26 German respondents in Exhibit 7.1(a) (labeled "A" through "Z") answered a survey about their likelihood of purchasing a case for their smartphone at different prices of 4, 6, 8, 10 or 12 EUR. Respondent A said she would "definitely" (=5 on a scale from 1 to 5) buy at a price of 4, 6 or 8 EUR, will "likely" (=4) buy if the price were 10 EUR, and "may or may not" (=3) buy at price of 12 EUR, leading to a set of responses: (5, 5, 5, 4, 3). Those responses can then be transformed into probabilities using the rule above as : (0.5, 0.5, 0.5, 0.2, 0) in Exhibit 7.1(b).

	Answer				
Customer	**€4**	**€6**	**€8**	**€10**	**€12**
A	5	5	5	4	3
B	5	5	5	4	4
C	5	5	4	3	3
D	4	4	4	3	3
E	5	5	4	3	2
F	5	5	4	3	2
G	4	4	3	2	2
H	4	4	4	3	2
I	5	5	5	4	3
J	5	5	5	4	4
K	3	3	2	1	1
L	3	3	2	1	1
M	4	4	4	3	2
N	5	5	4	3	2
O	2	2	2	2	2
P	5	5	4	3	2
Q	5	5	4	3	3
R	5	5	5	4	4
S	4	4	4	3	3
T	4	4	3	2	2
U	5	4	4	3	2
V	5	5	5	4	4
W	3	3	3	2	1
X	3	3	2	2	1
Y	4	4	3	2	2
Z	5	5	4	4	4

(a)

	Answer				
Customer	**€4**	**€6**	**€8**	**€10**	**€12**
A	0.5	0.5	0.5	0.2	0
B	0.5	0.5	0.5	0.2	0.2
C	0.5	0.5	0.2	0	0
D	0.2	0.2	0.2	0	0
E	0.5	0.5	0.2	0	0
F	0.5	0.5	0.2	0	0
G	0.2	0.2	0	0	0
H	0.2	0.2	0.2	0	0
I	0.5	0.5	0.5	0.2	0
J	0.5	0.5	0.5	0.2	0.2
K	0	0	0	0	0
L	0	0	0	0	0
M	0.2	0.2	0.2	0	0
N	0.5	0.5	0.2	0	0
O	0	0	0	0	0
P	0.5	0.5	0.2	0	0
Q	0.5	0.5	0.2	0	0
R	0.5	0.5	0.5	0.2	0.2
S	0.2	0.2	0.2	0	0
T	0.2	0.2	0	0	0
U	0.5	0.2	0.2	0	0
V	0.5	0.5	0.5	0.2	0.2
W	0	0	0	0	0
X	0	0	0	0	0
Y	0.2	0.2	0	0	0
Z	0.5	0.5	0.2	0.2	0.2
Average	**0.32**	**0.31**	**0.21**	**0.05**	**0.04**

(b)

EXHIBIT 7.1

Responses to likelihood of buying a smartphone case by 26 German consumers at 5 different prices with raw scores in (a) and transformed scores to actual purchase likelihood, and average purchase likelihood in (b).

Averaging across all 26 respondents, the total probability vector obtained from this sample is (0.32, 0.31, 0.21, 0.05, 0.04).

The next step is to fit a Logit model (see Chapter 2) which has a mathematical form of

$$\text{probability} = \text{max} / (1 + \exp(-(\beta_0 + \beta_1 \times \text{price}))),$$

where max, β_0 and β_1 are parameters to be estimated by regression or another procedure.

In this case, max = 0.33, β_0 = 8.30, and β_1 = -0.97. β_0 is the price at which half of the potential sales are obtained, and β_1 should be negative because it is the parameter that captures price sensitivity. Exhibit 7.2 plots the resulting "likelihood of purchase" curve.

EXHIBIT 7.2

The likelihood of purchase curve from the customer-data in Exhibit 7.1.

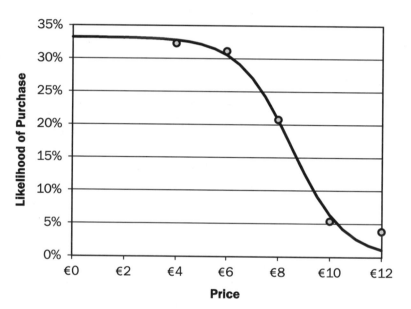

Now it is straightforward to find the price that maximizes revenues (or profits, if the cost structure is known). Suppose that the firm has fixed costs of 5000 EUR and marginal unit costs of 3 EUR/unit. Assuming a total market of 10,000 customers, then the price that maximizes profit is 7.5 EUR as shown in Exhibit 7.3.

The Gabor-Granger method is robust and easy to implement. Also, if many respondents answered the survey, it is possible to group these customers into different segments (based on demographics, usage patterns, discriminant variables, etc.), and estimate a response function for each group, hence allowing price discrimination as discussed below.

Price	Unit sold	Cost (€)	Revenues (€)	Profit (€)
€0.0	3,321	14,962	-	-14,962
€0.5	3,320	14,960	1,660	-13,300
€1.0	3,319	14,958	3,319	-11,688
€1.5	3,318	14,954	4,977	-9,977
€2.0	3,316	14,947	6,631	-8,316
€2.5	3,312	14,936	8,280	-6,656
€3.0	3,306	14,918	9,918	-5,000
€3.5	3,297	14,890	11,538	-3,352
€4.0	3,281	14,843	13,125	-1,719
€4.5	3,256	14,769	14,654	-115
€5.0	3,217	14,650	16,084	1,484
€5.5	3,154	14,463	17,349	2,886
€6.0	3,058	14,173	18,347	4,173
€6.5	2,913	13,738	18,931	5,194
€7.0	2,703	13,110	18,924	5,814
€7.5	**2,421**	**12,262**	**18,154**	**5,892**
€8.0	2,068	11,204	16,545	5,341
€8.5	1,672	10,016	14,211	4,195
€9.0	1,274	8,823	11,469	2,646
€9.5	919	7,756	8,727	971
€10.0	632	6,895	6,316	-579
€10.5	419	6,256	4,395	-1,860
€11.0	270	5,811	2,973	-2,888
€11.5	171	5,514	1,971	-3,543
€12.0	107	5,322	1,289	-4,084

EXHIBIT 7.3

Calculating the Profit Maximizing Price using the formula:

Profit= Total Market (10,000) x(Price-Marginal cost)xPurchase Probability(Price)-Fixed Costs

The method has some limitations, including:

- The results are sensitive to how survey responses are translated into purchase likelihood, e.g., if a "will definitely buy" is transformed into p=0.5, while in reality it is closer to 0.3, the model overestimates the optimal price point and sales potential.
- If the optimal price point falls outside the range of tested price levels, the model predictions are not reliable and the study should be conducted again to include those price levels.
- The model does not readily provide margins of error, or confidence intervals for the optimal price level.

An insight from the model is that at the optimal price point, sales never reach maximum potential. At the price level that optimizes profit, there will always be customers who do not buy the product because it falls outside their price range. Thus, if no customer complains that your prices are too high it means your product is priced too low for optimal profit.

EXAMPLE: PSYCHOLOGICAL PRICING USING THE VAN WESTENDORP (1976) METHOD

The Van Westendorp method uses easy-to-gather customer information to compute a price range that is psychologically acceptable to the market. The approach asks four questions: At what price would you say product X is:

- Too cheap (to be credible)
- A Bargain
- Expensive
- Too expensive (to be considered)

These responses are then ranked and plotted along the four dimensions above and the manager can check where the lines cross (Exhibit 7.4).

EXHIBIT 7.4

Psychological Pricing Graph using the Van Westendorp (1976) method, where the lightly shaded area is the psychologically acceptable range and the darkly shaded area is the range between the optimal price and the expected price.

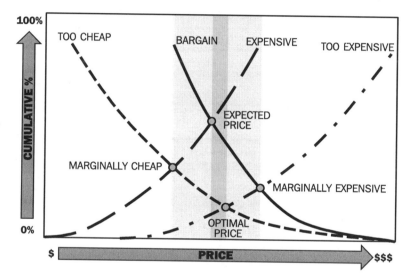

The optimal psychological price is where the "too cheap" and "too expensive" lines cross: that is where opinions are equally split between those who think it is too cheap and those who think it is too expensive at that point.

The expected price is where the "bargain" and the "expensive" lines cross. The "marginally expensive price" is where "too expensive" crosses "bargain" and the "marginally cheap" point is where "too cheap" and "expensive" cross, providing the borders of the psychologically acceptable range.

This approach is easy to apply and can provide a guiding framework when there is a lack of solid data. It may also be useful as part of an overall process of price-setting. There is little theory behind the approach, however, and no link between what customers say and what they will actually do.

Many sophisticated marketers, especially in B2B markets, practice value-based pricing by taking into consideration the product's value-in-use. A value-in-use analysis is based on the argument that a product's price should relate to the value a particular customer places on the product. This approach is particularly appropriate for large volume purchases when the salesperson has pricing discretion. The salesperson imagines him- or herself in the buyer's situation and determines whether the best investment would be for the buyer to adopt the product or replace its current product with a proposed new product. To implement this pricing scheme, firms can use tools such as value-in-use (Chapter 2) or conjoint analysis (Chapter 6) to assess the value that the specific customer or customer segment places on an offering and then use that information as the basis for their pricing decisions.

Exhibit 7.5 illustrates the value-based pricing idea. From the left, the supplier's production plus its distribution costs represent the zero-profit or minimum selling price. The customer won't pay more than its perceived value (maximum buying price) which, in this illustration, is below the true economic value that that customer is likely to realize. Note that good marketing communication closes the gap in perceptions between the customer's perceived value and its true value. Price, then, divides the total value created into the value captured by the seller (the profit margin) and the value captured by the buyer (what economists call consumer or customer surplus). The higher the price, the more profit the supplier gets, but the more reluctant the buyer is to make the purchase and the more attractive the customer or market appears to competitors.

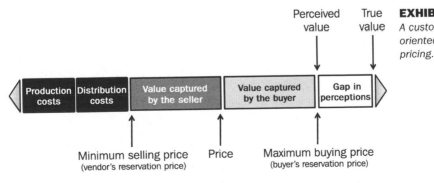

EXHIBIT 7.5
A customer-value oriented approach to pricing.

Competition-Oriented Pricing

When a company bases its prices chiefly on what its competitors are charging rather than on cost or demand, its pricing policy can be described as competition oriented. In the most common type of competition-oriented pricing, a firm tries to maintain its price at the average level charged by the industry, also called *going-rate* or *imitative pricing*.

Firms apply going-rate pricing primarily to homogeneous commodities like oil, even though the market structure may vary from pure competition to a pure oligopoly. The firm selling a homogeneous product in a purely competitive market actually has little choice in setting its price. However, in an oligopoly, in which a few large firms dominate (e.g., the plate glass industry), firms still tend to charge the same price as their competitors, though for different reasons. Because only a few firms exist in the market, each firm is aware of the others' prices—and so are customers. The firm with the lowest price will likely capture the most business, so competitors immediately move to decrease their prices to that lower level. On the flip side, this situation also discourages individual firms from increasing their prices.

However, in markets characterized by product differentiation, individual firms have more latitude in their pricing decisions. Product differences, whether in terms of styling, quality, or functional features, desensitize buyers to existing price differentials. Firms therefore make their product and marketing programs compatible within each pricing zone and respond to competitors' price changes in a manner that maintains their own relative prices.

In markets in which the firm competes with an unknown number of suppliers and has no way to determine their prices, pricing policies often employ competitive bidding. For example, manufacturers and service organizations that sell to the U.S. Defense Department, municipal governments, original equipment producers, and so forth must bid against others to receive a contract for the work; that contract usually goes to the lowest bidder. In addition, electronic price-discovery mechanisms in procurement auctions (e.g., www.ariba.com) have broadened the domain for competitive bidding. Therefore, sellers must carefully think through two issues surrounding each bidding opportunity: (1) Should the firm bid at all (the decision to bid), and (2) if so, what bid should it make (the bid-size problem)?

Price Discrimination

If a firm uses demand-based pricing, it faces the issue of how to implement price discrimination. In this case, the "discrimination" occurs between customers or segments of customers whose values (or, more technically, "reservation prices" or willingness to pay) differ from those of other customers or segments. A firm trying to implement direct price discrimination in practice faces several difficulties:

1. *Identifying customers' reservation prices is difficult.* Rarely are the observable characteristics of customers closely correlated with their reservation prices, and firms cannot obtain accurate estimates by simply asking customers how much they will pay.

2. *Targeting a particular price at a particular segment is difficult.* Most consumer goods, for example, feature posted prices and thus are available to every customer at an equal price.

3. *Preventing arbitrage is difficult.* Customers with low reservation prices may buy up a lot of the product and supply it to customers with higher reservation prices at a price higher than what they initially paid but lower than the reservation price of the latter group.

4. *Charging different prices to different segments for an identical product may be illegal* if based on certain grounds, such as sex and race discrimination. The Robinson-Patman Act governs discrimination by a firm among channel intermediaries.

5. *Customers may view price discrimination as unfair.* Those who pay a higher price for an item resent price breaks given to others, unless the firm can position a price break positively, such as by framing it as a form of charity (senior citizen discounts, student discounts). In many situations, sellers "throw" other items into the package—free service, beneficial financing, free software—that make the price discrimination less obvious and perhaps more acceptable.

EXAMPLE:

In September 2000, Amazon.com received headlines when customers found that the same DVDs were being offered to different buyers at discounts of 30, 35 or 40 percent. Amazon insisted the discounts were part of a random "price test," but critics suggested they were based on customer profiling. After weeks of bad press, the firm offered to refund the difference to buyers who had paid the higher prices. The company vowed it would not happen again.

Source: www.washingtonpost.com/wp-dyn/content/ article/2005/06/18/AR2005061800070_pf.html

Despite these difficulties, direct price discrimination schemes continue to exist. For example, telephone companies discriminate between residential and business users in their prices. Senior citizen and student discounts represent other forms of price discrimination. And many business products and services, whose terms and conditions of sale get customized, use discriminatory pricing policies. Services lend themselves particularly well to direct price discrimination, because the seller (e.g., a lawyer) deals with the customer one-on-one and provides services that are difficult to resell. All these cases satisfy the identification, targeting, arbitrage prevention, and legality requirements.

However, most price discrimination in practice is not as direct as these examples; the need for indirect price discrimination provides one source of the considerable variety in modern pricing schemes. The remaining challenge is to identify correlations between the reservation prices of different segments (Chapter 3) and their preferences for some specific product attributes. If the firm can discover such correlations, it can tie its different prices to the different levels of the attributes and allow customers to choose the level of the attribute they want to buy.

Consider, for example, the airline industry, which bases its pricing on revenue management. Airlines offer a variety of fares with various restrictions (and some with no restrictions). Options such as no advance purchase requirements, no Saturday-stay-at-destination requirement, and no cancellation penalties mean higher fares, whereas lower fares demand many such restrictions. The industry thus creates a product line differentiated according to the restrictions attribute, and different products in the product portfolio appeal to different segments. A business traveler likely finds the restrictions costly in terms of time or convenience and opts to pay more for the higher unrestricted fares; a vacation traveler, however, finds the lower fares appealing and does not mind the restrictions.

EXAMPLE

Airline pricing is based on sophisticated computer systems called revenue management systems. For every flight on every scheduled date, the airline creates various fare classes called "buckets" and dynamically controls the number of available seats it releases into each bucket on the basis of the actual bookings for that flight on preceding days, as well as estimated demand for the remaining seats in the different buckets.

Exhibit 7.6 summarizes the revenue that an airline would realize in three different situations if 138 passenger seats are available for a particular flight: (a) the maximum revenue potential possible if the airline knows the exact demand for each fare class in advance; (b) the revenue if the airline releases seats on a naive, first-come, first-served basis (i.e., low-price seats fill up first); and (c) the actual revenue realized with a revenue management system. The opportunity cost of the first-come first-served system is $6,561 (the difference between full prior knowledge and the naive system). In comparison, the opportunity cost of the revenue management system is only $2,916. Thus, the revenue management system can provide a gain in incremental revenue of $3,645 over the naive system.

If a market can be segmented by value and those segments can be identified (targeted), a clear opportunity for price discrimination exists. The institutional differences in different markets and legal restrictions have prompted various methods, but to implement any of them, the seller must analyze customer value carefully (through choice models, conjoint analysis, value-in-use analysis, or one of the other methods we have described), segment the market, and target the various segments (Chapter 3).

In other words, to implement price discrimination, the firm must understand how to separate the market segments and support the price discrimination program through advertising, distribution, and other marketing instruments. Some of the most common schemes rely on geographic and temporal variations in pricing, use nonlinear pricing (i.e., base prices on customer characteristics), and employ nonprice marketing instruments. As Patrick Kiernan noted in the *Wall Street Journal* (June 21, 2001, p. 1), "Before long the only one paying the posted price, or the 'insult price' ..., will be a stranger to the seller with no purchase history."

Really, the main limit to the effective use of price discrimination is the marketer's imagination. Even promotions and coupons represent means of price discrimination. Coupon users are more price sensitive than nonusers, so the manufacturer sets a price that is higher than the optimal price for the price-sensitive segment and uses coupons to promote sales to it. The manufacturer therefore can realize optimal prices for both the price-sensitive segment and the segment composed of customers who are willing to pay more.

EXHIBIT 7.6
Example of the opportunities associated with a revenue management system for airline pricing and fare class allocations.

Fare Class	Passengers		Revenue ($)	
	Demand	Boarded	Average	Total
Y0	12	12	313	3,756
Y1	6	6	258	1,548
Y2	10	10	224	2,240
Y3	3	3	183	549
Y4	59	59	164	9,676
Y5	21	21	140	2,940
Y6	64	27	68	1,836
Total	175	138		22,545

(a) Revenue when airline has full knowledge of demand for various fare classes.

Fare Class	Passengers		Revenue ($)	
	Demand	Boarded	Average	Total
Y0	12	0	313	0
Y1	6	0	258	0
Y2	10	0	224	0
Y3	3	0	183	0
Y4	59	53	164	8,692
Y5	21	21	140	2,940
Y6	64	64	68	4,352
Total	175	138		15,984

(b) Revenue when airline sells seats on a first-come, first-served basis (assuming that lower fare passengers book first).

Fare Class	Passengers			Revenue ($)	
	Boarded	Spilled	Total	Average	Total
Y0	12	0	12	313	3,756
Y1	6	0	6	258	1,548
Y2	10	0	10	224	2,240
Y3	3	0	3	183	549
Y4	40	19	59	164	6,560
Y5	20	1	21	140	2,800
Y6	32	32	64	68	2,176
Total	123	52	175		19,629

(c) Revenue for airline using a revenue management system to control the amount of seats it releases to different fare classes on the basis of actual and forecasted demand for a specific date prior to flight departure.

Customer characteristics also inform price discrimination, especially for services. The most common such characteristics include:

- *Age*—special prices for children, senior citizens.
- *Income/education status*—student prices for movies and journal subscriptions; income-linked membership fees in organizations.
- *Profession*—government employee discounts, teacher discounts.
- *Membership*—AAA discounts on auto rentals, employee discounts, Sam's Club.

Even the distribution outlet can serve as a mechanism for price discrimination. For example, specialty stores usually charge higher prices than supermarkets. And the products themselves can be differentiated; software companies, for example, often sell "student versions" of software packages that include all but a few features of the higher priced version for 10% or less than the price of the unrestricted software. Similarly, some companies use brand differentiation as a price discrimination mechanism, particularly by selling (unbranded) generics at a lower price than their branded counterparts.

Pricing Product Lines

Most firms market more than a single product, and if these products are not related, through either shared costs or interdependent demand, a price discrimination approach may be appropriate. In this case, the prescriptions arising from an analysis of single-product pricing may not be appropriate for several reasons:

- Products in a line may relate to one another on the demand side, whether as substitutes or complements.
- Cost interdependencies may mean shared production, distribution, or marketing expenditures.
- Some products might be sold together as a bundle (e.g., stereo system vs. its individual components), which creates complementarities.
- The price of one product in a line may influence the buyer's subjective evaluation of other products in the line.

In addition to information about demand (i.e., price elasticities), which the firm needs for pricing a single product, when pricing product lines, the firm requires further knowledge of cross-price elasticities—the changes in demand for one product when the price of a different product changes (e.g., demand for SUVs goes down when gas prices go up).

RESOURCE ALLOCATION AND THE MARKETING COMMUNICATIONS AND PROMOTIONS MIX

In the remainder of this chapter, we discuss some critical considerations firms must take into account when determining their marketing spending level (i.e., budget) and budget allocations across products, markets, or other entities. The guiding principle in these discussions is the unifying concept embodied in Exhibit 1.3 of Chapter 1. We focus on justifying a total marketing communications and promotions budget by addressing the following questions all firms should ask:

1. How much should we spend in total during a given planning horizon?
2. How should that spending be allocated to each marketing mix element? How much of our budget should be spent on advertising and other forms of impersonal marketing communications? On sales promotion? On the sales force?
3. How should those individual budgets be allocated? To customers? To geographies? To sub-elements of the marketing communications mix? Over time?

These three questions are closely interrelated. It is nearly impossible to address the question of how much to spend (budget) without determining how to spend the budget properly (i.e., allocated across the competing uses). Thus, these questions provide the perspective we use to explore each element individually. And, these questions have become increasingly important with the growing multiplicity of media and channel options available for marketers to allocate their budgets. A major trend is for companies to allocate a greater proportion of their marketing budget to online media because online marketing triggers higher response than traditional marketing from certain target segments (e.g., young people), and with respect to certain activities undertaken by customers (e.g., researching a product online before buying at a store). Also, customer response to online marketing is trackable (e.g., response to Google Adwords), and often costs less than offline to generate the same customer response.

Adidas is reallocating its marketing budget of about $1.5B (13% of its sales) to make online media the primary way to reach its target audience of 14-19 year olds, with the traditional media (TV and print) playing a supplementary role in the future. Nike and Puma are pursuing a similar strategy (Bachfischer 2010). In addition, as more customers go online first to research big purchases, marketers of such products are shifting their spending toward the online medium. For example, General Motors, among the top advertisers in the U.S., expects to spend half its $3 billion advertising budget on online advertising (Halliday 2008).

Even companies, such as Proctor & Gamble, that have strong brands and maintain a major presence in traditional media are increasing spending on online marketing. P&G had an advertising budget of about $10 billion in 2011 and is making major shifts of its budget to search and social media based advertising, with some of its brands such as Aussie and Secret spending 100% of their advertising budget on online media (Glazer 2012).

Advertising and Impersonal Marketing Communications

One of the most important yet bewildering promotional tools of modern marketing management is advertising. No one doubts that it can be effective in presenting information to, or persuading, potential buyers. Everyone also agrees that it can influence customers' preferences for a product, enhance a company's image, or affect customers' purchasing behavior. Even when advertising does not directly influence sales, it can alter images and preferences, which, in turn, influence sales. Small changes in people's preferences for a product can have lasting impacts that result in increased sales over time. Jedidi, Mela, and Gupta (1999) show that advertising's long-term effect reduces price sensitivity for a product, whereas promotions (e.g., sales, coupons) increase price sensitivity.

Advertising is bewildering, among other reasons, because its effects typically play out over time, may be nonlinear, and often interact with other elements in the marketing mix to create sales. Currently, no one can really say what advertising actually does in the marketplace. However, what firms want from advertising is fairly clear: Increase company sales and profits. But advertising can rarely create sales by itself. Whether the customer buys depends as well on the product, price, packaging, personal selling efforts, services, financing, and other aspects of the marketing program, as well as the customer's own decision process.

Even more than for the other elements of the marketing mix, advertising decisions and their effectiveness depend on their interaction with marketing objectives, product characteristics, and various other elements of the marketing mix.

Personal selling

When personal selling is an important element in the marketing mix (e.g., in industrial markets), advertising's direct role diminishes. Personal selling is a far more effective (though more expensive) communication method than advertising, but because of its extra expense, it is most effective only when the expected level of sales to a single prospect is large (generally, sales to B2B customers, wholesalers, and retailers).

Branding

If a company produces several variations of its product under a family or company name (Kellogg's cereal, Campbell soups), it can advertise the entire line and simply focus attention on a special brand from time to time. When a firm carries different brand names (Procter & Gamble's Tide, Bold, and Cheer detergents), the company must advertise each brand independently and make separate advertising budget, copy, and media decisions.

Pricing

The copy, or message, and media placement of any advertising must reinforce and be consistent with the brand's price position. Industry folklore suggests that advertising for a premium-priced brand should emphasize its differentiated qualities, whereas that for a low-priced brand should stress its low price.

Distribution channel

The complexity of the distribution channel and the overall marketing strategy dictate different targets for advertising messages. To influence wholesalers or retailers, a firm can use two different strategies: push or pull. With a push strategy, the firm directs its marketing efforts toward salespeople or the trade industry, with the objective of pushing the product through the distribution channel. A pull strategy requires the firm to aim its marketing strategy at the ultimate consumer in an attempt to stimulate consumer demand, which then pulls the merchandise through distribution channels.

Therefore, the three major decisions surrounding advertising are (1) setting objectives (e.g., increase awareness, reinforce current brand image) and budgeting (how much to spend), (2) developing copy (what message), and (3) choosing media and vehicles through which the message will be delivered. Although we address these three points separately here, they are closely interrelated; advertising objectives drive copy decisions, and copy effects, which vary by response group, affect media decisions. In addition, time remains an issue for all three decision areas. In developing an advertising budget, a firm must consider its spending over time by evaluating both pulsing (i.e., sporadic) and continuous spending policies. Furthermore, the effectiveness of advertising copy eventually wears out, so firms must create new copy (executions of the message) and phase it in. Finally, firms must decide which media to use, in conjunction with the timing and scheduling of their messages.

Advertising Decisions in Practice

To determine the spending level for advertising, one of the important decisions firms make, they rely on several common methods.

Affordable method

Many executives set the advertising budget according to what they believe their company can afford. Setting budgets in this manner is tantamount to saying that the relationship between advertising expenditure and sales results is tenuous, so the company should spend whatever funds it has available and use advertising as a form of insurance. The basic weakness of this approach is that it leads to a fluctuating advertising budget that makes it difficult to plan for long-range market development.

Percentage-of-sales method

Many companies set their advertising expenditures at a specified percentage of their sales (either current or anticipated) or the sales price. Automobile companies traditionally budget a fixed percentage for advertising on the basis of the planned price of each car, and oil companies normally set their appropriations as some fraction of a cent for each gallon of gasoline sold under their own label.

Practitioners claim a number of advantages for this method. First, advertising expenditures vary with what the company can afford. Second, it encourages managers to think in terms of the relationship among advertising cost, selling price, and profit per unit. Third, to the extent that competing firms spend approximately the same percentage of their sales on advertising, it encourages competitive stability.

However, the percentage-of-sales method really has little to justify it. It uses circular reasoning, in that it makes sales the determinant of advertising rather than its result. It also leads executives to set advertising appropriations on the basis of the availability of funds rather than the available opportunities. Furthermore, the method provides no logical basis for choosing a specific percentage, except historical precedent, competitors' actions, or costs. Finally, it does not encourage firms to appropriate funds for advertising constructively on a product-by-product or territory-by-territory basis but instead suggests that all allocations occur for the same percentage of sales.

Competitive parity method

Some companies set their advertising budgets specifically to match competitors' outlays—that is, to maintain competitive parity.

Two arguments support this method. One is that competitors' expenditures represent the collective wisdom of the industry, and the other is that maintaining competitive parity helps prevent advertising wars. But neither of these arguments is compelling. There are no a priori grounds for believing that competitors use logical methods to determine their outlays. For different companies, advertising reputations, resources, opportunities, and objectives likely differ so much that others' budgets provide poor guidelines. Furthermore, there is scant evidence that appropriations based on the pursuit of competitive parity actually stabilize industry advertising expenditures.

Knowing what the competition spends on advertising is undoubtedly useful information. But it is one thing to have this information and another to copy it blindly. And even if the advertising budget is set appropriately by competitors, how they use that budget can vary widely in this increasingly digital era.

Objective-and-task method

With the objective-and-task method, advertisers develop their budgets by (1) defining their advertising objectives as specifically as possible, (2) determining the tasks required to achieve these objectives, and (3) estimating the costs of those tasks. The sum of these costs provides the proposed advertising budget.

If they undertake this method, firms must develop their advertising goals as specifically as possible to guide them when they develop copy, select media, and measure results. For example, a goal stated as "to create brand preference" is much weaker than "to establish 30% preference for brand X among Y million women in the 18–34 age category by next year."

This method enjoys strong appeal and broad popularity among advertisers. However, it cannot indicate how to choose the specific objectives or how to evaluate them to determine whether they are worth the cost of attaining them.

The Marketing Engineering approach

As data, concepts, and software related to advertising have become more pervasive, setting and justifying an advertising and marketing communication budget has grown increasingly amenable to advertising response models. For example, online banner and keyword advertising offer firms the means to estimate the relationship between their advertising spending and results (e.g., clickthroughs, sales per click). This response model approach uses the following general structure:

Problem: Find a total budget B and sub-budgets (allocations) B_1, B_2, ..., B_{10} (assuming 10 geographies, products, or markets).

Step 1: Determine the market response to a spending level B_1, or S_1 (gross sales), denoted by the function $S_1(B_1)$. Do the same for each subgroup. (This step fills in Box 2 in Exhibit 1.3 in Chapter 1.)

Step 2: Determine the gross profit margin m_1 associated with sales S_1 by calculating the percentage of S_1 that represents profit BEFORE accounting for B_1. Perform the same calculation for all subgroups.

Step 3: Find the sub-budgets B_1–B_{10} to maximize profit:

$$\text{Profit} = m_1 \times S_1(B_1) + ... + m_{10} \times S_{10}(B_{10}) \\ - B_1 - B_2 - ... - B_{10}$$

= Sum of gross profits minus cost of the communications program,

and take into consideration the total budget available

$$B = B_1 + ... + B_{10} \text{ (total budget restriction).}$$

Other constraints also might limit minimum or maximum spending in a region, for a product, or for another unit of analysis.

Marketing Engineering models address the budget decisions for marketing communications using a similar framework.

Sales Force Decisions

Exhibit 7.7 highlights three major decision categories—organization, allocation, and control—for which sales force managers are responsible. The four boxes and the connecting arrows offer a simple way to conceptualize decisions regarding sales force management. The goals and objectives provide the link between the overall strategic plan for the firm and the three sales force decision areas. The bidirectional nature of this link indicates that goals and objectives determine, and are determined by, each decision. Furthermore, each decision area influences and is influenced by other decision areas. Decisions pertaining to the organization of the sales force determine the internal (firm-based) context and structure needed to deploy the sales effort; decisions focused on allocation partition the total sales effort among revenue-generating entities (e.g., market segments); and control decisions attempt to motivate salespeople to adopt the firm's objectives as their own.

Sales force sizing and allocation

The size (how many salespeople?) and allocation (how should total sales effort be allocated to different products, markets, and sales functions?) of the sales force represent fundamental management issues for every sales force. Fortunately, many well-tested models support decision making in this area. Despite their effectiveness, many firms continue to employ intuitive methods instead.

EXHIBIT 7.7

Conceptual outline of sales force management decisions, showing the overall relationships between sales force goals and objectives and the three major decision areas: organization, allocation, and control.

Intuitive methods. Firms often determine the size of their sales force by deciding what they can afford, based on a percentage of the forecasted sales for the company, historical norms, or selling expense ratios for competitors. By dividing the average cost of a salesperson into this figure, they get the size of their sales force:

$$\text{Number of Salespeople} = \frac{\text{Selling Expenses as \% of Sales}}{\text{Average Cost of a Salesperson}}$$

Data pertaining to selling as a percentage of sales are widely available; for example, Sinha and Zoltners (2001) indicate that average sales force expenditures across all U.S. industries is 6.8% of sales.

In another approach, known as the "breakdown method," firms divide the sales forecast for the planning horizon by the average revenues generated by a single salesperson during that length of time:

$$\text{Number of Salespeople} = \frac{\text{Forecasted Sales}}{\substack{\text{Average Revenues Generated} \\ \text{by a Salesperson}}}$$

When the firm has determined the total number of sales people, it allocates the total effort (e.g., total number of calls or visits available) to different accounts and prospects on the basis of their actual or forecasted sales. For example, salespeople may visit accounts with high sales levels every month but those with low levels of sales only once every six months.

The above intuitive approaches to sizing and allocating sales forces are unsatisfactory for two main reasons:

1. They do not account for the possibility that some accounts or prospects may respond differently than the way the "average" account does.
2. They fail to recognize that a firm cannot determine the best sales force size (i.e., total sales effort) without knowing how to allocate the total sales effort most effectively.

Market-response methods (ReAllocator approach). Market-response methods require firms to estimate response functions, which calculate the relationship between sales effort and sales in each sales entity of interest. We define a sales entity as anything that may be associated with potential sales for the firm—customers, prospects, market segments, geographic areas, products sold by the firm, and so forth. If the firm estimates sales response functions for each sales entity, it can calculate the level of effort it should allocate to each entity to maximize profits or achieve its other objectives. The sum of the sales effort across a set of non-overlapping entities reflects the total sales effort the firm needs; divided by the average effort of a salesperson (e.g., 750 calls per year), this sum provides an estimate of the necessary number of salespeople.

In particular, the ReAllocator model provides a general approach to the sizing and allocating problem. Lodish et al. (1988) developed a version of this model for Syntex Laboratories, and we use that application as the example in our discussion. Because of its generalizability, the ReAllocator model can be adapted for use by various multiproduct, multisegment firms that employ a field sales force.

When Lodish et al. developed the model in 1982, Syntex sold seven prescription drugs (e.g., Naprosyn, Anaprox) that it promoted to nine physician specialties (e.g., general practice, dermatology). Syntex considered increasing its sales force size substantially, with the expectation that doing so would increase the sales of its portfolio of products among the nine physician segments. Exhibit 7.8 outlines the process used to implement the Syntex model.

Syntex used a flexible, S-shaped response function to characterize the sales response of each sales entity (product or market segment), as shown in Exhibit 7.9. To calibrate the model—that is, to make it specific to a particular product or market—senior managers from the sales, marketing, and research departments, who together possessed several decades of experience in selling pharmaceutical products, estimated the response functions using a form of the Delphi method (Chapter 5). These managers separately answered several questions with respect to how sales of each product would respond to sales efforts and how each physician segment would respond to varying sales effort levels. The following introduction and questions illustrate the type of questions they answered:

According to Syntex's strategic plan, if sales force effort is maintained at the current level (indexed to 1) from 1982 to 1985, sales of product A will reach the planned level (indexed to 1). What would happen to product A's year 1985 sales (compared with a base of 1 for the present levels) if during the same time period it received

1. No sales effort? X_0
2. One-half the current effort? $X_{0.5}$
3. 50% greater effort? $X_{1.5}$
4. A saturation level of sales effort? X_{∞}

(The answers to these questions provide inputs that estimation software uses to draw a smooth, S-shaped curve like that in Exhibit 7.9)

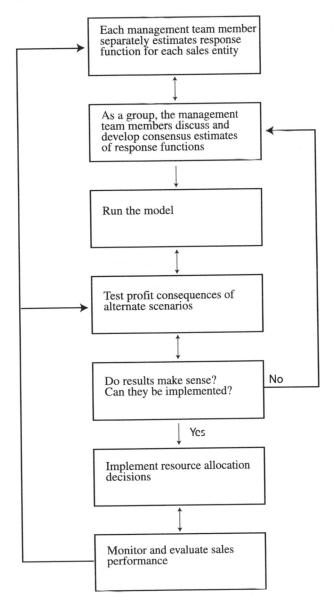

EXHIBIT 7.8

The sequence of steps for developing and implementing ReAllocator for Syntex Laboratories as a sales force resource allocation model.

EXHIBIT 7.9

An S-shaped sales response function that links current and other levels of selling effort to actual or anticipated sales.

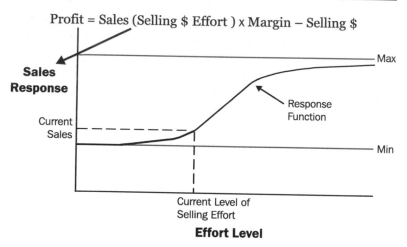

$$\text{Profit} = \text{Sales (Selling \$ Effort)} \times \text{Margin} - \text{Selling \$}$$

After a half-day training session, each manager privately answered this and similar questions; that is, each manager provided answers for X_0, $X_{0.5}$, $X_{1.5}$, and X_∞, respectively. The summarized answers, collated by computer, then went to each manager participant.

After studying this summary, the managers discussed the initial results, contemplated the differences between their own responses and the group mean, and then completed the same questionnaire again. In the Syntex study, this second round led to consensus estimates for the questions. On the basis of these inputs, they could generate an S-shaped curve for every response entity—product or physician specialty—of interest to the company. Thus, Syntex had the key information it needed to run the ReAllocator model.

The ReAllocator model takes these inputs and provides an answer to the following question: What spending level for each product (or physician specialty) will be most profitable, given the profit margins on these products (or from these physician specialties), the associated sales response functions (S-curves), and the investment costs associated with a unit of selling effort? The model allowed managers to consider various constraints (minimum and maximum levels of effort in total or for a particular product or physician specialty) when determining the budget and its allocation.

Syntex calibrated the model twice to allocate sales effort first to products and then to physician specialties. The company used these calibrations to plan for changes in the size of the sales force; Lodish et al. (1988) provide a fuller discussion of how the company used this model.

The ReAllocator model also can assess the overall value of a sales force. In the modern competitive environment, firms must justify every investment in terms of their opportunity costs, and one meaningful estimate in the context of sales force investment computes the difference between the profits derived from specific effort levels of a preselected sales force size and the profits the firm would earn if it expended zero sales effort toward all sales entities.

Because the ReAllocator model is quite general, if a salesperson wishes to allocate his or her time to customers or prospects, he or she could use the same model, with the customer/prospect as the unit of analysis. Lodish (1971, 1974) introduced just such a model, called CALLPLAN, designed as an interactive call-planning system that would help salespeople determine how many calls to make to each or each category of client and prospect in a given time period to maximize the returns on those calls. When United Airlines implemented CALLPLAN through a carefully designed field experiment, it increased sales by more than 8% with no increase in total sales force effort.

Sinha and Zoltners (2001), who summarize insights from various implementations of sales resource allocation models, find that the average results of 50 sales force sizing projects indicate that resource allocation models identify contribution improvements of 4.5% over a three-year base plan. Only 28% of this incremental improvement was attributable to a size change; the rest came from changes in resource allocation. That is, the bulk of the gains firms realize when they use resource allocation models occurs because they have gotten their sales forces to work smarter, and not work more. Exhibit 7.10 summarizes the results.

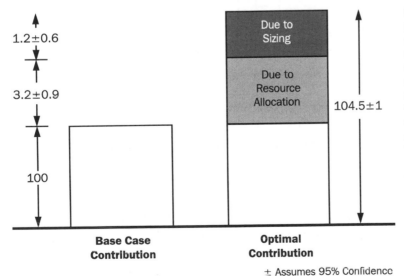

EXHIBIT 7.10

Compared with a company's base plan, model-based resource allocations generate an incremental contribution of 4.5%, with 1.2% of that attributable to changes in the size of the sales force and the rest to the reallocation of sales effort.

Response function estimation in online markets. Experimentation is another way to obtain response functions, especially in digital media. When experimentation is combined with a measurement approach called the "marketing funnel" it facilitates both marketing budgeting and resource allocation. The marketing funnel summarizes the mental stages that customers go through from first becoming aware of a product (or an offering) to eventually becoming loyal customers. The funnel provides a managerially useful tool to combine the psychology associated with customer behavior with an assessment of the business value of various marketing activities in influencing customers to move from the top of the funnel to the bottom. The funnel concept has gained increased use in the digital domain because the specific effects of a marketing action can often be isolated and measured there.

EXAMPLE

Exhibit 7.11 illustrates a funnel that starts with customer traffic to a website generated by a marketing mix activity (e.g., Google Adword placements) and ends when some of those customers buy products at the website. The funnel data includes intermediate measures such as percent that become aware of the product, percent that express interest in the product, and eventually the Return on Investment (ROI). Note that the funnel concept is similar to the chain-ratio method of forecasting we described in chapter 5.

In this example, 0.3% of the visitors to the company's website buy the product. That is, of 1,000 people who see the ad, 100 click it. Of those 100 who click it, 3 request a sample. And each of the three who request a sample only has one chance in 10 of buying. So this funnel says that it takes over 3,000 people to see the ad to obtain one customer at the bottom of the funnel.

Another measure of response could be those who express an interest in the product by clicking on the ad and purchasing a sample-sized version of the product (here 3% of those seeing the ad).

By knowing how much a firm paid to Google for the traffic it generated and the profit margin associated with the products sold, the firm can compute the level of market response (e.g., awareness, interest, sales, ROI) to the marketing spend. By varying the amount spent on a marketing mix activity in different time periods, or in different locations (e.g., different websites), a firm can calculate a response function associated with that activity. Digital media make this type of sales funnel response function estimation via experimentation relatively straightforward, providing a powerful tool for determining the optimal marketing budget and for allocating that budget to marketing activities that drive a specific business goal (e.g., awareness, sales).

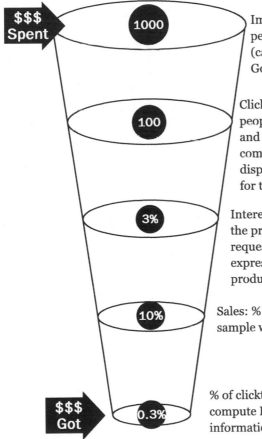

EXHIBIT 7.11

An example of a marketing funnel.

Impressions: Number of people who see the link (called paid placement) at Google's site.

Clickthroughs: Number of people who click on the link and are taken to a company's Web site that displays a more detailed ad for the product.

Interest: % of those who see the product ad and click to request a sample (i.e., they express an interest in the product).

Sales: % of those receiving a sample who buy the product.

% of clickthroughs who buy (can compute ROI using this information).

SALES PROMOTIONS: TYPES AND EFFECTS

Sales promotion comprises a wide variety of tactical promotion tools in the form of short-term incentives designed to stimulate earlier or stronger responses from customers in a target market. Most promotions refer to temporary, advertised price reductions, but promotions can take many other forms. Among the more popular forms are coupons, premiums, and contests for consumer markets; buying allowances, cooperative advertising allowances, and free goods for distributors and dealers; discounts, gifts, and extras for industrial users; and sales contests and special bonuses for members of the sales force.

Most promotions, when properly applied, complement other elements of the marketing mix and therefore require a coordinated effort among retailers, wholesalers, salespersons, advertisers, and (often) the people in charge of manufacturing and distribution. Exhibit 7.12 illustrates the types of complex flows that characterize promotions and suggests the importance of understanding and modeling both individual and combined effects of promotional activity at several levels.

EXHIBIT 7.12

Promotion types vary widely and can be directed at either the trade (retailer) or the consumer.

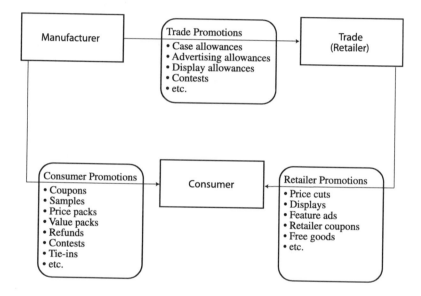

To model promotional effects, firms therefore must determine (1) the objectives of the promotion, (2) the characteristics of different promotion types and their purported effects on those objectives, (3) the effectiveness of different promotions, and (4) the range of promotion decisions.

Objectives of Promotions

Because sales promotion tools differ so much in form and function, they cannot all support the same objective equally. For example, free samples stimulate consumer trial, but access to a free management advisory service may cement a long-term relationship with a customer. In general, sales promotion techniques make three contributions:

    1. Communication: Gain attention and usually provide information that may lead the consumer to the product.

2. *Incentive:* Incorporate some concession, inducement, or contribution designed to represent value to the receiver.
3. *Invitation:* Include a distinct invitation to engage in the transaction immediately now.

Exhibit 7.13 provides a partial list of specific marketing objectives and some promotions that might enable a firm to meet them.

EXHIBIT 7.13

A range of marketing objectives and the promotions firms can use to meet those objectives. Source: Blattberg and Neslin 1990, p. 464.

Objective	Promotional Type
Increase repeat buying	In-pack coupons, continuity programs (e.g., frequent flyer, "N for" retail promotions)
Increase market share among brand switchers	FSI coupons, coupons targeted to users of other brands, retail promotions
Increase retailer's promotion frequency	Trade deals, combination of consumer promotions and trade deals (big-bang theory)
Enhance the product's image	Co-op image advertising with image-oriented retailers
Increase category switching	Retail promotions, FSI coupons, large rebates
Target deal-sensitive consumers	Coupons, "N for" retail promotions
Increase category consumption	Retailer promotions, promotions tied to events (e.g., back to school)
Increase trial among nonusers	Cross-couponing, free samples, trial packs, direct-mail coupons
Liquidate short-term inventories	Trade deals, rebates, inventory financing
Increase distribution	FSI coupons (increase demand), trade deals (increase DPP)

"N for" = multiple unit promotion (6 for 99¢)
FSI = free standing insert in newspapers and magazines
DPP = dealer price promotion

The range of possible objectives is broad, and the effects are numerous (and possibly confounding). For example, whereas a seller's primary purpose in a promotion may be to attract nonbrand purchasers, it also may want to reward brand-loyal users for their loyalty. Because both types of buyers purchase during a promotion, the seller accomplishes both purposes. In this sense, firms must set objectives and measure the effect of each particular promotion, regardless of whether those objectives pertain to the level of retail inventory, increased retail distribution, coupon redemption rates, sales effects, or any other effect.

Characteristics of Promotions

Marketing managers choose promotions for the cost-effective manner in which they enable them to accomplish their objectives.

The key considerations surrounding this approach vary with the promotional type.

For example, for sample promotions, firms often send sales people door to door, send the sample via mail, or offer it free with the purchase of another product. Furthermore, the size of the sample can vary. (A promotion to introduce Gainesburgers, a dog food designed to look like a hamburger, largely failed when General Foods only included half the recommended portion of a dog's meal in the sample pack.)

Although price-off offers from the manufacturer require the seller to determine the total quantity, promotion quantity depends partly on the amount the retailer will accept and that will prompt it to feature the item. The seller must carefully determine the percentage and frequency of such offers; when price-off offers appear too frequently, buyers may come to expect the discount or perceive the regular price as an increase.

One of the benefits of a coupon promotion is that the most important measure, redemption rate, is easy to determine, though it depends on the value of the coupon. Because few coupon promotions are profitable for the manufacturer, it might be more appropriate to focus on more difficult-to-measure effects of coupons, such as long-term sales and profitability effects. As is true in many sample promotions, the manufacturer has only limited control of the type of household it reaches with coupons.

For premium offers included in a package (i.e., with a purchased consumer good), the key factors are the premium type and the offer duration. The premium should be consistent with the quality image of the brand and, if appropriate, must remain in place long enough that a regular buyer can obtain a set (e.g., glassware).

Although in-store displays effectively move merchandise, for most sellers, display space is limited, and the display must pay for itself according to the retailer's criteria.

Therefore, each promotion type has specific dimensions that make it unique and that influence both its cost and its impact on short- and long-term brand sales.

Although marketers generally disagree about what promotions do and how they should be viewed, they seem to concur that promotions (unlike advertising) cannot build long-term brand customer loyalty or increase category sales (Nijs et al. 2001).

Blattberg, Briesch, and Fox (1995, pp. G123–G125) provide some other useful generalizations about promotional effects as well:

1. *Temporary reductions in retail price increase sales substantially*. Temporary retail price promotions (e.g., supermarket flyers) cause short-term sales to spike, a rare response to consumer advertising on television or in other media.

2. *Brands with higher market shares are less deal elastic*. Higher-share brands experience less sales response to deals, even though they may capture a greater proportion of switchers.

3. *Deal frequency changes consumers' reference prices*. Heavily promoted brands lose equity (i.e., consumers think they are less valuable), and the resulting lower consumer reference price reduces the premium the firm can charge for its brand in the marketplace.

4. *Greater deal frequency minimizes the sales spike in response to a deal*. As a result of consumer expectations about deal frequency, changes in consumer reference prices, and stockpiling effects from previous deals, the sales response simply is not as steep when deals are more frequent.

5. *Cross-promotional effects are asymmetric; promoting higher quality brands affects weaker brands (and private-label products) disproportionately*. Promoting Coca-Cola causes customers to switch from a store brand in greater numbers than promoting the store brand would cause them to switch away from Coke, likely because of brand equity differences. Extending this finding to brands' perceived type suggests that promoting higher tier brands generates more switching behavior than does promoting lower tier brands.

6. *Retailers pass less than 100% of trade deals on to consumers*. Because retailers represent the vehicles for passing trade promotional money on to consumers, sellers must be aware that most brands receive far less than 100% pass-through. (Pass-through is the percentage of funds a manufacturer offers to a retailer that get reflected in promotional discounts to the consumer. Greater than 100% pass-through would mean the retailer had offered discounts to the end user in excess of the compensating funds it received from the manufacturer.)

7. *Display and feature advertising influence item sales*. Feature and display advertising also interact synergistically.

8. *Advertised sales promotions can increase store traffic.*
   The weight of evidence indicates advertised promotions
   of some products and categories influence store traffic
   levels. Increased store traffic can lead to store switching or
   customer visits to multiple stores.
9. *Promotions affect sales in both complementary and
   competitive categories.* Practitioners understand the
   existence of this effect but not its magnitude. The impact of a
   promotion in one category on the sales of a complementary
   or competing category likely is a function of the type and
   characteristics of the categories themselves.

These general findings lead to the following observations for
modeling and evaluating promotional results:

- Brand loyalty may (or may not) be affected.
- New triers may (or may not) be attracted.
- Promotions interact with other elements of the marketing
  mix (especially advertising).
- Promotional results interact with production and distribution and thereby affect inventory levels rapidly and dra-
  matically.
- Promotional frequency influences promotional effects and
  relates to the average length of the product's purchase cycle.
- The type of promotion can have differential effects on
  brand loyalty and promotional attractiveness.
- Promotion size may have threshold and saturation effects,
  suggesting an S-shaped sales response relationship.
- Firms may experience different levels of success when implementing different promotions; a failure could be due to
  poor implementation, poor promotion design, or both.

Historically, the most common technique for evaluating consumer promotions has been a simple comparison of sales or market share before, during, and after the promotion. This technique
attributes any increased sales to the impact of the sales promotion
program, all other things being equal. Exhibit 7.14 depicts the results most manufacturers would love to see: During the promotion
period, the company's brand share rose to 10%, a gain of 4% that
consists of both deal-prone consumers who switched to take advantage of the deal and brand-loyal customers who increased their
purchases in response to the price incentive. Immediately after the
promotion ended, the brand share fell to 5%, because consumers

had overstocked and needed to work down their inventory. After this stock adjustment, brand share rose to 7%, with a 1% increase in the number of loyal customers. This ideal pattern might occur if the brand offers good qualities that many nonbrand users were not aware of.

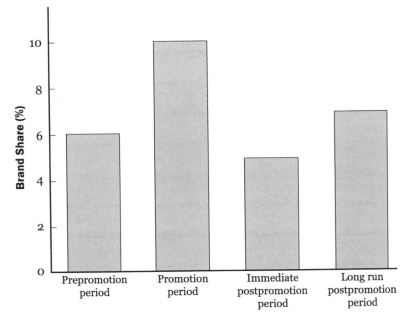

EXHIBIT 7.14

Potential effect of a consumer deal on brand share. Share increases during the promotion period, drops afterward (due to stockpiling), and returns to (perhaps) a different level in the long run.

If we assume that the effects of a promotion are short lived, then this method for analyzing promotional effects seems sound. However, even with the increased availability of retail scanner data, determining the effects of a promotion remains quite challenging. To obtain accurate measures of incremental sales, the seller needs accurate estimates of baseline sales—that is, the sales for the brand that would have occurred if the promotion had not taken place. If we were to assume sales in a nonpromotional period (prior to the promotion) function as the base (as in Exhibit 7.14) and then sales accelerate strongly, the baseline estimate is biased downward, and we wind up overstating the effect and profitability of the promotion. This assumption also seems to ignore the likelihood that the sales rate immediately following the promotion is much lower than the long-run postpromotional sales rate.

For a trade promotion, profitability also depends on how much of the promotional effect the retailer passes on to the end customer and how much it retains to stockpile for future use. As Blattberg and Levin (1987) point out, forward buying and stockpiling are such extensive retail practices that it may be impossible to infer a baseline from wholesale sales data. Therefore, manufacturers need good models of both consumer responses to retailer promotions and retailer responses to trade promotions to evaluate the profitability of their own trade promotions.

The wide availability of scanner data linked to individual characteristics has given a great boost to efforts to model individual choice behavior, including the effects of promotions. Because of the sophistication of these methodologies, building associated models requires expertise. Regardless of how complicated they may be, many models share the same goal: to estimate the likelihood that a customer will choose the brand as a function of the following variable categories (Blattberg and Neslin 1990, p. 220):

- Brand "dummy" variables to represent the intrinsic value of brands.
- Promotions.
- Last purchase effect on loyalty.
- Last purchase effect on promotion responsiveness.
- Personal and demographic characteristics.

Most approaches use some form of the multinomial logit model as a foundation, but more elaborate models also consider category choice, brand choice, customer loyalty (in terms of tendency to repeat purchase), quantity purchased, and purchase timing, then use that information to help determine which brands the retailer should promote, as well as the appropriate level and timing of those promotions.

SUMMARY

We use this chapter to address the marketing mix but focus primarily on price and marketing communications. Setting an appropriate price requires knowledge of the customer's willingness to pay, the production cost, probable competitor reactions, and any changes in these factors over time. Most pricing decisions rely fundamentally on costs, demand, or the nature of competition, and Marketing Engineering methods consider each of these factors.

Among the various forms of marketing communication, advertising is at once the most potent and the most problematic. New electronic forms of advertising likely will exacerbate its problematic nature, especially in the sense that advertising's overall effects remain hard to establish in practice. Nonetheless, managers demand whatever decision support they can obtain to make informed advertising decisions, including those related to budgeting. In this chapter, we provide several approaches that, though far from perfect, offer some systematic methods to apply to the sizing and budget allocation process.

Similarly, when determining sales force allocations, the best models enable managers to monitor sales activities and focus on encouraging salespeople to work smarter, not just harder. We address the ReAllocator model in particular as a proven means to address sales force allocation and budgeting issues. However, as the use of information technologies continues to expand, firms likely will find further applications for these models (and their variants).

Finally, knowledge of the effects of promotions is growing, and manufacturers and retailers use many effective models to design and implement them. The widespread availability of scanner data and procedures to analyze them permit a better understanding of the effects of promotions and the operational models that guide more effective promotional decision making.

CHAPTER 8

Harvesting Value from Marketing Engineering

Developments in modeling, computing, and communication technologies during the past couple of decades have provided the ingredients that allow marketing models to improve decision making in modern organizations. In this book, we use the term "Marketing Engineering" to bring together many of the concepts, tools, and insights that assist and ease marketing decision making.

In our ongoing efforts to develop, teach, and implement consulting projects using our Marketing Engineering material in the past 20 years or so, we have gained various insights, some of which surprised us. We therefore start this final chapter by summarizing 10 lessons that we hope help you become a better and more disciplined marketing decision maker.

THE 10 LESSONS

Marketing Engineering is Marketing

Analytics, though absolutely necessary in today's decision environments, exist to support marketing decisions. The Marketing Engineering approach helps users ask good questions and develop systematic, fact-based methods for answering those questions.

Therefore, the Marketing Engineering approach, when successful, helps you expand and improve the way you think about marketing.

Marketing Engineering is a Means to an End

Although Marketing Engineering enables marketers to take advantage of data, information, and computer models when they make important marketing decisions, it is not just about data, information, or analyses. Rather, you must remember that Marketing Engineering is a systematic, model-enabled process designed to help you make better marketing decisions, which then will lead to better actions and outcomes.

Marketing Engineering Frames the Opportunity Costs Associated with Alternative Actions (or Inaction)

The "what-if" capability of Marketing Engineering often represents the most useful aspect of systematic decision making. In many marketing contexts, "what-if" questions are difficult to answer without the help of a model. In such situations, if you lack strong Marketing Engineering support, you are forced to resort to familiar ways of doing things—ways that involve increasing risk and greater costs in fast moving or complex environments.

Marketing Models Require Judgment

This book contains various models that are relevant to both operational and strategic decisions. But models, no matter how sophisticated, complicated, or elegant, will always be simplified and incomplete representations of reality. Models developed to support strategic decisions (e.g., positioning) usually provide insights into the directions of actions you should take but no specific guidelines; models developed to support operational decisions tend to be both narrow and specific (e.g., how many sales calls should a salesperson make to a given account in the next quarter?). When you use either type of model, you must temper the model results with your own judgment. For strategic decisions, managers must use their judgment to translate broad guidelines into specific actions. For operational decisions, they must use their judgment to fine-tune specific recommendations to fit the overall strategy of the firm. Decision models are very useful, but they are too simple to be trusted entirely.

Another reason for exercising judgment arises from the business context within which you use a model. Model results often suggest changes to current plans, but decision makers can balk at implementing those changes because of the amount of organizational disruption and resistance that they would provoke. Models reveal the gaps between what organizations could accomplish and what they are actually prepared to do. Identifying such gaps is crucial for generating informed judgments about how best to implement potential actions suggested by the model.

Marketing Engineering as a Whole is Greater than the Sum of its Parts

As we hope this book has shown, to make decisions about a major business problem, you need a full Marketing Engineering toolkit to support you—including tools designed to help you segment a market, select a segment to serve, customize a product offering for that segment, target and position that product, and develop promotional plans and ad copy. The value of Marketing Engineering concepts, and the tools that support them, increase exponentially as the business problem broadens. Ideally, every Marketing Engineering concept and related tool would raise questions beyond its specific scope and expose unexplored areas of the overall marketing system. However, it is often better to build separate models and then link their insights and recommendations rather than attempt to build a complex, fully integrated model that simultaneously addresses all the issues. Together and in conjunction, the models provide a more complete and understandable set of action guidelines than any one of them could offer individually.

Data and Information Do Not Automatically Result in Value

We are past the era when firms could gain competitive advantage merely because they possessed market information. Today, large firms have access to more market and customer information than they can use (e.g., clickstream data generated through their websites). To gain the most value from that information, firms must try new approaches, such as

- Computer and communication technologies that make relevant information available in a timely manner to the entire workforce.
- New knowledge management techniques that help employees throughout the organization use specialized knowledge

(e.g., marketing decision models) to convert information into more effective decisions and actions.

For example, if a firm has a superior process for developing new products, it should make sure that market information feeds into that process, so that it can develop products carefully tailored to customer needs and introduce them sooner than its competitors. Marketing Engineering approaches that include firm-specific knowledge (e.g., customized conjoint analysis models) help firms transform market information into superior products. Such uses of information are not transparent to competitors and not likely to be replicated by them, which offer significant competitive advantage.

Modern Software Allows for Rapid Prototyping

Markets are changing so quickly that decisions must reflect and result from quick adaptation rather than careful optimization. Thus, to be useful, decision aids must be capable of rapid prototyping. Applying even simple, Excel-based models will enable you to explore the potential value of a Marketing Engineering approach in a particular decision context before you decide to invest more effort in developing customized models or use more traditional approaches.

Every Model Has its Downside

The deceptive simplicity of applying easy-to-use software and the presumed scientific credibility of the underlying models often give users a false sense of security. But there is also a real danger in having too much data and information without the analytic capabilities to make sense of those data. The growing availability of fine-grained data, such as those from scanner panels, Web logs, and customer relationship management (CRM) systems, has encouraged mechanistic applications of marketing models that often focus on finer details at the expense of exploring more difficult, strategic issues.

We also observe two interesting situations in this context: Users with strong quantitative backgrounds often feel drawn to the technical aspects of the results, which means they miss the big picture, whereas those with weak analytical skills either ignore model results and go with their gut or, contrastingly, accept the results uncritically. But the best outcomes come from teams that include people who possess different levels of analytical abilities and who pool their efforts while questioning and supporting one another. These teams use the model results as one input into a decision process that also includes common sense and educated judgments.

Marketing Engineering Requires Lifelong Learning

This book is brief, and the list of marketing problems and challenges is long; no book of this length could communicate the full richness of marketing problems or all the opportunities and challenges associated with Marketing Engineering. Do you recall ever watching "slicer dicer" demonstrations on TV? The demonstrator shows how the new and improved slicer can slice tomatoes perfectly in 15 different ways. But when you try it at home, you got less than perfect results, because learning to use the device takes time. In a similar vein, even after studying Marketing Engineering and using the associated software, you may underestimate the challenges associated with applying this approach in practice. Successful applications require a blend of modeling knowledge, common sense, judgment, good communication skills, patience, practice, and, most important, a willingness to learn through experimentation.

Marketing Engineering Instructors Should Be Coaches Rather than Teachers

Instructors must recognize that their pedagogic focus when it comes to Marketing Engineering should be to induce learning rather than simply to impart knowledge. Marketing Engineering cannot be taught through lectures alone; this topic is not one for the "sage on the stage," making pronouncements that students accept uncritically. However, just as you cannot learn how to ride a bicycle by listening to a lecture but can learn quickly under the direction of a guide or coach, the same holds true for Marketing Engineering. The more instructors act as guides, critics, and facilitators, the more students internalize and comprehend the concepts and methods we have described in this book.

A LOOK AHEAD FOR MARKETING ENGINEERING

When we look ahead, we see a future that is both bright and exciting for Marketing Engineering, especially when it is embedded in model-based marketing decision support systems (MDSS, in the shorthand we use in this section). As the boundaries blur among models, data, information, and the information systems that provide the interfaces, Marketing Engineering approaches will become core components of MDSS. Modern MDSS align only partially with the evolving decision support needs of managers and customers, and tomorrow's systems must develop differently and integrate alternative approaches, quite unlike those that many academics, and even some practitioners, use when it comes to MDSS today. Exhibit 8.1 summarizes the changes we expect between the MDSS frontiers as they currently exist and those frontiers in the next 5–10 years.

The major drivers of the change toward tomorrow's MDSS are the huge investments that firms are making in IT infrastructures linked to communication networks. The digital backbones that exist inside and outside firms today support technologies such as Java and cloud computing, which allow the execution of computer programs on any computer connected to the network, and XML, which easily aggregates data of various types and from various sources. These two developments alone enable decision makers to tap into vast amounts of computing power and data sources on demand and thereby have created a new supply and demand environment around MDSS and, more generally, marketing analytics.

In this new environment, digital networks (both Intranet and Internet) function essentially as a single, integrated, giant computer, and data repositories function as a giant filing cabinet. But these vast data and computing resources are just necessary ingredients; by themselves, they cannot improve decisions, increase productivity, or ensure competitive gains. Increasingly, firms recognize instead that their most important competitive capabilities include their ability to convert information into timely actions (Davenport 2006). Another marketing trend is moving decision making along more customer-focused and data-driven paths. Marketing analytics embedded within CRM systems and dashboards also enable firms to connect their data and knowledge with autonomous intelligent systems to facilitate timely decisions.

	MDSS Frontiers Today	MDSS Frontiers Tomorrow
Focus of MDSS	Support strategic decisions	Support both strategic and operations decisions
Time scale	Days and weeks, if not months	Move towards real-time data entry, data access, data analysis, implementation, and feedback
Mode of operation	Individual- and PC-centric	Organization- and network-centric to support multiple employees in multiple locations on multiple devices
Decision domain	Marketing	Marketing plus other functions, such as supply chain and finance
Company interface	Loosely coupled with company's IT systems	Woven into company's operations and decision processes
MDSS intervention opportunities	Discrete and problem-driven	Continuous and process-driven
MDSS goal	Support analysis and optimization	Support robust, adaptive organizational decision processes
MDSS design	Information and decision appliance	Productivity and business model appliance
MDSS operation	Interactive (user interacts with model)	Both interactive and autonomous (embedded)
MDSS outputs	Recommended actions; what-if analysis	Visualizations of markets and their behaviors (e.g., dashboards), extended reality (e.g., business model simulation), explanations (e.g., why?), and automated implementation (e.g., create alerts, automate actions)
MDSS implementation sequence	Intervention opportunity → decision implementation → integration with IT systems	Integration with IT → intervention opportunity → decision implementation

EXHIBIT 8.1
The frontiers of Marketing Engineering–focused MDSS today and in the mid- to long-term future. Marketing Engineering models gradually will be woven into the fabric of organizational processes and become core requirements for enhancing organizational productivity and business model success.

Consider the following examples that illustrate how successful companies such as Travelocity, Walmart, and Amazon.com have converted their IT infrastructure into profits by facilitating timely decisions and actions.

EXAMPLE

Travelocity, one of the Web's largest online travel sites, takes strategic advantage of its Web log data to improve its promotional programs. For example, in early 2000, TWA announced a special $360 round-trip fare between Los Angeles and San Juan, Puerto Rico. Typically, a traditional marketing pitch would have notified the whole Hispanic community in the L.A. area, including many people who had absolutely no interest in Puerto Rico. Instead, Travelocity analyzed its data warehouse, and within a few hours, it had identified 30,000 customers in L.A. who had inquired about fares to Puerto Rico within the past few days. An e-mail sent to these customers the next morning resulted in a remarkable 25% of the targeted segment either taking the TWA offer or booking another Caribbean flight!
Source: Forbes, July 9, 2001.

EXAMPLE

Walmart has developed the world's largest commercial data warehouse, reputed to comprise more than 500 terabytes of data. This centralized warehouse includes data on every transaction in every one of its stores for the past 65 weeks, as well as the inventories carried in each store. As we mentioned in a previous chapter, this database came in particularly handy on 9/11, when the company detected substantial increases in sales of flags, decals, and guns and ammunition within hours of the terrible event. Flag sales were up 1800% over the same date on the previous year, and sales of ammunition increased by 100% (Christian Science Monitor 2002). Detecting these changes early enabled Walmart to replenish each sold-out store quickly with the appropriate quantities of these items, as well as place additional orders with its suppliers before most of its competitors could even respond. As a result, Walmart not only helped meet customer demand but did so in a way that conferred competitive advantages on it.

EXAMPLE

Amazon.com may have collected more information about customer decision-making processes than any other company in the world. According to the company, at the end of the second quarter of 2012, it had over 150 million active customers (defined as those who have bought within the past year), and it collects information about what every one of those customers searches, buys, bids, and posts (e.g., wishlists, guest registries), as well as noting each time they participate in a contest or a survey or communicate with customer service. Amazon has built ever-more sophisticated recommendation tools for cross-selling that can dynamically generate a list of specific products each customer likely wants the most. It uses its database of customer information to make ongoing marketing decisions. For example, when Amazon.com offered the new "Amazon Prime" free shipping club program in 2005, investors gave the idea mixed reviews. Customers could buy, for $79 a year, unlimited free two-day delivery and discounted next-day delivery on in-stock items. Despite the investors' concerns, the Prime program enabled the company to differentiate its services, because few, if any, retailers would be able to match Amazon in terms of the scope of its product categories or its scale and thereby could not manage their transportation costs as tightly. Jeff Bezos, CEO of Amazon.com, reports that ongoing analyses of customer behavior before and after customers join the Prime program show that they increase their purchases with the company after joining, which means these customer relationships are deeper and their customer lifetime value is greater. Furthermore, continuous monitoring and analytics helps Amazon fine-tune its offerings and recommendations to strengthen relationships with these customers even further. In another compelling experiment, Amazon explored the option of offering both new and used books (at much lower prices) whenever a customer searched for a book title. Again, careful analyses of customer behavior indicated to the company that both Amazon and its customers would benefit if the customers had access to additional options, including listing offerings from other vendors, and the company implemented those options.

The real-time marketing analysis and implementation capabilities these examples describe will become even more important for most firms in the years ahead. As those examples demonstrate, increasingly, external events (e.g., customer visits to websites, customer requests for quotes, events like terrorist attacks) or planned tests (e.g., price changes, free offers) will trigger MDSS applications, which must connect closely with the operational processes of a company. At the same time, this new infrastructure should offer more opportunities for traditional, proactive MDSS applications. For example, at NetFlix, the online DVD rental company, approximately two-thirds of the films customers rent were recommended to them automatically by the recommendation agent (an MDSS) available through the website. Customers might never have considered these movies themselves, but as a result, 70–80% of NetFlix rentals come from the company's back catalog of 38,000 films rather than recent releases, which allows the company to manage its inventories better (Flynn 2006).

Decision support tools for real-time decision environments require new types of decision models, as well as new ways to make them successful in organizational settings. When marketing analytics such as those just described rely on IT processes, IT specialists and computer scientists serve as the model developers, not marketing modelers. Marketing modelers often lack the IT skills required by system integration and typically focus their attention on MDSS designed to address specific strategic problems (e.g., segmentation, targeting, new product forecasting). In this latter case, marketers develop and test traditional MDSS models to determine their potential value to resolve the problems before they get implemented within the IT infrastructure of the companies. If these initial model tests are successful, system specialists come in to deploy the models for broader use by integrating them into the company's IT architecture. Such traditional MDSS follow a specific sequence: Intervention (i.e., MDSS development) → Implementation → Integration with IT.

But modern MDSS must be developed with an understanding of the organizational and IT architectures in which the models will be deployed. In many firms, corporate decision environments consist of enterprise-wide systems, such as enterprise resource planning (ERP) and CRM systems. To succeed in those environments, MDSS design and development may have to follow a different sequence: Integration with IT systems → Implementation → Intervention. For example, to build an MDSS structured around a marketing dashboard, the builder must begin with an understanding of the company's infrastructure as it applies to information gathering and access, implement the underlying dashboard model to interface seamlessly with the IT infrastructure in order for it to access relevant data on an ongoing basis, support various types of ad hoc managerial queries and analyses with dashboard readings, and guide the deployment of corrective actions, as necessary. Thus, the MDSS intervention enhances managers' understanding of the market situation as a basis for their actions, which in turn enhances their "mental models" of customers and markets. Such enhanced mental models offer a basis for improved productivity and better quality marketing decision making in the future. As the influential Morgan Stanley economist Stephen Roach notes, "In the end, sustained white-collar productivity enhancement is less about breakthrough technologies and more about newfound efficiencies in the *cerebral production function* of the high value-added knowledge worker" (Roach 2002, quoted. in IDC report, italics added).

Several developments suggest how marketers and marketing engineers likely will move from the current MDSS and Marketing Engineering environment to the environments of the future.

Online Analytical Processing (OLAP)

The analytical tool most widely used by corporations is the spreadsheet, but typical spreadsheets are limited to analyzing only small databases (say, up to 255 columns of data) and primarily provide a two-dimensional view of data. Decision makers often want to cut data along several dimensions, such as across time (How are we doing compared with last year?) or products and geography (Which of our products are prescribed by family practitioners in rural communities?). In response, database vendors such as IBM, Oracle, and Sybase offer multidimensional analytical tools for use with their database-management systems. These tools provide online decision support for managers that do not require them to learn complex database query languages. For example, Walmart uses sophisticated decision support systems to help its store managers identify the top 10–20 products in each store on each day of the week; they then alter shelf and end-of-aisle displays to take advantage of the changing mix of top products by day of the week. If the Walmart managers in the Wheat Ridge, Colorado, store find that it sells more diapers on a given Thursday, they plan special displays of diapers for the following Thursday.

Currently OLAP tools are stronger in terms of online data retrieval (e.g., number of orders booked in the previous month, number of purchases made by a specific customer) than in their analytic capabilities (e.g., How much discount should we offer a specific customer? What is our best sales forecast for next month?), which attempt to detect unexpected market response patterns and diagnose problems. However, as firms integrate more Marketing Engineering models into OLAPs, those tools likely will gain the ability to support complex decisions online. For example, companies could integrate a library of models into their corporate data warehouses, which would support managers who need to answer such questions as, "Why is the promotion more profitable in New York than in Philadelphia?" and thereby help them decide whether to cut back on promotions in Philadelphia. For some decision areas, data warehouses will need to support enterprise-wide models rather than just end-user models. For example, revenue management requires the execution of complex optimization procedures in large, dynamic databases. However, end-user models remain useful for many small, localized applications and for the small- and medium-sized firms that do not have such large databases.

EXHIBIT 8.2

One way to implement an application service provider (ASP) approach for Marketing Engineering Models, data, and user interfaces, combined in traditional marketing models, get decoupled in a Web environment, which provides any Internet user with more flexibility for conducting marketing analyses and obtaining effective interpretations anywhere and anytime.

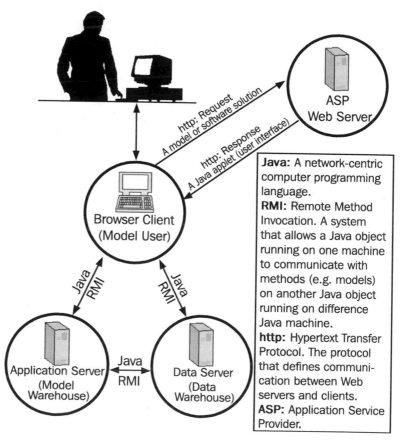

Models Offered as Web Services

Recently, new standards have emerged to support basic Web services architectures that define interactions between software agents (modeling applications) as exchanges of messages between service requesters and service providers. Requesters are those software agents that demand the execution of a service (in our case, a model), whereas providers refer to software agents that offer the service. For example, a forecasting service might provide instantaneous forecasts to authorized software agents that request such a service, and deliver the services on a mobile device to the exact location where the results will be used. Web services standards enable communication among different software applications that run on a variety of platforms and/or with different frameworks. Discovery services let anyone on the Web find the services for which they are looking and also offer the potential that multiple services might compete to satisfy a service request. In the near future, we expect to see many more Web services for marketing analytics, whereby service vendors offer on-demand online access to various types of knowledge resources and implementation tools (e.g., software, data, content, models, back-end analysis, implementation such as e-mail solicitations).

These Web service providers will convert knowledge resources into services (e.g., analysis, process control, order management, billing) accessible over the Web instead of being packaged as products and systems that run as client installations. For example, salesforce.com offers a Web service model for sales force automation that includes online contact management, forecasting, e-mail communications, customized reports, and synchronization of wireless devices. Google Earth provides the interfaces necessary for anyone to exploit its huge geographic database and obtain various value-added services (e.g., bed and breakfast offerings located in a particular geographic area). Zillow.com, an online real estate database, uses a proprietary algorithm called the "Zestimate" to appraise property values. Zillow.com has estimated the value of more than 57 percent of the U.S. housing stock, which it makes available on its website at no cost. We anticipate many more model-supported services (e.g., what are forecasted home delivery pizza sales when a snowstorm hits a store's target geographies?), made possible by dynamically linked data retrieval from multiple sources with appropriate software providing analytics. Exhibit 8.2 shows one possible way to implement a Web service model for analytical support. With these developments, the emerging capability offers marketing analytics to anyone, anytime, anywhere.

The Internet also could drive the prices of digital products down to near their marginal production costs—$0. As a result, many Web analytic services may be available for extremely low costs (or, alternatively, for limited free usage or in exchange for viewing advertisements, like Zillow.com which generates its revenue by selling advertising on its website), making them even more attractive for both analysts and managerial users. Thus, in the next decade, we expect an explosion in the availability of customizable, scalable, and (possibly) embedded decision models on the Internet that are available everywhere, anytime, and for every interested user.

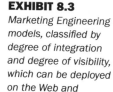

EXHIBIT 8.3

Marketing Engineering models, classified by degree of integration and degree of visibility, which can be deployed on the Web and accessed over the Internet.

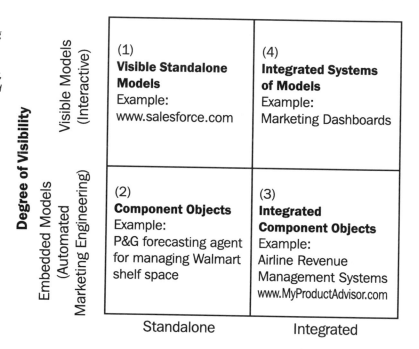

Degree of Integration

Exhibit 8.3 summarizes our view of how Web services will influence marketing modeling in the years ahead. We classify marketing models along two dimensions: On the horizontal axis (degree of integration), we distinguish between standalone models that support a single user for a single task on one extreme and integrated models that encompass organizational processes, databases, and other aspects of the decision environment at the other (e.g., single user, multiple tasks or multiple users, single task). On the vertical axis (degree of visibility), we distinguish between models embedded inside systems (i.e., a "black box model" that works in the background) that require few inputs or interactions with the user and those that are highly interactive and employ visible structures. We discuss four categories of models that represent the extremes of these two dimensions and indicate how the emerging networked economy will encourage their use.

Visible standalone models

Highly visible but less integrated, these models can exist on application servers (several Web services already do this, such as www.salesforce.com) for easy access by client browsers. Increasingly, such analytics services, including our Marketing Engineering models, will be available via remote, "cloud-based" computing facilities. In such an environment, software renditions of marketing models remain in central locations, which minimizes updating and distribution costs. Model users also benefit because they have constant access to the latest versions of the software.

Visible models with user interactions can also become more valuable online. For example, applications ranging from simple computational devices, such as lease versus buy (www.leaseguide.com/leasevsbuy.htm) and cost-of-living (www.homefair.com) calculators, to sophisticated programs, such as Web analytics (www.google.com/analytics), are available on a 24/7 basis. These applications could be supported by online technical help and live support, improved content (e.g., help files, tutorials), and links to related applications that are available elsewhere on the Internet. Many traditional marketing models, such as the Bass or GE/McKinsey Portfolio models, would benefit from being redesigned or re-implemented in newer software packages for deployment over the Internet.

Component objects (automated Marketing Engineering)

Embedded, standalone models can be deployed more widely on the Internet because they can be structured to monitor continuously and optimize various aspects of how an organization functions. Component objects support only a few well-defined tasks (e.g., assessing whether the caller is a valuable customer) and generally operate in self-contained, standalone environments. They also are likely to be deployed in systems that enable interfaces between companies, particularly in situations where security and strategic considerations often prevent the deployment of more comprehensive systems. For example, Proctor & Gamble's access to purchase data for its products at Walmart allows it to deploy automated models that forecast demand, schedule production and delivery, optimize inventory holdings, and even assess the effectiveness of specific promotions.

Integrated component objects (automated integrated Marketing Engineering)

Integrated, embedded models exploit the blurred lines between software, content, services, and applications to deliver more complete decision solutions. For example, an integrated segmentation system not only would run standard clustering algorithms but could also access data from elsewhere on the Web, and then, after the execution of the model, distribute customized communications to customers in different segments. Revenue management systems at the world's major airlines exploit such capabilities by dynamically optimizing schedules, prices, and seat inventories and sending messages to targeted customers about new travel opportunities they might find attractive. Similarly, recommender systems such as MyProductAdvisor.com or Amazon's product recommendations fall into this category, because they link multiple data and knowledge sources in automatically generated recommendations, as well as enable customers to act on those recommendations by offering them the means to purchase products. Although integrated component objects may be used by unsophisticated users, the models themselves are likely to be quite sophisticated (akin to autopilot for an aircraft) and require frequent updating and validation by highly skilled modelers.

Integrated systems of models

Finally, highly visible, highly integrated models link logically, share databases and knowledge bases, and support common and recurring decisions (e.g., marketing planning) among managers who may be in different locations. Such marketing systems include dashboards that integrate multiple sources of data and analyses to provide managers with detailed views of the entities and activities for which they are responsible, as do GE Capital's dashboard for senior executives (Whiting 2002) and Harrah's dashboard for marketing executives (Brown 2002). Using Harrah's dashboard, a marketing executive can determine whether a particular high-value customer is likely to respond better to a free meal or a free night's stay in the hotel. More opportunities continue to emerge for marketing's use of integrated systems, as our subsequent descriptions of groupware systems detail.

Intelligent Marketing Systems

Current uses of MDSS often take place in a reactive mode, that is, after managers have identified decision problems. This limits their usefulness and value. Herbert Simon (1977) notes that problem solving consists of three phases: intelligence, design, and choice. In the intelligence phase, the decision maker identifies problems and situations that call for decisions. In the design phase, the decision maker generates many potential solutions to the problem, and then finally selects specific solution(s) in the choice phase. Historically, decision models have emphasized design and choice phases, but information-intensive environments call for decision support systems that also apply to the intelligence phase.

Many marketing organizations generate millions of pieces of data daily. For example, a firm might distribute 20 products to 10 accounts in each of 300 markets and employ 300 salespeople. The only way it can interpret and use the resultant large amounts of data it accumulates is by deploying intelligent models that automate the data interpretation process. Various firms are experimenting with data mining, a process that relies on automated analysis agents to sift through the data to find nuggets of insight.

As a means to identify patterns in the data that indicate problems that require managers' attention and decisions, data mining comprises correlations and associations (e.g., people who bought Enid Blyton's *Best Stories for Five-Year-Olds* also bought J.K. Rowling's *Harry Potter and the Chamber of Secrets*), sequences (people who bought fresh salmon fillets also bought bananas in the same grocery shopping trip), data grouping through classification and clustering (e.g., more men than women buy CDs by Red Hot Chili Peppers), and forecasting (e.g., people who bought most recently are likely to purchase again next week). Data mining also involves many methodologies, including statistical analyses, neural networks, and rule-based systems. We expect to see many interesting marketing applications of data mining in the coming years.

Data mining: *Analyses designed to discover (unexpected) relationships in a set of data.*

A promising data mining application pertains to real-time customization of websites, in which the content dynamically adjusts as users interact with the site. For example, Facebook allows an advertiser to target the reach for its ad by location, gender, age, and interests. As the advertiser adds filters, Facebook will automatically update the count of people fitting the selected criteria to gauge the size of the target market on Facebook. Modern systems can continuously monitor, measure, and simulate banner ad effectiveness across a network of partner sites and dynamically optimize ad deployment. If a newsworthy event during a golf tournament suddenly increases traffic at golf-related sites, the banner ads on that site automatically become more effective, and a good data mining analysis could tell the advertiser to redirect more of its advertising expenditures to such sites. This capability will become more important as firms are challenged to act effectively in an increasingly dynamic, digital, networked economy.

Another intelligent marketing system that interprets and employs large amounts of data is appropriately named *autonomous intelligent systems (agents)*. These systems help managers automate both the analysis process and the implementation of model results. For example, an automated segmentation and targeting system can identify attractive segments and then arrange to send members of those segments e-mail messages or arrange for a sales call. Agents can be particularly useful for repetitive decision problems that have highly varying input conditions (e.g., credit authorization, automated analysis, report writing). In such situations, it is possible to specify the structure of the problem and the range of variation in inputs reasonably well in advance, but the exact combination of input conditions that might occur is very difficult to anticipate. That is where agents prove helpful.

Among the most important autonomous software agents being developed for marketing use are the recommendation agents several websites currently deploy, automated help desk/call center agents, and automated report generators. Partially automated systems (i.e., they use human intervention when they cannot make independent judgments) offer textual analysis of blogs to sift nuggets from vast quantities of trivia (Bulkeley 2005), like ACNielsen's Buzzmetrics (www.nielsenbuzzmetrics.com, formerly www.intelliseek.com). Likewise, we expect that automated systems soon will search the Web to generate customized reports that help salespeople prepare for sales calls or generate role-specific, top-line reports that detail recent events for company managers, such as a customized version of Twitter's What The Trend service (www.whatthetrend.com). Commercial applications that support customer service representatives (a form of help desk) offer another usage avenue for agents within MDSS. For example, a customer service representative at a help desk supported by an autonomous agent could find out if a customer is likely to be a prospect for other offerings, update information about the customer's new needs (product design feedback), and provide early warning about major problems. Such computer agents are most useful when marketers need models that (1) explain behavior or recommendations (e.g., why the model produced a specific conclusion in a report), or (2) simulate the recommendations of expert decision makers in well-specified decision areas.

Simulations

Managers use market simulations to learn about marketing concepts and explore and understand the possible outcomes of potential decision options. With simulations, marketing managers can experiment with a simulated representation of the marketplace and observe the likely result of these potential actions. And even better, they can do so at low cost and more rapidly than any real market experiment would allow. Organizations can also use simulations effectively to spread learning and new thinking among their employees (Senge and Lannon 1990). The objective of marketing simulation is not necessarily to predict the future but rather to help managers understand what they should do to adapt to various possible futures, given their beliefs about the likelihood of the occurrence of each of those futures. Thus, simulation facilitates backcasting—what we should do now to bring about a certain kind of future or to adapt in some way if that future actually were to occur. It is immaterial whether the simulated scenarios actually occur; what matters most is that executives learn about how their company, and the industry, will react to alternate futures. Marketing Engineering should provide models of the marketplace that form the core of such simulations.

Groupware for Decision Support

Groupware is a general term used to describe varied computer-and communications-based systems that enhance the efficiency and effectiveness with which a group of people make decisions, either synchronously or asynchronously.

Using groupware, project teams can share information (e.g., reports, presentations) and make and record decisions (e.g., on-line voting). Such systems can circumvent temporal, geographic, and organizational barriers in support of more collaborative work. For example, Price Waterhouse Cooper uses one of the world's largest installed bases of Lotus Notes to support its collaborative decision making. Thousands of the firm's employees (consultants) maintain their own Lotus Notes program, with which they access both corporation-wide Lotus Notes databases and databases specific to individual projects. With this system, Price Waterhouse Cooper makes its consultants' specialized expertise widely available across the company and can quickly form and support ad hoc teams to take advantage of emerging opportunities. Even simple asynchronous groupware that gathers, aggregates, and processes data from several people can be very useful for decision support.

Groupware:
Communication- and computer-based systems designed to help a group of people make decisions, whether synchronously or asynchronously.

For example, Toubia and Flores (2007) describe an "idea processing system" that structures the methods used to gather and employ customer inputs to screen new product ideas and cost effectively identify the most promising ones.

We expect groupware to evolve soon to the point at which it significantly influences marketing decision making and implementation in both ad hoc groups and well-defined project teams. Groupware can promote brainstorming and collaborative problem-solving activities among geographically dispersed persons and groups (e.g., developing a global promotion plan using modeling templates) and across different functions within a company (e.g., the CMO's and CFO's offices work on a common spreadsheet model to present the business case for a proposed marketing plan). Groups also might use groupware to create agendas (e.g., problems to be resolved), record ideas generated simultaneously and anonymously by participants, obtain votes on action items, produce reports summarizing discussions, and maintain records for future use. Participants may gather in the same room or, more likely, log in from remote locations. Groupware also can collect the judgmental inputs required to support many Marketing Engineering models. Commercial software such as SharePoint Workspace and the workgroup applications built into Microsoft Office 2010 are greatly increasing the availability of collaborative decision-making tools to a wide range of users and enable companies to leverage their intellectual assets more broadly within the company and with their outside partners. For example, SharePoint applications support such activities as voice over Internet protocol (VoIP), instant messaging, text-based chats, file sharing (text, pictures, spreadsheets), drawing, brainstorming, threaded discussions, tracking meeting agendas, determining action items, and defining schedules. Finally, groupware can greatly enhance the implementablility of marketing analytics by providing a common platform that the implementation team uses to access model results, compare actual outcomes with expected outcomes, send alerts to appropriate team members, revise model inputs, and update model results.

Improved Model Outputs

As the managerial uses of computing increase, the need for user interfaces that operate in an intuitive manner becomes ever more critical. To be successful, decision models must serve users who have very little time and those with poor computer skills. Many decision models fail to attract users because the systems in which they are incorporated are difficult to use. For example, several systems designed to automate lead generation have not met their performance goals because they require salespeople to accept black box recommendations or adapt to a non-intuitive software design. The developers of this software should have employed familiar, existing sales processes as their design foundation, rather than an imagined notion of how salespeople work. Our own research (Kayande et al. 2009) suggests that different types of feedback (namely, suggested corrective actions, and potential upside of different actions) must be embedded in such systems if users are to accept and actually use MDSS.

Along similar lines, visual representations of data and model outputs, such as Google Earth, should greatly increase the chances of model use. Three examples that suggest the potential for such outputs are:

1. www.babynamewizard.com, which offers a visual means to explore the popularity of various baby names from 1880 onwards;

2. www.smartmoney.com/map-of-the-market, which offers an aerial view of 1,000 U.S. and international stocks, all at once, and thereby provides the "big picture" as well as more specific details about the current performance of individual stocks; and

3. www.americanbulls.com, which offers automated reports about the likely performance of every stock the following day, along with recommended trading strategies.

As people get accustomed to these better designed software packages, they will expect greater ease of use from every software package they encounter. The best software hides those aspects novices do not need (i.e., they cover the engine with a streamlined hood) and highlight the most important inputs and outputs to that user at that specific time. To ensure that increasing numbers of managers adopt their products, MDSS vendors must focus on continuously improving the user-friendliness of their products.

INSIGHTS FOR BETTER IMPLEMENTATION OF MARKETING ENGINEERING

As we noted at the outset of this chapter, the potential benefits of MDSS are exceptional. Yet good Marketing Engineering and related MDSS are akin to the "better mousetrap"—if you build them, customers still may not come. A significant literature details the implementation barriers to the adoption and use of MDSS, as well as ways to lower them. Here, as elsewhere, we accept Pareto's 80–20 rule: A few simple insights can drastically increase the likelihood of a successful application of Marketing Engineering. We propose six.

Be Opportunistic

Select problems or issues that have a good chance of rapid and demonstrable success. The successful application of a model that favors a negative decision (e.g., do not introduce the new product) will have less impact than the application of a model that favors a positive decision (e.g., introduce the new product). When managers agree that the firm needs drastic improvements in a particular area, you have the opportunity to prove the value of Marketing Engineering if you set precise, defensible goals and expectations. If you remain open to new approaches in such situations, noticeable improvements are possible. When Sinha and Zoltners (2001) scrutinized hundreds of projects in which they had used marketing decision models, they realized their models had the biggest impact in situations characterized by moderate complexity and high measurability. They therefore offer the following guidelines for developing models that succeed in organizational settings:

1. Build realistic models.
2. Build adaptive models.
3. Generate implementable solutions.
4. Get it done quickly.
5. Solve the right problem.

Start Simple; Keep It Simple

The famous KISS (Keep It Simple, Stupid) principle: Start with problems that are understandable and familiar. For example, if your firm possesses a large customer database and wants to determine how to identify and target its efforts to the most profitable accounts, choice segmentation software likely offers a quick and intelligent solution. It is easy to explain, "We will target customers who, based on their previous purchase behavior, are more likely to respond favorably to our future selling efforts." You can program the software to tag promising accounts and update predictions regularly. In this case, everybody wins: The sales force increases its sales per salesperson and thus commission incomes, managers find satisfaction in the more effective use of the firm's resources, and even less responsive accounts get turned over to a newly created telemarketing sales force that then offers a new source of revenue. A simple model serves its purpose if it leads to a novel insight or unearths an unexpected option. Marketing Engineering helps you use your imagination and expand your decision options, even if a particular model does not definitively state the proper decision.

Work Backward: Begin with an End in Mind

Start with an understanding of the goal of your modeling effort. Do you need to provide justification for a course of action? Who in the organization are likely to benefit the most from the use of the Marketing Engineering model? Do you want to resolve an issue because your judgment seems inadequate? Is your goal to facilitate a group decision? To forecast (what will happen?) or explain something (why did it happen?)?

In addition, you should try to undertake any Marketing Engineering effort with target dates for meetings and presentations in mind. This scheduling ensures discipline in completing the modeling effort, and the required meetings provide a forum for discussing modeling results and facilitating follow-through efforts.

Score Inexpensive Victories

Look for areas in which the model development costs are low compared with their potential benefits. For example, the sales force allocation model that Lodish et al. (1988) describe is fairly inexpensive to implement and functions effectively with just judgmental data. Not only is it efficient; it also offers the potential to increase current sales revenues by 5–10% simply by reallocating efforts. People and organizations alike use models when the opportunity costs of not using them are clearly higher than the costs of using them.

Develop a Program, Not Just Projects

There is no doubt that well-designed projects can have important organizational impact, but in essence, they remain one-time modeling exercises that cannot leave a permanent mark on the organization. A program of analytics (see Exhibit 8.2), in contrast, can bring about enduring changes to organizational structures and processes that have lasting impacts. A CRM system, for example, is not just a software system but is really a change agent that

makes sustainable improvements to business processes, measurements, and managerial accountability. The Syntex model is a one-
time implementation; the Rhenania model is a tool to change the
direct mailing processes of the company completely (Chapter 1).
Although the former may have been temporarily useful, the latter type enables the company to realize benefits over an extended
time horizon.

Let us be clear: We describe the Marketing Engineering applications at both Syntex Labs and ABB Electric as successful. But
there is one important difference between them: The Syntex application is a project, and turnover in the original team and management prevented Syntex from getting the most out of this effort.
If it had properly monitored and adapted its implementation of
the recommendations, the firm could have increased the profits
derived from the project by more than 10% and at no additional
cost. In contrast, at ABB, Marketing Engineering had been an integral part of the organization for more than two decades and influenced the allocation of sales and promotional efforts, the development of new products and advertising copy, the positioning of
products, and decision making for manufacturing. Its Marketing
Engineering program saved ABB and then helped it survive and
prosper; ABB's president, Daniel Elwing, recognized, "It had to
be a program; it could not be a project." Much of the benefit and
usefulness associated with Marketing Engineering involves the
related activities that surround modeling implementations. Sinha
and Zoltners (2001), in reflecting on more than 2,000 projects undertaken by several hundred firms during a 25-year span, report
that more than 95% of the total effort often gets spent on issues
such as problem finding, database management, change management, and implementation. The benefits of modeling are subtle—
for example, a problem framed as a sales force sizing issue may be
more profitably viewed as a sales force reallocation problem.

Make Marketing Engineering a Team Sport

At the beginning, we noted that effective implementation of
Marketing Engineering demands a supportive organizational culture, fostered by top management team involvement. The good
news is that we are beginning to find evidence (e.g. Germann,
Lilien and Rangaswamy 2011) that deployment of Marketing Engineering leads to improved organizational performance, potentially putting Marketing Engineering on the good side of the top
management team. The not so good news is, at least to date, that
the supportive business case for Marketing Engineering has been

made only in a small fraction of organizations. The team must be educated, motivated and coached to make the changes needed to see the full benefits of Marketing Engineering.

SUMMARY

And so, the future is very bright for Marketing Engineering. By providing a bridge between marketing concepts and disciplined marketing decision making and implementation, it joins the ranks of critical management tools for successful 21st century firms. Moreover, it provides a link between today's marketing decision context and the marketing decision-making world of tomorrow. Despite all this remarkable promise, the potential of Marketing Engineering remains largely untapped. We hope the experiences and insights summarized in this chapter will inspire you to develop and deploy Marketing Engineering to benefit both you and your firm.

Chapter 1

Lilien, Gary L. and Arvind Rangaswamy, 2004, *Marketing Engineering*, Trafford Publishing: Victoria, Canada.

Kotler, Philip and Kevin Lane Keller, 2005, *Marketing Management, 12th ed.*, Prentice Hall: Upper Saddle River, NJ.

Schrage, Michael, 1999, *Serious Play: How the World's Best Companies Simulate to Innovate*, Harvard Business School Press: Boston, MA.

www.decisionpro.biz

www.statsoft.com/textbook

www.askpedia.com/q/525/Install_Base_of_Microsoft_Office_Worldwide_and_in_the_US

www.smartplanet.com/blog/business-brains/marketing-chiefs-not-prepared-for-data-explosion-ibm-study/19518

Chapter 2

Anderson, James C. and James A. Narus, 2003, *Business Market Management: Understanding, Creating and Delivering Value*, 2d ed., Prentice Hall: Englewood Cliffs, NJ.

Gupta, Sunil and Donald Lehmann, 2005, *Managing Customers as Investments: The Strategic Value of Customers in the Long Run*, Wharton School Publishing: Philadelphia, PA.

Rust, Roland, Valerie Zeithaml, and Katherine Lemon, 2000, *Driving Customer Equity: How Customer Lifetime Value is Reshaping Corporate Strategy*, The Free Press: New York.

www.neurometrix.com

Chapter 3

McDonald, Malcom and Ian Dunbar, 2004, *Market Segmentation: How to Do It, How to Profit from It,* Butterworth-Heinemann: Burlington, MA.

Myers, James H., 1996, *Segmentation & Positioning for Strategic Marketing Decisions,* 1st ed., South-Western Educational Publications: Belmont, CA.

Waaser, Ernest, Marshall Dahneke, Michael Pekkarinen, and Michael Weissel, 2005, "How You Slice It: Smarter Segmentation for Your Sales Force," *Harvard Business Review,* Vol. 82, No. 3, pp. 105-11.

Yankelovich, Daniel and David Meer, 2006, "Rediscovering Market Segmentation," *Harvard Business Review,* Vol. 84, No. 2, pp. 122-31.

www.slideshare.net/sapient/sapientnitro-gfk-roper-ho

Chapter 4

Ries, Al and Jack Trout, 2000, *Positioning: The Battle for Your Mind,* McGraw-Hill: New York.

Chapter 5

Armstrong, Scott J., 2001, *Principles of Forecasting,* Kluwer: Boston, MA.

Linstone, Harold A. and Murray Turoff, 2002, *The Delphi Method: Techniques and Applications*, available at http://www.is.njit.edu/pubs/delphibook/.

Makridakis, Spyros G., Steven C. Wheelwright, and Rob J. Hyndman, 1997, *Forecasting: Methods and Applications*, 3d ed., John Wiley & Sons: New York.

Ringland, Gill, 2006, *Scenario Planning: Managing for the Future*, 2d ed., John Wiley & Sons: New York.

www.forecastingprinciples.com

Chapter 6

Cooper, Robert G. (2001), Winning at New Products: Accelerating the Process from Idea to Launch, 3d ed., Perseus Books: Reading, MA

Kahn, Kenneth B., 2005, The PDMA Handbook of New Product Development, John Wiley & Sons: New York.

Ulrich, Karl and Steven Eppinger, 2003, Product Design and Development, 3d ed., Mcgraw-Hill/Irwin: New York.

Verganti, Roberto, 2006, "Innovating through Design," Harvard Business Review, Vol. 84, No. 12, pp. 114-23.

www.sawtooth.com

www.infinn.com

www.thoughtrod.com

www.imaginatik.com

www.whynot.net

www.innocentive.com

www.gyronix.com

www.branddelphi.com

Chapter 7

Bower, Joseph L. and Clark G. Gilbert, eds., 2006, *From Resource Allocations to Strategy*, Oxford University Press: Cambridge, MA.

Dolan, Robert J. and Hermann Simon, 1996, *Power Pricing*, The Free Press: New York.

Matson, Eric, 1995, "Customizing Prices," *Harvard Business Review,* Vol. 73, No. 6, pp. 13-14.

Nagle, Thomas T. and John Hogan, 2005, *The Strategy and Tactics of Pricing: A Guide to Growing More Profitably,* 4th ed., Prentice Hall: Englewood Cliffs, NJ.

Sharpe, Paul and Tom Keelin, 1998, "How SmithKline Beecham Makes Better Resource-Allocation Decisions," *Harvard Business Review,* Vol. 76, No. 2, pp. 45-52.

www.ariba.com

Chapter 8

In addition to the resources available at www.decisionpro.biz, you may find the following Web sites useful to keep up with developments in marketing analytics:

www.decisionsupportsciences.com

www.marketinganalytics.com

www.marketingnpv.com

www.msi.org

www.marketingprofs.com

www.sas.com

www.spss.com

www.wrcresearch.com

SUBJECT INDEX

F

Factor analysis, 83, 103-107
  Attribute-based perceptual mapping, 103 107
  In segmentation, 83, 106
Field value-in-use assessments, 37
First choice rule, 112-113
Focus groups, 41-42
Forecasting
  Causal analyses, 120
  Judgmental methods, 121-125, 140, 149
  Market and survey analyses, 120
  Methods of, 120-136
  Time-series analyses, 120

G

Gabor-Granger method, 180-183
Gatekeepers. *See* Organizational buying center
GE/McKinsey multifactor matrix model, 160-162, 229
Growth
  Product life cycle, 132-136

H

Heterogeneity, customer, 61-62, 65, 82
Hierarchical methods in cluster analysis, 85
Hybrid conjoint model, 170

I

Idea generation and idea evaluation
  Models for, 158-160
Ideal-point models, 107-108
Imitation effect. *See* Bass Model
Importance ratings, 42, 81
Independent variables, 18-19, 66, 149
Influencer. *See* Organizational buying center
Innovation effect. *See* Bass Model
Interactive decision process, 2

J

Joint-space mapping method
  Ideal-point, 107-108
  Vector models, 107-109
Judgmental forecasting methods, 121-125, 140, 149
  Chain ratio method, 123-125
  Delphi and related methods, 122-123

Jury of executive opinion, 122
Jury of executive opinion forecasting method, 120-122

K

K-means partitioning clustering method, 86

L

Latent class customer segmentation, 70-72
Law of demand for pricing, 177-179
Life cycle, product (PLC), 132-136
Logit choice rule, 45-47
Loyalty, 52-58, 63, 69, 73, 137, 207-212

M

Market
  Response models, 10-15, 17-21, 123, 197. *See also* Response models
  Segment, 30, 61-65, 75, 110-111, 119, 200
  Simulations, 171, 233
Marketing
  Reengineering of, 5
  Strategies, 194
Marketing management support systems (MMSSs), 2
Market-share models, 16
Maturity, product life cycle (PLC), 133-135
Maximum utility in choice rule, 171
Mental models, 1, 7, 23-25, 225
Model-based marketing decision support systems (MDSS), 220-221, 224-225, 231-232, 235-236
Model-building software, 5
Models
  ASSESSOR, 127, 137, 144-149
  Averaged ideal-point, 108
  BASES, 144
  CALLPLAN, 203
  GE/McKinsey portfolio, 160, 229
  Ideal-point, 107-108
  Integrated systems of, 230
  Interactive decision, 2, 25
  Logit, 45-47
  Market response, 10-22
  Market share, 16
  MDSS, 220-221, 224-225, 231-232, 235-236
  NEWS, 144
  Offered as Web services, 227-230

COMPANY INDEX

NAME INDEX

REFERENCES

Accenture Report, 2002, *Insight Driven Marketing*, (January), available at www.accenture.com.

Anderson, Eric and Duncan Simester, 2003, "Mind Your Pricing Cues," *Harvard Business Review*, Vol. 81, No. 9, pp. 96-103.

Anderson, James C. and James A. Narus, 2003, *Business Market Management: Understanding, Creating and Delivering Value*, 2d ed., Prentice Hall: Englewood Cliffs, NJ.

Armstrong, Scott J., 2001, "Selecting Forecasting Methods," in Scott J. Armstrong, ed., *Principles of Forecasting*, Kluwer: Norwell, MA.

Bachfischer, Nikola (2010), "Adidas: Marketing budget reallocation to digital channels," http://www.aquarius.biz/en/2010/11/29/adidas-marketing-budget-reallocation-to-digital-channels/ (accessed April 4, 2012).

Bass, Frank M., 1969, "A New Product Growth Model for Consumer Durables," *Management Science*, Vol. 15, No.4 (January), pp. 215-27.

Blattberg, Robert C., Richard Briesch, and Edward J. Fox, 1995, "How Promotions Work," *Marketing Science*, Vol. 14, No. 3, Part 2 of 2: Special Issue on Empirical Generalizations in Marketing, pp. G122-32.

Blattberg, Robert C. and John Deighton, 1996, "Managing Marketing by the Customer Equity Test," *Harvard Business Review*, Vol. 74, No.4 (July), pp. 136-44.

Blattberg, Robert C. and Stephen J. Hoch, 1990, "Database Models and Managerial Intuition: 50 Percent Model + 50 Percent Manager," *Management Science*, Vol. 36, No. 8, pp. 887-99.

Blattberg, Robert C. and Alan Levin, 1987, "Modelling the Effectiveness and Profitability of Trade Promotions," *Marketing Science*, Vol. 6, No. 2 (Spring), pp. 124-46.

Blattberg, Robert C. and Scott A. Neslin, 1990, *Sales Promotions: Concepts, Methods and Strategies*, Prentice Hall: Englewood Cliffs, NJ.

Bower, Joseph L. and Clark G. Gilbert, eds., 2006, *From Resource Allocations to Strategy*, Oxford University Press: Cambridge, MA.

Brown, Erika, 2002, "Analyze This," *Forbes* (April 1), pp. 96-98.

Bulkeley, William M., 2005, "Marketers Scan Blogs for Brand Insights," *Wall Street Journal* (June 23), p. B1.

Business Week, "What Should you Spend on Advertising?" February 10, 2009.

Cooper, Robert G (2001) *Winning at New Products 3d* Edition Perseus Books: New York.

Davenport, Thomas H., 2006, "Competing on Analytics," *Harvard Business Review*, Vol. 84, No. 1 (January), pp. 98-107.

Day, George S., 1981, "The Product Life Cycle: Analysis and Application Issues," *Journal of Marketing*, Vol. 45, No. 4 (Autumn), pp. 60-67.

Dolan, Robert J. and Hermann Simon, 1996, *Power Pricing: How Managing Price Transforms the Bottom Line*, The Free Press: New York.

Elliott, Stuart (2012), "Marketing Budgets Rise for Some Giants," *New York Times* (February 21, p. B1).

Elsner, Ralf, Manfred Krafft, and Arnd Huchzermeier, 2004, "Optimizing Rhenania's Direct Marketing Business through Dynamic Multilevel Modeling (DMLM) in a Multicatalog-Brand

Environment," *Marketing Science*, Vol. 23, No. 2 (Spring), pp. 192-206.

Flynn, Laurie J., 2006, "Like This? You'll Hate That. (Not All Web Recommendations Are Welcome)," *New York Times* (January 23), p. C1.

Forrester Research (2010), "The State of Business Intelligence Software and Emerging Trends."

Fuld, Leonard, 2003, "Be Prepared," *Harvard Business Review*, Vol. 81, No. 11, pp. 20-25.

Gabor, A and C. W. J. Granger,(1964) "Price Sensitivity of the Consumer," *Journal of Advertising Research,* Vol. 4, No. 4, pp. 40-44.

Garvin, David A. "Competing on the Eight Dimensions of Quality." *Harvard Business Review* 65, no. 6 (November-December 1987).

Gensch, Dennis H., Nicola Aversa, and Steven P. Moore, 1990, "A Choice-Modeling Market Information System that Enabled ABB Electric to Expand its Market Share," *Interfaces*, Vol. 20, No. 1 (January-February), pp. 6-25.

Germann, Frank, Gary L. Lilien and Arvind Rangaswamy (2012), "Performance Implications of Deploying Marketing Analytics," Working Paper.

Glazer, Emily (2012), "P&G's Marketing Chief Looks to go Digital," *Wall Street Journal*, (March, 14, p. B7).

Griffin, Abbie, 1993, "Metrics for Measuring Product Development Cycle Time," *The Journal of Product Innovation Management*, Vol. 10, No. 2, pp. 112-25.

Gupta, Sunil and Donald Lehmann, 2005, *Managing Customers as Investments: The Strategic Value of Customers in the Long Run*, Wharton School Publishing: Philadelphia, PA.

Halliday, Jean (2008), "GM Roars Forward Into Digital Ad Channels," *Ad Age Digital* (March 17).

Hise, Richard T., Larry O'Neal, James U. McNeal, and A. Parasuraman, 1989, "The Effect of Product Design Activities on Commercial Success Levels of New Industrial Products," *Journal of Product Innovation Management,* Vol. 6, No. 1, (March), pp. 43-50.

Hogarth, Robin M., 1987, *Judgment and Choice*, 2d ed., John Wiley & Sons: New York.

IDC (2010), "State of the U.S. Business Analytics Market."

Jamieson, Linda F. and Frank M. Bass, 1989, "Adjusting Stated Intention to Predict Trial Purchase of New Products," *Journal of Marketing Research*, Vol. 26, No.3 (August), pp. 336-45.

Jedidi, Kamel, Carl F. Mela, and Sunil Gupta, 1999, "Managing Advertising and Promotion for Long-Run Profitability," Marketing Science, Vol. 18, No. 1, pp. 122.

Kahn, Kenneth B., 2005, *The PDMA Handbook of New Product Development*, John Wiley & Sons: New York.

Kahney, Leander, 2006, "Straight Dope on the IPod's Birth," *Wired* (News), accessed October 17, 2006, available at http://www.wired.com/news/columns/cultofmac/0,71956-0.html.

Kannan, P K, Barbara Kline Pope, and Sanjay Jain (2009), "Pricing Digital Content Product Lines: A Model and Application for the National Academies Press," *Marketing Science,* Vol. 28, No. 4, pp. 620-638.

Kayande, Ujwal, Arnaud De Bruyn, Gary L. Lilien, Arvind Rangaswamy, and Gerrit Van Bruggen (2009),"How Incorporating Feedback Mechanisms in a DSS Affects DSS Evaluations," *Information Systems Research*, Vol. 20, No. 4, December pp. 527–546.

Kotler, Philip and Kevin Keller, 2005, *Marketing Management*, 12th ed., Prentice Hall: Upper Saddle River, NJ.

Kumar, V. (2008) *Managing Customers for Profit* Wharton School Publishing, Philadelphia, PA.

Lilien, Gary L. (2011) "Bridging the Academic-Practitioner Divide in Marketing Decision Models" *Journal of Marketing,* Vol. 75, No. 4, pp. 196-210.

Lilien, Gary L. and Arvind Rangaswamy, 2004, *Marketing Engineering*, Trafford Publishing: Victoria, Canada.

Lilien, Gary L., John Roberts and Venky Shankar (2011) Effective Marketing Science Applications: Insights from ISMS-MSI Practice Prize Finalist Papers and Projects. MSI Working Paper.

Lindgren, Mats and Hans Bandhold, 2003, *Scenario Planning: The Link Between Future and Strategy*, Palgrave Macmillan: New York.

Linstone, Harold A. and Murray Turoff, 2002, *The Delphi Method: Techniques and Applications*, available at http://www.is.njit.edu/pubs/delphibook/.

Lodish, Leonard M., 1971, "Empirical Studies on Industrial Response to Exposure Patterns," *Journal of Marketing Research*, Vol. 8, No. 2, pp. 212-18.

Lodish, Leonard M., 1974, "'Vaguely Right' Approach to Sales Force Allocations," *Harvard Business Review*, January-February, pp. 119-25.

Lodish, Leonard M., Ellen Curtis, Michael Ness, and Kerry M. Simpson, 1988, "Sales Force Sizing and Deployment Using a Decision Calculus Model at Syntex Laboratories," *Interfaces*, Vol. 18, No. 1 (January-February), pp. 5-20.

Makridakis, Spyros G., Steven C. Wheelwright, and Rob J. Hyndman, 1997, *Forecasting: Methods and Applications*, 3d ed., John Wiley & Sons: New York.

Matson, Eric, 1995, "Customizing Prices," *Harvard Business Review*, Vol. 73, No. 6, pp. 13-14.

McDonald, Malcom and Ian Dunbar, 2004, *Market Segmentation: How to Do It, How to Profit from It*, Butterworth-Heinemann: Burlington, MA.

McKinsey & Co. (2009), "McKinsey Global Survey Results: Measuring Marketing," *McKinsey Quarterly*, (March), pp. 1-8.

Moore, William L. and Edgar A. Pessemier, 1993, *Product Planning and Management: Designing and Delivering Value*, Mc-Graw Hill: New York.

Meulman, Jacqueline, Willem J. Heiser, and Douglas J. Carroll, 1986, *PREFMAP-3 User's Guide*, available at www.netlib.org/mds/prefmap3a/manual.ps.

Myers, James H., 1996, *Segmentation & Positioning for Strategic Marketing Decisions*, 1st ed., South-Western Educational Publications.

Nagle, Thomas T. and John Hogan, 2005, *The Strategy and Tactics of Pricing: A Guide to Growing More Profitably*, 4th ed., Prentice Hall: Englewood Cliffs, NJ.

Natter, Martin, Andreas Mild, Thomas Reutterer, and Alfred Taudes, 2006, "An Assortment-Wide Decision-Support System for Dynamic Pricing and Promotion Planning," *Marketing Science*.

Navasky, Victor S. and Christopher Cerf, 1998, *The Experts Speak: The Definitive Compendium of Authoritative Misinformation*, Villard Books: New York.

Nijs, Vincent R., Marnik G. Dekimpe, Jan-Benedict E. M. Steenkamp, and Dominique H. Hanssens, 2001, "The Category-Demand Effects of Price Promotions," *Marketing Science*, Vol. 20, No. 1 (Winter), pp. 1-22.

Nijs, Vincent, Shubha Srinivasan, and Koen Pauwels, 2006, "Retail-Price Drivers and Retailer Profits," *Marketing Science*.

Rangaswamy, Arvind and Gary L. Lilien, 1997, "Software Tools for New Product Development," *Journal of Marketing Research*, Vol. 34, No. 1, Special Issue on Innovation and New Products (February), pp. 177-84.

Ries, Al and Jack Trout, 2000, *Positioning: The Battle for Your Mind*, McGraw-Hill: New York.

Ringland, Gill, 2006, *Scenario Planning: Managing for the Future*, 2d ed., John Wiley & Sons: New York.

Robertson, S. Thomas and Howard Barich, 1992, "A Successful Approach to Segmenting Industrial Markets," *Planning Review*, Vol. 20, No. 6, pp. 4-11.

Rust, Roland, Valerie Zeithaml, and Katherine Lemon, 2000, *Driving Customer Equity: How Customer Lifetime Value Is Reshaping Corporate Strategy*, The Free Press: New York.

Schrage, Michael, 1999, *Serious Play: How the World's Best Companies Simulate to Innovate*, Harvard Business School Press: Boston, MA.

Senge, Peter M. and Colleen Lannon, 1990, "Managerial Micro-worlds," *Technology Review*, Vol. 93, No. 5 (July), pp. 62-68.

Shapiro, Benson P., 1985, "Rejuvenating the Marketing Mix," *Harvard Business Review*, Vol. 63, No. 5, pp. 28-32.

Sharpe, Paul and Tom Keelin, 1998, "How SmithKline Beecham Makes Better Resource-Allocation Decisions," *Harvard Business Review*, Vol. 76, No. 2, pp. 45-52.

Shocker, Allan D. and William G. Hall, 1986, "Pretest Market Models: A Critical Evaluation," *The Journal of Product Innovation Management*, Vol. 3, No. 2, pp. 86-107.

Silk, Alvin J. and Glen L. Urban, 1978, "Pre-Test Market Evaluation of New Packaged Goods: A Model and Measurement Methodology," *Journal of Marketing Research*, Vol. 15, No. 2 (May), pp. 171-91.

Silva-Risso, Jorge and Irina Ionova (2008), "A Nested Logit Model of Product and Transaction-Type Choice for Planning Automakers' Pricing and Promotions." *Marketing Science*, Vol. 27, No. 4, pp. 545–566.

Simon, Herbert A., 1971, "Designing Organizations for an Information-Rich World," in Martin Greenberger, ed., *Computers, Communication, and the Public Interest*, The Johns Hopkins Press: Baltimore, MD, pp. 37-72.

Simon, Herbert A., 1977, *The New Science of Management Decision*, Prentice Hall PTR: Upper Saddle River, NJ.

Sinha, Prabhakant and Andris A. Zoltners, 2001, "Sales-Force Decision Models: Insights from 25 Years of Implementation," *Interfaces*, Vol. 31, No. 3, pp. 8-44.

Tirenni, Giuliano, Abderrahim Labbi, Cesar Berrospi, André Elisseeff, Timir Bhose, Kari Pauro, and Seppo Pöyhönen, (2007), "Customer Equity and Lifetime Management (CELM) Finnair Case Study." *Marketing Science* 26 (4), 553-565.

Toubia, Olivier and Laurent Flores (2007), "Adaptive Idea Screening Using Consumers," *Marketing Science*, Vol. 26, No. 3, pp. 342-360.

Ulrich, Karl and Steven Eppinger, 2003, *Product Design and Development*, 3d ed., Mcgraw-Hill/Irwin: New York.

Urban, Glen L., Thomas E. Hatch, Gerald M. Katz, and Alvin J. Silk, 1983, "The ASSESSOR Pre-Test Market Evaluation System," *Interfaces*, Vol. 13, No. 6 (December), pp. 38-59.

Urban, Glen L. and Gerald M. Katz, 1983, "Pre-Test Market Models: Validation and Managerial Implications," *Journal of Marketing Research*, Vol. 20, No. 3 (August), pp. 221-34.

Urban, Glen L. and Steven H. Star, 1991, *Advanced Marketing Strategy*, Prentice Hall: Englewood Cliffs, NJ.

Urban, Glen L., 1993, "Pretest Market Forecasting," in J. Eliashberg and G.L. Lilien, eds., *Handbook in OR and MS*, Vol. 5, Elsevier Science Publishers, pp. 315-48.

Urban, Glen L. and John R. Hauser, 1993, *Design and Marketing of New Products*, Prentice Hall: Englewood Cliffs, NJ.

Van Westendorp, P (1976) "NSS-Price Sensitivity Meter (PSM)- A new approach to study consumer perception of price." *Proceedings of the ESOMAR Congress.*

Verganti, Roberto, 2006, "Innovating through Design," *Harvard Business Review*, Vol. 84, No. 12, pp. 114-23.

Waaser, Ernest, Marshall Dahneke, Michael Pekkarinen, and Michael Weissel, 2005, "How You Slice It: Smarter Segmentation for Your Sales Force," *Harvard Business Review*, Vol. 82, No. 3, pp. 105-11.

Wack, Pierre, 1985, "Scenarios: Uncharted Waters Ahead," Harvard Business Review, Vol. 63, No. 5, pp. 72-89.

Whiting, Rick, 2001, "Virtual Focus Group," *Information Week*, July 20, available at http://www.informationweek.com/.

Whiting, Rick, 2002, "GE Capital's Dashboard Drives Metrics to Desktops," *Information Week*, April 22, available at http://www.informationweek.com/.

Wind, Jerry, Paul E. Green, Douglas Shifflet, and Marsha Scarbrough, 1989, "Courtyard by Marriott: Designing a Hotel Facility with Consumer-Based Marketing Models," *Interfaces*, Vol. 19, No. 1 (January-February), pp. 25-47.

Wind, Yoram J., 1978, "Issues and Advances in Segmentation Research," *Journal of Marketing Research*, Vol. 15, No. 3 (August), pp. 317-337.

Yankelovich, Daniel and David Meer, 2006, "Rediscovering Market Segmentation," *Harvard Business Review*, Vol. 84, No. 2, pp. 122-31.

Zangwill, Willard I., 1993, "Lightning Strategies for Innovation," *Success*, Vol. 40, No. 7, pp. 42-45.

ISBN 978-0-9857648-0-7

90000>

9 780985 764807